PREACHING AND TEACHING DIFFICULT TEXTS OF THE NEW TESTAMENT

BRYAN MURAWSKI

PREACHING AND TEACHING DIFFICULT TEXTS OF THE NEW TESTAMENT

HENDRICKSON

Preaching and Teaching Difficult Texts of the New Testament

Published by Hendrickson Publishers
3 Centennial Drive
Peabody, Massachusetts 01960
www.hendricksonpublishers.com

ISBN 978–1-4964–7659–3 (print)
ISBN 979-8-4005-1334-3 (Kindle ebook)
ISBN 979-8-4005-1335-0 (epub)
ISBN 979-8-4005-1336-7 (Apple epub)

Printed in the United States of America

First Printing — August 2025

Library of Congress Control Number: 2025933856

I dedicate this book to my siblings: Bill, Alan, and Joy.

Contents

Acknowledgments

Many people have helped shape both my preaching and my writing. I am honored to serve as one of the pastors at Riverstone Church in Yardley, Pennsylvania. I am grateful for the elders who have given me the opportunity to preach many challenging texts on a regular basis and the members who have encouraged me in this ministry.

My colleagues at Cairn University have been a great support and encouragement. I am especially indebted to Gary E. Schnittjer, who made many helpful comments on the Apocrypha chapter, as well as Kevin W. McFadden, who helped with some of the more technical Greek issues and a few other areas in the manuscript. All errors that remain are my own. Ally Bliven and Lauren Raab, two of our student workers in the department of divinity, saved me from numerous errors and gave feedback on many of my bad jokes. I am grateful to Cairn's administration for providing the department with these important roles.

As usual, the staff at Hendrickson has offered excellent feedback and careful editing. It has been a pleasure working with all the folks there, but I am especially grateful for Patricia Anders, Phil Frank, and Madi Cannon for their work on this manuscript.

I am increasingly grateful to the Lord for providing me with a beautiful, supportive, and faithful wife who encourages me to continue carving out time to write. Thank you, Janice. And Chelsey, Nathan, Micah, and Adam—thanks for being patient with your Pastor-Professor Dad.

I do hope and pray that this book will continue to encourage pastors and teachers to preach and teach all of Scripture. The world needs it.

κήρυξον τὸν λόγον
Preach the word!

Introduction

Digging for Treasure

I must start this book with a confession. Over the last few years, I have become something of an addict.

Since childhood, I've been addicted to reading, which has only expanded over time (what pastor-professor isn't?). Since my teenage years, I've been addicted to cheesy B-grade monster movies. But these are nothing new.

My most recent addiction is rockhounding and fossil collecting.

I can't get enough of it. In the summer of 2023, as my hobby was growing into a full-fledged addiction, I dragged my family up and down the state of New York to dig for all sorts of buried treasures. After a brief trip to Niagara Falls, we stopped at Penn Dixie Fossil Park and Nature Reserve in Blasdell, New York. There, we spent a hot afternoon chipping away at several hundred pounds of slate rock. Even my youngest son, who was three years old at the time, found himself swinging a hammer and surface hunting for fossils.

Over the course of several hours, we moved hundreds of pounds of rock . . . for what?

For a few trilobites.

A trilobite—in case you aren't a nerd—is an extinct arthropod.

An arthropod—in case you aren't a nerd—is the phylum of creatures in the animal kingdom that includes lobsters, crabs, spiders, millipedes, and insects.

A phylum—in case . . .

Never mind. Back to trilobites. Imagine a pill bug (or, as we used to call them when I was a kid, a "roly-poly bug") but with a cooler head. Penn Dixie famously offers visitors a chance to release trilobites from their rocky prison by chiseling open slate.

After pocketing a few pounds of trilobites entrapped in rock, resembling weird miniature Han Solos, we ventured across the state to camp in Herkimer, New York.

There, we also chiseled and moved hundreds of pounds of rock. But this time, we did it to uncover Herkimer diamonds, a special kind of double-terminated quartz crystal that grows in pockets of the abundant dolomite bedrock in the area.

Even my daughter enjoyed this activity! For Christmas later that year, I had a jeweler make her a pair of beautiful dangling earrings from two of her best finds.

But once again, hundreds of pounds of rocks, this time for a few ounces of treasure that could fit in the palm of my hand.

That's the life of a rockhound enthusiast or any fossil collector. Whether it's scouring miles of beach at the Calvert Cliffs in Lusby, Maryland, for that one epic shark tooth, or wading through thousands of gallons of water and sifting millions of particles of sand to uncover that perfect belemnite at Big Brook Nature Preserve in Colts Neck, New Jersey, the joy of the hunt is the treasure that comes from the search. Hours of backbreaking labor and sweaty, grimy work become worth it when you uncover that flawless display piece.

The reward is worth the effort.

Scriptural Treasures

Mining the pages of Scripture shares many similarities with rockhounding and fossil hunting. There are days when surface hunting yields plentiful results. My wife and I went down to South Carolina on a dig (on our anniversary—what a wife!) and spent the entire day surface hunting, hardly lifting a shovel at all. We came away with hundreds of shark teeth, whale and dolphin bones, and all kinds of other goodies.

Scripture can be like that too. Open the page to Romans 12, and you'll find that nearly every verse is of the "surface hunt" variety. It does not take much digging to explain and apply commands like "abhor what is evil" (v. 9) or "be constant in prayer" (v. 12). I'm not recommending ditching the commentaries, but wise teachers could probably spend more time on application than explanation in such a fertile field.

On other days, preparing a sermon is more like working the fields in Mohawk Valley, New York. My oldest son, Nathan, and I spent eight grueling hours breaking rock—hammer, chisel, the whole nine yards. Eight hours of backbreaking work for a small pocket full of gemstones.

Totally worth it, though.

All passages require hard work for the responsible interpreter and preacher, but some passages require *really* hard work to uncover the treasure.

To put it another way, not all passages are Romans 12. Some passages require disproportional digging.

Which texts do I mean?

I'm thinking about that long list of names in Romans 16. How do you preach *that*? Or 1 Peter 3:18–22, where Peter mentions Jesus proclaiming *something* to the spirits in prison (whoever they are!). Or maybe Matthew 24–25, the Olivet Discourse, a passage notorious for its difficulty of interpretation. If you crack open ten commentaries on the passage, you're sure to get twenty opinions. And what about those hidden reefs of text-critical issues that plague books like Acts, or the two major ones at the end of Mark and in the middle of John?

Just like mining for buried treasure—whether shiny or fossilized—mining these difficult texts yields great results in personal Bible study, in a small group study, and even in a sermon. They not only *can* be taught and preached, they *must* be, for the sake of your church and your commitment to preach and teach the whole counsel of God's word (Acts 20:20).

Why Preach and Teach Difficult Texts?

My basic thesis for this book is that every single verse of Scripture is inspired and relevant for the sanctification of a believer. It therefore can and should be taught and preached.

In my first book on this topic, *Preaching Difficult Texts of the Old Testament*, I leaned heavily into a New Testament passage that informed and motivated my understanding of this thesis: 2 Timothy 3:16–4:2.[1] In this passage, the apostle Paul writes to Pastor Timothy,

---

1. Bryan Murawski, *Preaching Difficult Texts of the Old Testament* (Peabody, MA: Hendrickson, 2021).

> All Scripture is breathed out by God and profitable for teaching, for reproof, for correction, and for training in righteousness, that the man of God may be complete, equipped for every good work. I charge you in the presence of God and of Christ Jesus, who is to judge the living and the dead, and by his appearing and his kingdom: preach the word; be ready in season and out of season; reprove, rebuke, and exhort, with complete patience and teaching.

Since I don't expect that every reader of this New Testament volume will have read the Old Testament volume (though I do hope that is the case!), a brief flyby over this passage will solidify the point.

Paul tells Timothy that *all* Scripture is God-breathed and is not only profitable for a believer's sanctification but also preachable. What does "all Scripture" include?

In a word, *everything*.

It includes those seemingly throwaway-able introductory verses that most of the epistles begin with. It includes those interpretive enigmas, like when Paul mentions people being "baptized on behalf of the dead" (1 Cor 15:29). It even includes those inspired texts that appear to quote or reference uninspired texts, like Jude's reference to 1 Enoch (Jude 9).

The only thing "all Scripture" may not include are those verses or passages that may not be inspired after all (we will get to those in the chapter on textual criticism). But preachers or teachers will have to say *something* about these passages in sermons, even if they hold them to be late, uninspired additions. Therefore, preachers need to know how to preach these texts.

But let's not stray too far from the point. Every verse of Scripture is inspired, profitable, and preachable.

This doesn't mean it's always easy for us to understand *how* the Bible is profitable. Sometimes good treasure requires digging. It doesn't mean every passage of the Bible is equally as profitable for every individual or church on any given Sunday. Sometimes a church needs the coddling of Philippians more than the rebuke of Galatians, or vice versa. But every passage always has some benefit.

This means that when teachers skip or skim or sidestep or ignore the more challenging texts in the Bible, they unwittingly heap on themselves and their church a lot of negative side effects.

When they ignore difficult passages, they teach their congregants to do the same in their own devotions. This reveals a lazy pulpit, which indeed reflects their character. They functionally seat themselves on the throne of God, deciding what is best from the pages of the good book.

Maybe I'm overstating some of this, but I don't think so. It's a dangerous thing to play fast and loose with the text of Scripture. We wouldn't dare cut out words from our favorite memory verses because they are too hard to memorize. Why do we do the same with entire books or passages in the Bible from our pulpits?

A Word on Teaching Versus Preaching

Unlike the Old Testament volume, which focused primarily on preachers, I intentionally broadened the scope of this book to include both preachers and teachers. I found that many of the people who benefited from the first book were laypeople volunteering their time to teach Bible studies, lead Sunday school classes, and facilitate small groups. Many of my students who may not necessarily go on to pastoral or pulpit ministry benefited from the read.

Therefore, my sights in this volume are set not just on the preachers but on teachers as well. I'm *not* primarily thinking about "professional" teachers, such as those in a college classroom or a Bible teacher in a Christian school (though again, I do hope they would find some benefit to this book!). Instead, much of the homiletical advice in this volume relates to those who find themselves teaching in a church ministry setting, to one degree or another.

That being said, I will often toggle between talking to "preachers" and "teachers." Don't be offended if you're on one side or the other. Much of the advice works in both camps. Advice specific to one or the other will be so labeled.

Who Should Teach and Preach Difficult Texts?

Maybe you're still not sold. After all, why do the dirty work of digging through hardened rock when surface hunting yields profitable results with much less effort? Here are three more reasons to preach and teach difficult texts.

Reason #1: Preaching difficult texts is a requirement for those committed to expository preaching.

I cannot conceive of any logical reason for a pastor to dig through challenging texts of Scripture other than a firm commitment to expository preaching.

Bryan Chapell defines expository preaching as "a message whose structure and thought are derived from a biblical text, that covers the scope of the text, and that explains the features and context of the text in order to disclose the enduring principles for faithful thinking, living, and worship intended by the Spirit, who inspired the text."[2]

Such preaching should be guided by controlled hermeneutics that study the passage in its literary, historical, and theological context.[3] I am still convinced that what I wrote in my first volume remains true today: No other method of preaching upholds the profitability of all Scripture in such high regard as expository preaching, working chapter by chapter, verse by verse through entire books of the Bible.[4]

Yes, there is room in all pulpits for topical sermons. But topical sermons should also be expository in the sense that they are drawn from a careful exegetical study of each text used in the sermon.[5] That means that when done correctly, topical sermons will likely take *more* time and preparation than an expository sermon, because the preacher must study numerous texts and contexts to ensure that any principles are derived from the au-

---

2. Bryan Chapell, *Christ-Centered Preaching: Redeeming the Expository Sermon* (Grand Rapids: Baker Academic, 2005), 31. Technically speaking, his definition relates to an expository sermon, but I'm using the definition as it relates to both teaching and preaching.

3. This leans on some of the nuances from Haddon W. Robinson's definition in *Biblical Preaching: The Development and Delivery of Expository Messages*, 3rd ed. (Grand Rapids: Baker Academic, 2014), 5.

4. This book isn't the place to give a robust argument for the benefits of expository preaching. Readers should consult the homiletical resources already noted. I can also commend the excellent transcript by D. A. Carson, "The What and Why of Expository Preaching," *The Gospel Coalition*, 1 June 2003, https://www.thegospelcoalition.org/sermon/the-what-and-why-of-expository-preaching/.

5. I once heard my homiletics professor say, "I'm convinced that if you know how to preach an expository sermon, you'll know how to put together a topical sermon." There's a lot of truth in that statement!

thor's intent, not the preacher's own design for the sermon. Proper topical sermons do not begin with preachers identifying three to five points they want to make on a particular topic and then finding verses to support those points. That's not expository topical preaching, nor is it the proper method of sermon preparation. Instead, preachers should study what the Bible says about the topic, *then* derive principles from whatever they see in the text. In that way, the text itself remains the controlling guide for the sermon. Often, the principles that come from such a study surprise even the preacher.[6]

Preachers committed to giving their congregations a steady diet of verse-by-verse preaching through a book of the Bible will find difficult passages inescapable. In contrast, preachers who pick and choose which passages to preach can avoid any unpleasant topic or text. Though this "surface-hunting" convenience may feel right and yield some fruit from the pulpit, it denigrates the passages skipped or skimmed over and brings a host of other problems, some of which have already been mentioned.[7]

The more I preach, the more convinced I become that *every* book of the Bible has some unique challenge to it. Matthew begins with a genealogy and, among other things, has two solid chapters of eschatology toward its end.[8]

---

6. One of the most challenging sermon series I've ever preached was in Proverbs. After doing an expository study of chapters 1–9, I spent ten weeks or so in the middle of the book preaching on various topics (laziness, God's sovereignty, marriage, money, etc.). Because I endeavored to allow a careful study of the text to drive the points of the sermon, my time in sermon preparation was disproportionately more intense than almost any other message series I have preached. That's how I knew I was doing something right.

7. After writing these thoughts with such strong conviction, I feel the need to offer an apologetic of sorts for my two volumes on Isaiah: *The Preacher's Hebrew Companion to Isaiah 1–39: A Selective Commentary for Meditation and Sermon Preparation* (Peabody, MA: Hendrickson, 2024); *The Preacher's Hebrew Companion to Isaiah 40–66: A Selective Commentary for Meditation and Sermon Preparation* (Peabody, MA: Hendrickson, 2025). Noting the selective nature of these volumes (each one covers only twelve passages in a sixty-six-chapter book), readers might wonder if I have hypocritically committed the same homiletical sin that I'm denouncing here. But the aim of that commentary series is not to cover the book exhaustively like other commentaries or series; rather, the aim is to give preachers a selection based on which passages the authors think preachers would most likely preach (xii).

8. Though I believe genealogies are certainly one of the most challenging kinds of texts to preach, I don't deal with them in this volume, as they were covered in my previous Old Testament volume. Since my volume was published, I can also

Mark has a "deleted scene" kind of ending that requires careful study and explanation. Luke also has a genealogy and a few of its own eschatological sections. John's Gospel is ripe with rich and challenging theology and controversial statements. Acts has its fair share of textual and historical issues. As for Romans—there's a reason some preachers take years to work through it! And don't get me started with the difficulties in 1 Corinthians. And so on through each book. Every biblical book offers unique challenges. If we want to preach through them, we can't avoid them.

The hope of this book is to help preachers and teachers fill in the gaps between what they've learned in their homiletics classes in seminary and what challenges await them in the pulpit. Many seminaries have done well to prepare preachers to preach Pauline epistles and maybe even some narratives. This is good, since you'll find plenty of both in the New Testament. Even within these genres, however, we find genealogies, extensive use of Old Testament Scripture, references to noncanonical works, people lists, sticky text-critical issues, and other challenges.

I had two homiletics classes with an excellent professor.[9] My first semester taught me the basic scaffolding of a sermon. It culminated in a sermon from a Pauline text (mine was Phil 2:1–11). During my second semester, I had to preach five sermons from five different biblical genres, including an Old Testament narrative, a parable, a psalm, and a topical sermon in Proverbs. I left feeling well-equipped to preach.

To no fault of my professor or any others who teach such courses, there wasn't much focus on some of these challenging in-between passages. After all, how much can you squeeze into two semesters? My seminary training equipped me to deal with most passages hermeneutically, but I had some homiletical gaps to fill.

That's where this volume helps. It guides where other good, more general resources do not. After all, as you work through the Bible in your commitment to expository preaching and teaching, you can't miss the difficult texts.

---

recommend Nancy S. Dawson, *All the Genealogies of the Bible: Visual Charts and Exegetical Commentary* (Grand Rapids: Zondervan Academic, 2023).

9. Don Cheyney at Cairn University (formerly, Philadelphia Biblical University). I dedicated my first volume to him and owe a great deal of insight in this volume to his teaching.

Reason #2: Preaching and teaching difficult texts communicate a high view of Scripture's inspiration.

Most of this point has already been made, but just in case you missed it: *All* Scripture is God-breathed, inspired by God. Every last verse. Few teachers or preachers would deny this, yet too few teachers and preachers practice it like they believe it.

Take, for example, Romans 16. It is no exaggeration to say that some preachers spend *years* working through Romans from the pulpit. Oftentimes it comes with a strange kind of boast. "I spent five years in the book!" "I only spent two. Shame."

However, most preachers spend nowhere near the time on the final chapter as they did on the others. Is it because the final chapter is not as rich in theology? I doubt it. Rather, the final chapter may not be so rich in *surface-hunting* theology, but it's rich indeed.

Pastors spend a whole sermon in Romans 1:16, perhaps understandably so. But why not a whole sermon in 16:14—"Greet Asyncritus, Phlegon, Hermes, Patrobas, Hermas, and the brothers who are with them"? If their methodology is consistent with how they handle the rest of the book, they might zoom in on the word *brothers* and consider the theology of being adopted into the family of God.[10] Which verse is more inspired: Romans 1:16 or 16:14?

The answer, of course, is neither. They are both equally inspired.

Now again, does this mean that both verses command equal *time* from the pulpit? Or that each verse has an equal impact on most people? I'm going to guess that Romans 16:14 has not inspired as many people to preach the gospel as Romans 1:16. And that's fine. But I would suggest that this still does not permit the preacher to dismiss, sidestep, or neglect the more obscure verse. A high view of inspiration causes the preacher to say, "I know God wrote this verse just as much as God wrote any other verse of the Bible. It's infallible, inerrant, and useful for my sanctification. How so? And how do I communicate that to the church?"

---

10. I'm not arguing that this methodology is *correct*, but I'm arguing that if they're consistent with the way many preachers treat the book as a launching pad to enter discussions on systematics, then this might be how they would apply that methodology to this more obscure verse.

Demonstrating a commitment to expository preaching and a high view of inspiration might lead the preacher to spend extra time learning how to pronounce these individuals' names instead of just guessing or mumbling through them on the spot. A high view of inspiration causes the preacher to study each individual name to see if there is any further significance to their mention, either in the more immediate context of the letter or the far context of other Scripture. A high view of inspiration forces the preacher to remain with the text until the questions of "What does it mean?" and "How does it apply?" have been answered.

Reason #3: Preaching and teaching difficult texts exalt Christ and teach the gospel.

I mean it. This comment is not an exaggeration. When we preach and teach difficult texts, we exalt Christ. And we preach and teach the gospel. How so? We know that doing anything with excellence glorifies the Lord (1 Cor 10:31). So certainly in that manner we exalt Christ by boldly facing challenging texts.

More specifically, as Paul writes in 1 Corinthians 2:2, "For I decided to know nothing among you except Jesus Christ and him crucified." Paul's obsession, his one driving goal, and his passion and ministry focus above all was to preach Christ. To exalt Jesus through word and deed.

Paul spent many hours reasoning to the Jews from the Scriptures. Surely this included some difficult passages. It would be reasonable to assume, then, that Paul found a means to exalt Christ and continue the spread of the gospel in preaching these difficult texts.

I have argued elsewhere that every passage of Scripture should point to the gospel.[11] When we preach challenging texts, we don't do so to boost our ego or proudly show everyone how great an exegete or orator we are. That's the wrong kind of boast, the wrong kind of foolishness. Instead, we do so—like with every other passage we preach—to exalt Christ and teach the gospel.

Let's go back to Romans 16:14 and put it into practice. How does this obscure verse exalt Christ and teach the gospel? Does not the inclusion of so many Greek names in this verse highlight the power of the gospel to cut

11. Murawski, *Preaching Difficult Texts*, 6–9.

through the former dividing lines of Jew and Gentile? That Paul calls these men "brothers"—using Old Testament terminology for non-Israelites—has profound significance and relates to everything he just argued for in the middle of his letter. The fact that he can speak of these men as being part of the family of God certainly reveals the powerful effects of the gospel, and the gospel itself can only be understood along with the effective sacrifice of Jesus Christ. Praise Jesus that his death and resurrection enabled all people of every race and nationality to have access to the gospel!

What This Book Is Not

Before a quick overview of what to expect from this book, it may help to set aside aims that tangentially relate to this work. The aim of this book is primarily homiletical. The goal extends beyond helping preachers and teachers understand the *meaning* of difficult texts—that is the work of commentaries and appears to be the actual function (though not always the stated function) of many similarly titled books. Rather, this book's goal is to equip preachers and teachers with their ability to bring these texts to light in the pulpit. Though many chapters will necessarily speak to hermeneutical issues, this is only to help the end goal of better preaching. After all, if you don't understand what a passage is doing or why it's there, how will you know what to do with it in the pulpit? Too many resources stop short of that final step. I know how to put together a three-point sermon on Romans 12:1–2; how do I put together a three-point sermon on Mark 16:9–20, which I may or may not trust is original to the Gospel? It's the difference between knowing what Romans 16 teaches and knowing how to teach Romans 16.

Because of this primary goal, just like my earlier Old Testament volume, I organized this book not by texts but by topics. If you ask, "What texts does *Preaching and Teaching Difficult Texts of the New Testament* cover?" you're asking the wrong question. If you ask "What *kinds* of texts does *Preaching and Teaching Difficult Texts of the New Testament* cover?" you're a bit closer to the goal. It will do little homiletical good to list a bunch of challenging texts and spend a few pages talking about the meaning of each of them. That's what commentaries are for. It will be much more productive to group these difficult texts into common "types" and recommend advice for understanding and preaching them. That's what this book is for.

As such, if you are looking for a book that deals with more common New Testament genre categories—such as the parable or narrative or epistle—keep looking. You won't have to look far, because many excellent resources exist to help in these areas.[12] This book fills in the cracks that those other resources typically overlook. Sometimes, I'll take specialty examples within those categories to help a preacher with a specific type of challenge.

To summarize: Think homiletics, not hermeneutics. Think genres, not specific texts. And think unusually challenging niches within those common genres rather than the usual fare. Add to this that our goal is not to help the preacher with preaching to different audiences, preaching under challenging circumstances,[13] or giving long examples of sermons. With this clarification, you may have a better understanding of the book in your hands.

Overview

What "genres" of difficult texts does this book wrestle with?

The first chapter focuses on "people lists" in the New Testament, usually found at the end of Paul's letters. I've already noted Romans 16 as an example, which mentions by name more than thirty different people in a list-like fashion. Are we to look for hidden clues in the meaning of these names, or does the preacher need to do additional work to discern the meaning between the lines? Can a sermon on names really stand on its own at the end of a book that dealt with magnificent topics such as justification, atonement, and election?

Chapter 2 deals with "entrances and exits," a clever way of saying epistolary introductions and conclusions. "Paul, called by the will of God. . . . To the church of God that is in such and such a city. . . . Grace to you and peace from God our Father and the Lord Jesus Christ." Should preachers

12. Two of my favorites are from Steven D. Mathewson: *The Art of Preaching Old Testament Narrative* (Grand Rapids: Baker Academic, 2002); *The Art of Preaching Old Testament Poetry* (Grand Rapids: Baker Academic, 2024).

13. For example, Bryan Chapell, ed., *The Hardest Sermons You'll Ever Have to Preach: Help from Trusted Preachers for Tragic Times* (Grand Rapids: Zondervan, 2011), covers a host of difficult circumstances in which preachers find themselves, such as preaching a funeral for the death of a child or preaching after a national crisis. This is an incredible resource that I would highly recommend, but this topic is outside the aims of this text.

lump these opening lines into the first *actual* paragraph of the epistle, or are these lines *actually* the first paragraph? Here, I hope to equip preachers to treat these openings and closings as carefully as they would any other text in the middle of the book.

The third chapter will handle a topic that you would be hard-pressed to find elsewhere: well-worn stories. Some biblical stories seem to have been preached a hundred times over. Who hasn't heard the story of Zacchaeus, or Jesus feeding the five thousand, or Peter trying to walk on water? How do preachers keep well-worn stories like these fresh in the ears of their audience? Even more challenging may be the texts typically used for Christmas and Easter, texts that must be preached once or twice a year, every year, year after year! Even seasoned pastors may tire of preaching the same stories over and over. This chapter gives several suggestions to keep old things fresh in the pulpit.

Next up are the "nuggets." My Old Testament book dealt with the "Goliaths"—long texts that defy easy division into multiple sermons. This volume will treat the opposite: short pericopes just a few verses long. Too often preachers and teachers use shorter texts to launch into topical sermons rather than preaching the actual text in front of them. How does a preacher stick to the text when it is so short?

Chapter 5 tackles a fearsome area indeed: textual criticism. Every seminary-trained pastor has wrestled with textual criticism in Greek or Hebrew (if not, get a new seminary). Most of the time, those discussions stay out of the pulpit. But what happens when a preacher faces John 8 or Mark 16 and wonders what to do with a text that may or may not be inspired? And what about those passages where the point of the text hinges on a word that has textual issues? This chapter seeks to equip preachers to speak to textual problems without losing their audience or becoming an accidental heretic.

Some texts present challenges not because of what they say but because of what they *use*. The New Testament frequently quotes, alludes to, echoes, and references the Old Testament. It also, at times, does similar things to noninspired, noncanonical books like 1 Enoch or 2 Maccabees or a Greek poet. Chapters 6–7 will show preachers and teachers how to help an audience with the hermeneutics of allusions and quotations, without either denigrating the Old Testament or excessively elevating a noncanonical text.

Other texts do indeed present challenges because of what they say. Chapters 8 and 9 will focus on enigmatic statements (such as women wearing head coverings "because of the angels" in 1 Cor 11:10) and politically incorrect texts—passages that are clear but also clearly offensive to those in our modern age and political climate. These chapters help preachers to speak confidently, yet with appropriate humility and sensitivity, when dealing with these potentially explosive topics.

The final chapter fittingly focuses on the end times. Most Christians are either overly fanatic about studying eschatology or too timid to even try—too few fall in between! Many preachers find Revelation way too intimidating to ever preach, and they may shudder when they come to the Olivet Discourse, wishing to just skip it and move on to Jesus's death. This chapter will encourage preachers and teachers to humbly, yet boldly, go where few dare to trod—into the realm of eschatological texts. I am not seeking to push a single eschatological scheme or agenda here. Other books are written to convince you of such things. Rather, I hope to play strictly in the field of homiletics—how do I *preach* these texts?

The New Testament is 260 chapters long. This book has ten chapters. Unsurprisingly, I cannot say everything there is to say about every difficult text of Scripture. But I hope that this book will give preachers and teachers some valuable insight on how to handle the many challenges that they will indeed encounter, if they are committed to biblical expository preaching.

So, if you're ready, grab your shovel and pick and let's begin excavating some gems from the people lists in the New Testament!

1

Preaching and Teaching People Lists

I used to watch a lot of MMA (mixed martial arts). Even in the days before it became uber-popular, I enjoyed watching the likes of Matt Hughes, Randy Couture, Chuck Liddell, and Anderson Silva make mincemeat of their opponents in the octagon.

Perhaps it indulged my flesh a bit too much, but we can argue the ethics of Christians watching fighting sports another day. My enjoyment of the sport turned into a monthly social event for my friends and me. As many as a dozen people would pile into my small living room and cheer late into the night for the pay-per-view cards.

The worst part of each night was the post-fight interview with famed announcer-turned-podcaster Joe Rogan.[1] After fighting for three long rounds, the exhausted winner would undergo an interview with Rogan. Though breathless and often injured, the competitor had to face a barrage of questions about his strategy and emotions after his fight. Most of these guys couldn't string together an intelligent sentence on their best days, so you can imagine how these conversations sounded after getting punched in the face for fifteen minutes.

We would all groan when, at the end of the interview, the fighter would inevitably hijack the microphone from Rogan and spew off a list of people he wanted to thank—everyone from the trainers, his fellow gym rats, his

---

1. Actually, the worst part was being subjected to endless commercials for video games, movies, beer, snack nuts, or whoever sponsored the event that evening. With a $80 plus pay-per-view price tag, why did I also have to sit through an hour of commercials?

mother, and wife and kids. Every now and then someone would throw Jesus Christ a bone and mention him (usually after dropping a few choice four-letter words).

This thirty-second "thank-you" tag at the end of the interview was something we endured, not enjoyed. Most of us used the time to refill our drinks or use the bathroom.

The end of some New Testament letters—especially of the Pauline variety—can feel like those post-fight "thank-you" lists. It's like reading aloud the end credits of a movie. You only endure the end credits if you know there's an extra scene at the end.

Consider the preacher who has worked through an exciting and challenging ten-week series in Colossians. Though only four chapters long, the book packs in quite a bit of theology and application. It spans Paul's rich prayer in the beginning (1:3–14) to his exaltation of the preeminent Christ (1:15–23) to his practical applications and commands that flow from believers' new identity in Christ (3:1–17)—and even includes a section on marriage, children, and slavery (3:18–4:1). What an exciting sermon series! It's a four-round UFC main event.

And then, the post-fight speech. The last major section of Colossians has eleven verses (4:7–17) and lists just as many personal names. A few we recognize, like Mark, Barnabas, and Luke. But who in the world are Tychicus, Aristarchus, Nympha, and Archippus? Are we supposed to have remembered these people from Acts?

It feels like time to refill my drink and go to the bathroom.

More Than Just a "Thank-You"

There are only a handful of extensive "people lists" in the New Testament, and most are found at the end of Pauline texts.[2] I do not include in this category those many places in the New Testament letters where the author mentions an individual outside of a formal list. Usually those come

---

2. Though the appendix in the back of this book has a list of each kind of difficult text, the "People Lists" is small enough to reproduce in full here: Rom 16:1–16, 21–23; 1 Cor 16:10–18; Col 4:7–17; 2 Tim 4:9–21; Titus 3:12–14; Phil 23–24; 1 Pet 5:12–13. You'll notice only the last one on this list comes from a non-Pauline source.

with a paragraph or a few verses of commendation or rebuke, which makes them easier to preach.[3] This chapter handles lists that are generally more extensive. These lists typically have less extensive discussion on each individual mentioned. They usually come at the end of the book. Thank-you speeches at the end of UFC main events are skippable; people lists at the end of New Testament epistles are not. Far from a "I want to thank" speech after a prize fight, these New Testament lists are inspired texts with a purpose.

These lists certainly have great historical and sociological value.[4] They add proof and reliability to the New Testament texts, demonstrating that they were not written in a vacuum and that real, contemporary people could confirm the words and authenticity of the letters. Today, a namedrop could lead to a quick Google search to find public information about that individual. Back in the apostle Paul's day, Google was not a thing, but data could still be fact-checked. Mentioning the well-known and well-off Aquila and Prisca at the end of 1 Corinthians (16:19) may lend some weight to Paul's contentious words and some reliability that Paul indeed wrote this letter. Paul is saying, "Don't believe me? Just ask Aquila and Prisca!"

But as preachers and teachers, we recognize that these lists have a function beyond just their historical value. One challenge in preaching these lists is figuring out what their purpose is. Like most things in the Bible, scholars divide over how these endings relate to the rest of the letter. We can boil down their opinions into two main views.

In one corner of the octagon, you have folks like Anders Eriksson, who argues that these letter endings should be read through the rhetorical func-

---

3. A few examples from Philippians: Paul mentions Epaphroditus in 2:25, followed by a few verses of commendation letting readers know more about him (2:25–30). Preachers can easily structure a sermon around Epaphroditus with all that Paul says of him. Later in the letter, Paul mentions two women notorious for their divisiveness—Euodia and Syntyche (4:2)—along with Paul's fellow worker Clement, whom he commends (4:3). Though only two verses, it's also possible and much easier to structure a sermon around these three people since Paul has much to say about them in such a short space.

4. Douglas J. Moo writes, "The list of names in this section does not make very interesting reading for most students of Romans," then he qualifies this by saying, "But for those few who are especially interested in the socioeconomic composition of the early church, it is a gold mine." *The Epistle to the Romans*, NICNT (Grand Rapids: Eerdmans, 1996), 918.

tion of a *peroration*, traditionally the final part of a speech.[5] The peroration has two main functions: to recapitulate the main points of the letter and to make one final emotional appeal to follow the contents of the letter.[6]

So, some scholars see a tight and purposeful connection between the ending of the letter and the content therein. To take Eriksson's own argument as an example—he sees six main themes in the body of 1 Corinthians:[7] Paul's redefinition of the Corinthians' charismatic giftedness, the building metaphor for the church community, the divine calling to be an eschatological people of God in fellowship with Jesus, the eschatological framework for the Christian life, the christological theme, and the issue of factionalism and unity.[8]

Eriksson then demonstrates how the last chapter of 1 Corinthians recaps these themes. For example, 16:15 recommends Stephanas to the church, which speaks to the theme of factionalism and unity by recommending him as an authoritative church leader. In another example, the imperative "stand firm in the faith" (16:13) reintroduces the building metaphor.[9] To follow this approach, preachers and teachers will need to be convinced that the letter's closing closely relates to the body of the letter.

And that's just the problem: In the opposite corner of the octagon, we have commentators like David E. Garland, who does not see a sustained argument in these lists but rather views them as a smattering of different exhortations and greetings.[10] At one point, Garland even argues that these lists have become like a Rorschach test—interpreters end up seeing exactly what they want to see.[11] This is a good caution. We must be careful not to

---

5. Anders Eriksson, *Traditions as Rhetorical Proof: Pauline Argumentation in 1 Corinthians* (Stockholm: Almqvist & Wiksell International, 1998). Eriksson's work is more recently championed by others like Anthony C. Thiselton, *The First Epistle to the Corinthians: A Commentary on the Greek Text*, NIGTC (Grand Rapids: Eerdmans, 2000), 1348–51.

6. Eriksson, *Traditions*, 283.

7. The technical term for the body of the letter is called the *argumentatio*. I would not recommend using such words from the pulpit unless you want to sound like a stuffy snob.

8. Eriksson, *Traditions*, 285–88.

9. Examples taken from Eriksson, 289–90.

10. David E. Garland, *1 Corinthians*, BECNT (Grand Rapids: Baker Academic, 2003), 764.

11. Garland, 764.

overread the theology of the entire book into the final greetings.[12] Couldn't Paul have greeted a few partners in ministry without having to stuff his theology into every "hello"?

Keeping both of these viewpoints in mind, I think we can at least agree that these people lists have some unifying themes, whether or not they relate so closely to the letter's body. Take a moment and skim through the people list in Romans 16.

> I commend to you our sister Phoebe, a servant of the church at Cenchreae, that you may welcome her in the Lord in a way worthy of the saints, and help her in whatever she may need from you, for she has been a patron of many and of myself as well.
>
> Greet Prisca and Aquila, my fellow workers in Christ Jesus, who risked their necks for my life, to whom not only I give thanks but all the churches of the Gentiles give thanks as well.
>
> Greet also the church in their house. Greet my beloved Epaenetus, who was the first convert to Christ in Asia.
>
> Greet Mary, who has worked hard for you.
>
> Greet Andronicus and Junia, my kinsmen and my fellow prisoners. They are well known to the apostles, and they were in Christ before me.
>
> Greet Ampliatus, my beloved in the Lord.
>
> Greet Urbanus, our fellow worker in Christ, and my beloved Stachys.
>
> Greet Apelles, who is approved in Christ. Greet those who belong to the family of Aristobulus.
>
> Greet my kinsman Herodion. Greet those in the Lord who belong to the family of Narcissus.
>
> Greet those workers in the Lord, Tryphaena and Tryphosa. Greet the beloved Persis, who has worked hard in the Lord.
>
> Greet Rufus, chosen in the Lord; also his mother, who has been a mother to me as well.

---

12. E.g., in the above example given by Eriksson, *Traditions*, 289–90, on the imperative "stand firm," 1 Corinthians 16:13 is the only place in the epistle where the word στήκω appears. This weakens the case that this is a purposeful revisit of Paul's previous arguments. If Paul intended to remind readers of his key arguments in 3:9–17 with the building metaphor, why not reuse a word from that text to strengthen the connection?

> Greet Asyncritus, Phlegon, Hermes, Patrobas, Hermas, and the brothers who are with them.
>
> Greet Philologus, Julia, Nereus and his sister, and Olympas, and all the saints who are with them.
>
> Greet one another with a holy kiss. All the churches of Christ greet you.

What did you notice? You can't help but hear a drumbeat throughout this passage:

> Greet Prisca and Aquila. (16:3)
>
> Greet Mary. (16:6)
>
> Greet Andronicus and Junia. (16:7)

And so on. Are you beginning to see the picture? Paul uses the word *greet* (ἀσπάζομαι) seventeen times in verses 3–16 and an additional four times in verses 21–23.

Is that not enough to say there's a unifying "theme" tying this section together?

Now, this does not mean that your "big idea" is necessarily, "Greet one another with a holy kiss"—though that might make an interesting end to the service! But if your message's main point has *nothing* to do with the warm fellowship that results from hard labor in ministry through the bond of Jesus Christ, then perhaps you have missed something.

How do we find the main point in each people list? It's simple: Preachers and teachers, you will need to study diligently enough to make your own determination. What is the point of the people list in 1 Corinthians 16? What about Romans 16? How much does it relate to the body of the letter?

Frankly, I don't care to give you my answers to those questions. That would be cheating. This book is not a commentary, nor do I hope it is used as a shortcut for your sermons. You've got to do the dirty work of exegesis yourself.

It's reasonable to assume that most preachers will not pick up 1 Corinthians and only preach chapter 16. It's not exactly the first passage from that book you would choose as a standalone sermon! This means, for the vast majority of preachers, you will have already worked through the book of 1 Corinthians and considered its main themes and subthemes.

Therefore, you should spend as much time studying 1 Corinthians 16 as you would any other challenging chapter in the book. Use good resources. This means you may need to shelve the cheaper, softcover application-oriented commentaries and use something with a hardcover that requires two hands to lift. Often these yield the best results.[13]

Once you've (1) preached through 1 Corinthians over several months and (2) carefully studied the final chapter, you should be able to reasonably conclude whether or not chapter 16 truly reflects the themes of the body. Now you're all set to preach.

Well, not quite. Maybe read to the end of this chapter to pick up a few more tips on dealing with these kinds of lists.

Preaching and Teaching People Lists

Let's step up to the pulpit now and consider some practical, focused advice on how to handle people lists homiletically.

Don't Get Caught Up in the Weeds

If you study as you should, you'll find *plenty* of buried treasure within these tedious lists. Probably too much for a single sermon. As is normally the case for any passage you study, if you put the proper amount of work into the text, much more of what you learn will land on the cutting room floor rather than making it into the sermon. No preacher can say everything they *could* say on any given Sunday with any given text.

When it comes to people lists, one of the unique temptations is to regurgitate all the historical and sociological data that you've uncovered in your studies throughout the week. A great deal of print in commentaries will focus on the following:

- What is the meaning of this name?
- Does this name have a Greek or Jewish background?

---

13. Please understand I'm not dismissing the value of the cheaper, softcover brands. They have their place on a pastor's shelf. But I fear a tendency for busy pastors and Bible teachers to shortcut the richer, more detailed resources in favor of resources that do too much of the work for them (sometimes, unsurprisingly, with results not tethered as tightly to the text itself).

- Was this name common among slaves/freedmen or perhaps part of the upper class?
- Where else is this individual mentioned in Scripture?

Only some of these questions matter sometimes. Which ones and when? You'll have to be the judge of that!

An example will help. Romans 16:8 reads rather simply, "Greet Ampliatus, my beloved in the Lord." Not exactly anyone's life verse or favorite Bible hero, but a quick survey of a few commentaries will nonetheless turn up a mini treasure trove of information.

Ampliatus was a Greek name. It was a name found among slaves, so he was probably a slave or freedman. This Ampliatus could possibly be the same individual as the name found on a catacomb inscription.[14] Romans 16:8 is the only place he shows up in the Bible. Paul uses the phrase "beloved of God" (NASB) in 1:7 to speak of all believers in Rome. Paul is fond of the word *beloved* (ἀγαπητός), and it shows up twenty-six times in his letters, always in reference to believers. Four believers are singled out in Romans 16 as "beloved": Epaenetus (16:5), Ampliatus (16:8), Stachys (16:9), and Persis (16:12).

I suppose a pastor *could* say all that. There would be at least one eager college student in the pew furiously writing it all down in her church journal.

But to adapt a quote from the brilliant mathematician Ian Malcolm, "Your pastors were so preoccupied with whether or not they *could*, they didn't stop to think if they *should*."

Ask yourself: Am I giving this historical information to make myself sound smart and well-studied or perhaps to give the audience a cool little tidbit? Does this serve some greater theological or practical purpose to mention this? Will this information lead to life change?

Yes, preacher, you *could* note that Ampliatus was probably a slave or a freed slave based on the use of his name in antiquity. You *could* comment on how archaeologists found his name in a catacomb. But does this really matter for the sermon?

Sermons are not running commentaries intended to share all the facts one could share about that verse. They also aren't exhaustive historical or sociological lessons.

---

14. Moo, *Romans*, 924.

But here's the tricky part: Sometimes, you *should* indeed say a few words about this kind of thing!

Let's back it up with a verse from Romans 16:7: "Greet Andronicus and Junia, my kinsmen and my fellow prisoners. They are well known to the apostles, and they were in Christ before me."

In this verse, names become *very* important.

The controversy centers around Junia—whoever he or she is. I say "he or she" because that's controversy number one. Does the verse say Junia, a female, who is probably the wife of Andronicus (see ESV, KJV)? Or does the verse say Junias, a male, who is probably the ministry partner of Andronicus (see NASB)? The difference is in the accents.

- Junias (male) is spelled'Ἰουνιᾶν.
- Junia (female) is spelled'Ἰουνίαν.

Both words have the same consonants. The difference is in the accent over the latter pair of vowels.

What's the big deal? Normally, not much. But in some translations, the text says of the two individuals that they are not just well known "to" the apostles but rather "are outstanding *among* the apostles" (emphasis mine; NASB; cf. KJV; NLT).

The word "among" *may* imply that they are included with the other apostles. If so, and if the text reads "Junia" instead of "Junias" (which seems most likely, in my examination of the evidence), then we have here a female apostle. That's controversy number two.

Now, "apostle" doesn't necessarily mean "apostle" in the official sense of the word. It sometimes refers to messengers (2 Cor 8:23). So even if controversy number one settles on female Junia and controversy number two settles on "among" the apostles, it still does not necessitate that "apostle" means "apostle" and Junia is a female apostle.[15]

Again, the goal here isn't to solve the problem for you. You've got to study deep enough to know where the issues lie and which comments to

---

15. For further information on this debate, see the excellent discussion by John Piper and Wayne Grudem, "An Overview of Central Concerns: Questions and Answers," in *Recovering Biblical Manhood & Womanhood: A Response to Evangelical Feminism*, ed. John Piper and Wayne Grudem (Wheaton, IL: Crossway, 2006), 79–81.

make as you preach. Taking five minutes to discuss Ampliatus's slavery background may not be the best use of pulpit time. In Junia(s)'s case, wherever the preacher lands on the issue significantly impacts one's belief in apostolic authority and the complementarian/egalitarian debate. Thus, it may be necessary to spend a few minutes here.

But, once more I caution, *briefly*. The point of the sermon is not to argue for a complementarian view of apostolic authority. Save that for the theology classroom. If you can get there quickly, fine. But don't lose sight of the bigger picture. Become an expert at weeding out what is ancillary from what is necessary.

Watch Carefully for Unifying Themes

How do we avoid getting lost in the weeds of historical and sociological details? For each passage, think about the unifying theme. Some call this the "big idea."[16] Often it's not *who* Paul mentions, but *what he says* about who he mentions that becomes the unifying theme of the people list.

I already gave one example of the multitude of "Greet so-and-so" statements in Romans 16. But this isn't the only approach one could take with this passage. Nearly all the people in this list have Greek names, most of whom were likely slaves, freedmen, or their descendants. What does this tell us about the advance of the gospel? A quick refresher on verses such as Romans 1:14, 16, and 10:12 will remind the congregation why it's so significant that Paul ends his epistle by listing more than two dozen names, most of whom were probably not Jewish.

Paul's list in 2 Timothy 4 sounds quite different. There, it's not just a lovefest. Along with ministerial gems like Titus and Priscilla and Luke, in the twilight hours of the apostle's life, he's wrestling with knuckleheads like Demas and Alexander the coppersmith.[17] This mix of godly servants and

---

16. This term was popularized by Haddon Robinson's book on expository preaching, *Biblical Preaching*. Though recently some have pushed against this concept of preaching the "big idea" (e.g., Abraham Kuruvilla, "Time to Kill the Big Idea? A Fresh Look at Preaching," *JETS* 61 [2018]: 825–46), Robinson's book is still a standard that should occupy the shelf of every preacher.

17. If you don't know who these men are, pastors, stick around in your pulpit for a few more years. You'll meet them soon enough.

challenging opponents speaks not only into the realities of ministry but reflects some of Paul's previous warnings in the same epistle (e.g., 4:3–4).

Consider the larger themes that bind together the list of names. There, preacher, is your sermon.

Two Contradictory Rules of Thumb

How do I know if I should spend three minutes or thirty minutes on any given person in these lists? Generally speaking, use two rules of thumb to guide your sermon or lesson: (1) Spend proportionate time on each individual based on how much space the text devotes to them, and (2) spend more time on more notable figures in the New Testament.

Regarding the first rule of thumb, it may sound like a no-brainer to spend more time on the individuals the text focuses on. But put it to the test in the 2 Timothy 4 list and you'll see why it's important.

In 2 Timothy 4:19, Paul writes, "Greet Prisca and Aquila, and the household of Onesiphorus." This verse is loaded with famous people! It has the wealthy couple who make cameo appearances in several New Testament books and letters[18] and also Onesiphorus, who (along with Philemon) is the subject of an entire New Testament letter (albeit a short one). What *could* a preacher say about these three individuals? Plenty, if we collect all the different things the New Testament says about them.

But what does *Paul* say? Eight words total (in Greek), including two "ands."

Do preachers need to spend a whole sermon on this verse, or half a sermon, or even ten minutes of a sermon? Certainly not if they are preaching half of the final chapter of 2 Timothy. If Paul does not stop to spend time fleshing out these characters, why should we? It might help to give a *little* background to them—after all, Paul's audience would've known a thing or two about their ministry and history. But we should be careful not to allow things to dominate the sermon that do not dominate the text.

The second rule of thumb (spend more time on more notable figures in the New Testament) has potential to totally contradict everything I just wrote about the first rule of thumb! However, notice that key word "*more* time," not "*most* of the time" or "*all* of the time." Consider again Prisca,

---

18. Acts 18:1–3, 18, 26; Rom 16:3; 1 Cor 16:19; 2 Tim 4:19.

Aquila, and Onesiphorus. I would be shocked to sit through a sermon that mentions these individuals without elaborating on their rich history at all. Shocked and perhaps a bit disappointed.

The epistle's original audience would have had a number of facts flash through their minds at the mention of these names. If I said the name, "Mike Tyson," a number of word associations might instantly pop into your mind—heavyweight boxing champion, face tattoo, ear biter, etc. These associations would be immediate and almost subconscious.

Fast-forward two thousand years from now. If I said the name "Mike Tyson" to people living in AD 4025, they would probably have no clue to whom I was referring. I may need a moment to explain what would inspire a man to get a face tattoo.

That's how some of these names work. Mention Prisca and Aquila to a first-century Christian and they would know who you're talking about. They've had dinner with them. The couple visited their church and taught a Bible study. Paul doesn't need to elaborate on them because not only do the other letters and books of the New Testament do so, but Paul's readers *know* them.[19]

But *our* people—twenty-first-century people—don't always know them. So a word of explanation sometimes is needed.

Now, the wise reader will notice the potential for contradiction between these two rules. To illustrate, compare 2 Timothy 4:11 with 4:14–17. In 4:11, Paul writes, "Luke alone is with me." In 4:14–17, Paul details the horrors of dealing with Alexander the coppersmith, the damage the man did to his ministry, and the result of the believers deserting him.

If you're just preaching the text in 2 Timothy 4, you'll have a lot more to say about Alexander than you will about Luke. But if you lean on the rest

19. I would encourage preachers to use caution and restraint with names that appear multiple times but could potentially be different people. Remember, just like in today's culture, some people share a name! For example, there are at least three different people named "Justus" in the New Testament: the one in Acts 1:23 (also called Barsabbas; he was the runner-up for the vacant twelfth apostle position); the one in Acts 18:7 (Titius Justus, who lived next door to the synagogue); and the one in Colossians 4:11 (also called Jesus, but not *that* Jesus, which only further illustrates my point!). See Douglas J. Moo, *The Letters to the Colossians and to Philemon*, PNTC (Grand Rapids: Eerdmans, 2008), 340.

of the New Testament, you'll have a lot more to say about Luke than about Alexander.[20] If this were a *Choose Your Own Adventure* story, which path would you take?

My advice: When there's a potential contradiction between these two rules of thumb, lean on the text in front of you. Preach the text, not the person. Remember that to preach the passage is not to get hung up on saying all you can say about each individual. An expository sermon on Romans 16 does not spend thirty to forty minutes tracing every cameo appearance of Aquila and Priscilla in the Bible. You'll naturally give the couple a few extra minutes; after all, they *are* sort of Bible-famous, or at least much more famous than Phlegon (whose name sounds like something stuck in my throat) or Patrobas, who are both found in Romans 16:14.

In fact, all the advice in this chapter assumes that you are actually preaching or teaching a passage, not doing a topical sermon on an individual. Therefore, even if you can potentially say a whole lot about a person, if the text does not give you much reason to dive into their background and history, it may be better to season the sermon with just a hint of historical flavor before moving on to the individuals the text *does* indeed spend more time on.

Focus on Potential Application

If you haven't caught the point yet, I'll say it one more time: These people lists in the New Testament were not written to give preachers an opportunity to exercise their historical or biblical knowledge about what each name in the list means or to do a "Where's Waldo?" search throughout the Bible to find other places where these people pop up. The biblical authors mention these people for a reason. Here are a few potential roads to application in these sermons:

(1) *Commendations reveal behaviors that all believers should emulate.* Apparently, Paul had plenty of friends. I'm sure he would've had a large

---

20. Some scholars believe Alexander the coppersmith from 2 Timothy 4:14–17 could be the same Alexander mentioned in 1 Timothy 1:20. This could very well be the case, considering what terrible things Paul says about each Alexander. However, it cannot be proven, and either way, my point remains the same: The New Testament still says a lot more about Luke than Alexander, even if both 1 and 2 Timothy refer to the same Alexander.

following on Facebook had he lived in the digital age (assuming he would have a Facebook page, which admittedly does assume a lot). He has lots of pleasant things to say about these friends, all of which we would hope someone could say about us. Though I caution my students against undiscerningly replicating the behavior of the characters in a biblical narrative, the epistles actually invite us to consider these lists in this way. Near the end of the people list in 1 Corinthians 16, Paul says, "Give recognition to such people" (v. 18). This invites us to consider these individuals as examples to emulate.

Paul calls Tychicus a "beloved brother" and "faithful minister" and "fellow servant in the Lord" (Col 4:7). Who wouldn't want these things to be said about them? Every one of these titles will preach. Tychicus is not just a brother—he's a *beloved* brother. Beloved by the Lord, certainly, but the thrust here is beloved by Paul and all those who came in contact with him. I'm sure there are a few people like this in your church. If so, don't be afraid to mention them, maybe even in the sermon. (At least write them an email letting them know you thought of them!)

Tychicus is not just a minister—he's a *faithful* minister. There are plenty of ministers out there today, many of whom are far from faithful. Faithful ministers stick around when the going gets tough. Faithful ministers show their commitment not only to the Lord but also to other people. They faithfully show up, faithfully preach, faithfully love and forgive and shepherd through good times and bad times. If you have a faithful minister among you, make sure to let your congregation know—unless that minister is you. It's usually wise not to be the hero of your own sermon; it's better to let someone else recognize this about you.

Tychicus is not just a servant—he's a *fellow* servant *in the Lord*.[21] That means he serves together with Paul in the same gospel ministry. There are many servants in the church, but a servant who serves alongside you, sharing your sorrows and your joys and your hardships, is a true brother indeed. If you have a few fellow servants that come to mind, praise the Lord for them.

---

21. Moo, *Colossians*, 335, notes that the phrase "in the Lord" actually connects with both "faithful minister" and "fellow servant" in Greek.

These commendations, you see, will preach. We have here with Tychicus a potential three-part sermon—or at least a three-part application within a sermon—to encourage your church.[22]

(2) *Condemnations reveal behaviors that all believers should avoid and be aware of.* Sometimes a biblical writer mentions a person for the exact opposite reason of those he commends to the church. These are not only behaviors to avoid in our own lives; they are behaviors to which we should be alert and guard against encroaching into our church. After all, though wolves do come from outside, more often they rise up from *within* (Acts 20:29).

We've already talked about Alexander the coppersmith, that dirty rascal (2 Tim 4:14–15). But consider Demas, about whom Paul says he was "in love with this present world" and he "has deserted me and gone to Thessalonica" (2 Tim 4:10). The behavior of Demas has caused a gap in Paul's ministry world. Paul needs help. He needs friendship and support. In the previous verse, Paul urges Timothy, "Do your best to come to me soon" (4:9). Notice that verse 10 begins with "For" (γάρ), indicating the reason that Paul is so urgently asking Timothy to join him. Demas has left him hanging.

Why did Demas leave? Because the man was in love with this present world. His love for the world and its values and its temptations overcame his love for Christ and Paul and the ministry of the gospel. His love for the world revealed his true heart. His desertion speaks to his true allegiance.

It happens all the time. Men and women leave ministry positions to run after all kinds of temporal pleasures. Maybe ministry gets too hard for them; maybe they never really were committed to Christ but only involved because of the initial "rush" of acceptance into the Christian community. God will be the judge. But the world entices people out of their pastorates daily. The church should be warned to keep their thoughts on the cross, not on the world. Be in the world, not of it. Keep your eyes on the finish line.[23]

---

22. There's a lot more that we can say about Tychicus from other parts of the New Testament (Acts 20:4; Eph 6:21; 2 Tim 4:12; Titus 3:12). But the preacher needs to consider what fits within the context of the larger sermon to know how much to say about him.

23. Demas's behavior also came at a terrible time, as at least two others in Paul's ministry circle had recently left, though they left for different reasons than Demas. It is clear that Demas was the only one who is said to have "deserted" Paul, while Paul describes Crescens leaving for Galatia and Titus going to Dalmatia (2 Tim 4:10).

Churches need to be aware of people untested in ministry. We must all be vigilant and watchful for people who seem to be tempted by the world. It's a great ministry to help a brother or sister who is straying from the truth and pull them back to reality.

So, even statements of condemnation or censure have value for modern audiences.

(3) *Paul's relationships with his colleagues and friends reveal how to properly relate to friends, missionaries, and even enemies.* How Paul thinks of and interacts with these people reveals a lot. The names in 2 Timothy 4:9–21 speak to how much Paul appreciates his ministry colleagues and fellow believers in Christ. The fact that he's lonely reveals how much he values these people in his life. He can't do ministry the same without them. He may not *need* them, but he certainly *wants* them around. Though I'm sure Luke was a great companion to Paul, he alone is not enough to supply what Paul needs to reach the finish line (4:11).

Do we value friendship in the same way? Have we built ourselves a network of friends (real friends, not social media friends) who support, encourage, and uplift us as much as Paul's? These are questions that the church is increasingly challenged with as the world replaces meaningful relationships with clicks and likes and conversations hidden behind a screen. Christians value true relationships.

Consider how often Paul views these friendships through the eyes of ministry. They are not there simply to serve him or make him feel more comfortable or help him pass the time in jail until his next stint of persecution. They are "fellow" workers and "fellow" servants and "fellow" prisoners. He often mentions a brother or sister coming to visit (e.g., 1 Cor 16:10, 12). In 1 Corinthians 16:10–11, he shows concern about how Timothy will be received by the Corinthian church and how they can help him as he travels in dependence on the churches.

These are missional concerns. They model what our partnerships between churches and between missionaries and other pastors should look like. Too often we treat other churches or denominations like competition in town. Rather (assuming they are evangelicals preaching the gospel), we

---

Even though these latter two left for presumably good reasons, the timing of their departures along with Demas's desertion left Paul feeling quite lonely.

should strive to cooperate for the sake of furthering God's kingdom. Take a page out of Paul's book and urge your church to consider how they're doing in this area.

Even Paul's relationship with his persecutors and opponents in ministry has edifying value for the church. Paul isn't afraid to call out a person by name and warn the churches of these potentially divisive or heretical individuals. Some churches need to grow bolder in the way they protect their flock from dangerous individuals. Every church has or will have wolves, if they're faithful in ministry. Paul keeps his churches aware of the threats arising from both within and outside the flock. So should we.

(4) *People lists give examples of healthy fellowship.* Churches love to throw around the word *fellowship*. It makes everything sound more biblical. Inviting men out to a "fellowship" sounds like we accomplished something more spiritual than if we invited them to what actually takes place—gorging ourselves on roasted pig flesh while throwing bean bags through holes in a slanted slot of wood. It's a good time, but are we doing the Lord's work? Is it actually fellowship?[24]

The people lists in the New Testament give us a glimpse into what true, healthy fellowship looks like. True fellowship results in a spirit that is refreshed (1 Cor 16:18). True fellowship is coated in love (16:14). True fellowship is immersed in rich encouragement, like when Paul can't help but note how certain individuals "worked hard in the Lord" (Rom 16:12) or "risked their necks for my life" (16:4). Biblical fellowship is rich, meaningful, and all about Christ, and it's modeled in the people lists in the New Testament.

Several times Paul ends his letters with a command for believers to give one another a "holy kiss" (Rom 16:16; 1 Cor 16:20; 2 Cor 13:12; 1 Thess 5:26; Peter calls it "a kiss of love"; 1 Pet 5:14). This, of course, was a symbol of fellowship and love and family among the churches. It was holy, not sexual, though at times it was perverted toward that end.[25] This expression of love

24. I'm not saying that true fellowship can't be enjoyed over bacon burgers and cornhole. I'm only pointing out that true fellowship in the Bible seemed to center on ministry and even at times suffering rather than mindless fun activities.

25. Thiselton, *1 Corinthians*, 1346. As a teenager, I used to joke that giving one another a holy kiss was best partnered with the biblical practice of using "tongues." Thankfully, I have matured out of those kinds of jokes and would never put them in print today.

reveals the appropriate intimacy among the believers. There is a feeling of celebration and joy in these lists that should contagiously affect your sermons and, in turn, contagiously affect your church. If your church leaves the sermon bored to death because of the history lesson on names you just delivered, you have missed the appropriate *pathos* of the list.

(5) *People lists model spiritual concern*. These lists reveal a concern from the writer to the audience that penetrates much deeper than our typical surface-level "How ya doin'?" Hardly a word is spoken of the physical ailments of these people—ailments that paradoxically tend to dominate most of our prayer requests today.[26] Instead, we see a much more concentrated focus on spiritual issues, like the refreshment of someone's spirit (1 Cor 16:18), or the urge for proper encouragement (Col 4:8), or the need to show grace where it is necessary (2 Tim 4:16).[27]

Paul's focus was often ministry related. He was concerned for these people as it related to the successful fulfillment of his ministry and theirs. "Get Mark and bring him with you, for he is very useful to me for ministry" (4:11). Beware of Alexander the coppersmith, "for he strongly opposed our message" (4:15). Help Timothy on his way in peace, because he is doing the work of the Lord (1 Cor 16:10–11). And so on.

These are not just people Paul wanted to give a special shout-out to at the end of his championship fight with Rome. After going three rounds with the Colossians, a few warnings and thank-yous were most appropriate. Through these individuals, he continued his encouragement to the church, his warnings, his admonitions. Though these people are all long dead, may their names continue to edify our churches today.

---

26. Again, not that physical problems are unimportant to God and not that they're too "unspiritual" to pray about. We do see a few mentions of physical issues in these lists, like when Paul leaves behind Trophimus in Miletus because he was ill (2 Tim 4:20). But these concerns are few and far between.

27. Let's not forget the concern to read more books (2 Tim 4:13). I'm pretty sure that's my life verse.

2

Preaching and Teaching Entrances and Exits

It was pouring rain on my thirty-ninth birthday. Because of the weather, we decided to stay in town and settled on eating my birthday dinner at a local seafood restaurant.

I love seafood. I can eat it all day. I enjoy just about every kind of fish, crustacean, and mollusk in God's good ocean. That's why it was so challenging to choose just one entrée on the menu. Do I go with something classic, like a salmon or rainbow trout? Am I feeling the shrimp and scallop skewer? Maybe a nice lobster tail or seafood pasta? Truth is, it all looked good! But I eventually settled on an appetizer. Two, in fact: the crab soup and bang-bang shrimp. The appetizers were enough to fill me—with leftovers for the next day. And I knew that when I returned home, a nice cake was waiting for me.

Appetizers and desserts are not a meal's normal main course. Traditionally, they are the entrances and exits of the meal, not the meal itself. A well-chosen appetizer shared across a table awakens the palate and whets the appetite for the rest of the courses to come. And a delicious sugary dessert concludes the meal with the proper touch of sweetness.

Appetizers and desserts can sometimes overshadow the main course due to their greatness. I'm sure you can remember a meal or two where you left talking about the stuff that came before or after the main dish. Some restaurants pride themselves on their appetizers, and some diners show up just for the dessert.

What opens or closes a meal should complement the main course. Appetizers should excite the diner for what is to come, and desserts should leave one feeling full and satisfied. The same should be the case with the appetizers and desserts of the epistolary world: the entrances and exits of a letter.

A Grand Entrance

"Entrances and exits" is a clever way of saying epistolary introductions and conclusions. Most epistles have both to some degree.

Right out of the gate, I want to clarify what kind of entrances this chapter will *not* cover. This chapter will not focus on introductions like Hebrews 1:1–4. Preacher, if you can't build a sermon around the first four verses of Hebrews, this isn't the homiletics book you need right now. The same applies to other theologically packed "cold openings" like 1 John 1:1–4. Both texts have more than enough for a sermon, although they may be difficult for other reasons. This chapter, however, focuses on the more seemingly mundane openings.

Also, this chapter will primarily deal with epistles, particularly Pauline epistles, with some exceptions. The Gospels and Acts have entrances, but they are decidedly different from Paul's typical letter introductions. Matthew's begins with a genealogy.[1] Mark apparently hates Christmas and skips right past Jesus's birth story, starting his Gospel right at John the Baptist's ministry. Luke devotes a few verses to his opening, both in his Gospel and in Acts; but again, these have quite a different flavor from Paul's introductions. And John—you can build a whole sermon series around John's introduction! John 1:1–18 is one of the most theologically rich statements in the entire Bible.

The introductions to narratives all contribute something unique and obvious to the stories that follow. For that reason, we will focus on the epistolary introductions of the New Testament, most of which follow a standard formula.

Consider Paul's entrances. Every single Pauline book begins with the same word: Paul.[2] Sometimes Paul has a coauthor or amanuensis who joins him, like Timothy (2 Cor; Phil; Col; 1–2 Thess; Phlm) and Silvanus (1–2 Thess). Non-Pauline texts start similarly, with the exception of Hebrews and 1 John.[3]

---

1. For preaching genealogies, see Murawski, *Preaching Difficult Texts*, 15–33.

2. I am assuming all thirteen letters traditionally assigned to Paul are his. This is not the place for an extended defense of this subject. For more on Pauline authorship of individual books, most academic commentaries have extended discussions in their introductions and are a good starting point for those new to the conversation.

Also contrary to some modern scholarship, I attribute Petrine authorship to 2 Peter. On this, see the excellent discussion in Thomas R. Schreiner, *1, 2 Peter, Jude*, NAC 37 (Nashville: B&H, 2003), 255–76.

3. Second and 3 John do not identify "John" as the writer but "the elder," churning up considerable debate regarding his identity. For a helpful, brief summary of

After identifying the author and coauthor(s), Paul often has a further tag identifying himself: "a servant of Christ Jesus, called to be an apostle, set apart for the gospel of God" (Rom 1:1); "an apostle of Christ Jesus by the will of God" (2 Cor 1:1; Eph 1:1; Col 1:1; 2 Tim 1:1); etc. James, Peter, and Jude do the same: "James, a servant of God and of the Lord Jesus Christ" (Jas 1:1); "Peter, an apostle of Jesus Christ" (1 Pet 1:1); "Jude, a servant of Jesus Christ and brother of James" (Jude 1).

The next step is usually to address the audience. Sometimes this is short and sweet: "To the churches of Galatia" (Gal 1:2); "To Timothy, my beloved child" (2 Tim 1:2); "To the twelve tribes in the Dispersion" (Jas 1:1). Sometimes it comes with considerably more flourish, like the description of the Corinthians as "those sanctified in Christ Jesus, called to be saints together with all those who in every place call upon the name of our Lord Jesus Christ, both their Lord and ours" (1 Cor 1:2).

Paul's introductions then end with a variation of his typical greeting: "Grace to you and peace from God our Father and the Lord Jesus Christ." Others, like James, take a more abbreviated route: "Greetings!" (Jas 1:1).

Though introductions are fairly predictable, exits show a little more variety.

A Graceful Exit

Like the entrances, this chapter will put aside the narrative books and focus on the epistles. Narratives have their own unique exits that work differently than the epistles. Matthew closes with the Great Commission. If you can't build a sermon on that, please step down from the pulpit. Mark's exit will be dealt with in chapter 5 due to its infamous textual issue. Luke and John both have extended post-resurrection appearances of Christ. Acts just kind of ends.[4]

There are a few common conventions in epistolary closings. They are nowhere near as consistent and orderly as the entrances. Because of this

---

the debate, see D. A. Carson and Douglas J. Moo, *An Introduction to the New Testament* (Grand Rapids: Zondervan, 2005), 670–75. I take "the elder" to be a moniker for John the apostle.

4. Or rather, it just kind of keeps on going. The closing word of the book is ἀκωλύτως, "without hindrance," indicating the continual progress of the gospel that extends far beyond the events narrated.

variation, this chapter will focus mostly on entrances, as the exits often offer enough of a doxology or unique well-wishes to give the preacher something meaty to wrestle with in the pulpit.

However, it might help to mention a few commonalities many exits share. Four of Paul's letters have a form of the command "Greet one another with a holy kiss" (Rom 16:16; 1 Cor 16:20; 2 Cor 13:12; 1 Thess 5:26).[5] Apparently, Paul liked to smooch.

Many letters—especially Paul's—end with a few personal greetings to specific individuals or churches. We already dealt with these in the last chapter. These personal greetings are often interspersed with some final commands—sometimes delivered in staccato fashion.

Except for Romans and 2 Corinthians, every letter of Paul ends with some variation of "The grace of the Lord Jesus be with you." Romans ends with an explosive doxology; 2 Corinthians ends with a barrage of imperatives and a final greeting. Many of the General Epistles end similarly.[6]

Preachers must learn to leverage these seemingly skippable entrances and exits to their advantage in a sermon series. There are better ways to handle them than simply breezing past entrances to get to the "good stuff" that comes after or skipping exits in order to close out a series. For smaller epistles, the entrances and exits make up a significant portion of the letter itself. Second John has thirteen verses. Five of these verses are introduction and closing, consisting of more than one-third of the letter!

How Do They Work?

We have seen that most New Testament authors begin their epistles with a noticeable pattern: author(s), audience, greeting. This corresponds to typical Greco-Roman letter introductions. If you've ever mailed a physical letter (and that's a big *if*, considering the digital age in which we live), you probably put the name of the recipient at the top, included the date in the right corner, and started with some kind of greeting before moving to

5. Peter also has a variation: "Greet one another with the kiss of love" (1 Pet 5:14).

6. Revelation ends with the words: "The grace of the Lord Jesus be with you all. Amen" (22:21). I chose not to include Revelation in my examples in this chapter since it gets much attention in chapter 10.

the body of the letter. Then you signed your name at the bottom, perhaps after a few XOXOs.

We have conventions; Paul and his ministry partners did too. But did these entrances have any more significance than just following a typical pattern? Some think so.

In his book *Neglected Endings: The Significance of the Pauline Letter Closings*, Jeffrey A. D. Weima convincingly argues that though the Pauline closings followed many of the rhetorical conventions of the day, the grace benediction of many of Paul's letters was a new development and uniquely Pauline.[7] Furthermore, similar to Greco-Roman and Semitic letter endings, which demonstrate a general relationship between the closings and the contents of letters, Paul's letters also show a correlation between their closings and the arguments within. However, Paul's endings are decidedly more focused on echoing major themes addressed in his letters.[8]

Many would reason that at least some of the epistolary introductions work in the same way, though as chapter 1 cautioned regarding the people lists, we must guard against eisegeting themes into the entrances. But it's hard to dispute that when Paul begins his fiery letter to the Galatians with a firm statement about the origin of his apostleship—"Paul, an apostle—not from men nor through man, but through Jesus Christ and God the Father, who raised him from the dead" (Gal 1:1)—he is establishing his authority to speak as forcibly as he does throughout the letter.

Personally, I find that in some cases—like Galatians—Paul's introductions do directly relate to the rest of the letter. But there are times that they

---

7. Jeffrey A. D. Weima, *Neglected Endings: The Significance of the Pauline Letter Closings*, JSNTSup 101 (Sheffield: Sheffield Academic, 1994), 154.

8. Weima, 237–39, writes in his conclusion: "Paul's letter closings consist of several epistolary conventions, all of which exhibit a high degree of formal and structural consistency, thereby testifying to the care with which these final sections have been constructed. . . . For although Paul clearly was influenced by the epistolary practices of his day, he did not at all feel bound or limited to existing writing practices. . . . The most significant feature of Paul's letter closings, however, is the way in which they echo major concerns and themes dealt with in their respective letter bodies. . . . The closings serve as an hermeneutical spotlight, highlighting the central concerns of the apostle in his letters and illuminating our understanding of these key themes and issues. The letter closings of Paul, therefore, can no longer be ignored. Instead, they must play an important role in any examination and interpretation of Paul's letters."

may not. For example, consider Paul's opening statement to the Philippians: "Paul and Timothy, servants of Christ Jesus, To all the saints in Christ Jesus who are at Philippi, with the overseers and deacons: Grace to you and peace from God our Father and the Lord Jesus Christ" (Phil 1:1–2). Paul also calls himself a "servant of Christ Jesus" in Romans 1:1 and a "servant of God" in Titus 1:1. He addresses five other churches as "saints."[9] His "grace to you and peace" line shows up in some form in nearly every epistle.

The only major standout of this greeting is "with the overseers and deacons." If all of Paul's openings relate directly to the body of the letter, we might expect to hear something in the letter about overseers and deacons. Yet we do not. Not one word. And it does not seem that Paul needs to wield the authority of these church leaders to address the Philippians, since this is such a "happy" letter with much encouragement and little rebuke.

The point is that we find more evidence of the exits relating to the body of the letter than the entrances. Some entrances indeed have a lot to say and anticipate the author's arguments. Some probably not so much. Either way, far from being just a mundane way of opening and closing a letter, each entrance and each exit gives a unique gift and opportunity for the preacher to introduce and close an expository series. Here is some advice on how to leverage these portions of letters.

Preaching and Teaching Entrances

Consider Whether to Treat Entrances Separately or with Additional Content

The New Testament has twenty-one separate letters, not counting the narratives and Revelation. For each letter, preachers and teachers will need to determine whether to treat an entrance as a stand-alone sermon or to preach it along with whatever comes after it. I have twenty-one opinions on how I would deal (and have dealt) with each epistle's opening, but you'll have to apply wisdom to your unique style and congregational context. Maybe a few examples, though, wouldn't hurt to illustrate how this might work.

All preachers needs to preach Ephesians at some point in their life. I'm convinced of it. But how do you begin a series in the book? The first two

9. Romans 1:7; 1 Cor 1:2; 2 Cor 1:1; Eph 1:1; Col 1:2.

verses are fairly standard: "Paul, an apostle of Christ Jesus by the will of God, To the saints who are in Ephesus, and are faithful in Christ Jesus: Grace to you and peace from God our Father and the Lord Jesus Christ" (Eph 1:1–2).

It's the next sentence that slays.

If you've taken Greek past the first year, you're probably aware that Ephesians 1:3–14 is a single mega-sentence (and you've probably had to diagram it).[10] It is the longest in Ephesians, and if I remember my Greek class correctly, the longest in the New Testament. And it's every bit as magisterial as it is long, dwelling on topics like predestination, spiritual blessings, adoption, redemption, and eternal security, just to name a few.

Even though it's a single sentence, and thus a single contained thought, preachers can easily spend several weeks on it before moving to the next mega-sentence: 1:15–23.

It is challenging enough to determine if and how to break up 1:3–14 in the pulpit. Do you really want to add two more verses (1:1–2) as well as introduce a sermon series on top of that? Often, introducing a series includes giving reasons for why you've chosen this book out of all sixty-six options and providing some historical and cultural context to put the book's message into perspective, along with a few other odds and ends.[11] Thus, for Ephesians, it would probably be better to focus on the first two verses as a stand-alone sermon or lesson than rush into the first paragraph or sentence of material.

I would give the same advice for Romans for a different reason: Paul's "normal" introduction is seven verses long! It covers a range of issues: apostolic calling, Old Testament prophecies, the Davidic Messiah, the resurrection, and the gospel mission to the nations. You might actually be hard-pressed to get through the introduction in a single sermon.[12]

---

10. Our English translations tend to break up 1:3–14 into multiple sentences and sometimes even multiple paragraphs.

11. At the beginning of a sermon or teaching series, I often give the church an idea about how long I anticipate the series will run and hint about what kind of theological themes will be found in the book, along with what practical topics it will address. The goal is to get them excited about committing to read and study the book over the next few weeks and months. Additionally, I often like to challenge the church to memorize a significant portion of the book, which might take a few minutes of explanation. Sometimes, however, I punt that to another week.

12. John Piper took five weeks to work through Romans 1:1–7. D. Martyn Lloyd-Jones spent more than a dozen!

Now time for the opposite advice. Don't feel pressured to spend a whole sermon on two verses. Not every introduction to a letter requires a whole sermon. Does every sermon series in a Pauline epistle need to open with a detailed theological explanation of what grace, mercy, and peace mean? Maybe, considering the number of times we use those words from our pulpits. It can't hurt to have frequent reminders. But does it need to be a forty-five-minute reminder? Probably not.

I've taught through the book of James several times. Yes, it's helpful to spend time thinking about how the half-brother of Jesus started a book calling himself the "servant" (lit. "slave," δοῦλος) of his older brother. It's necessary to say a few words about his audience, the "twelve tribes in the Dispersion" (1:1). But do we need a whole sermon on it? Probably not, considering the first unit in the book is rather small, especially if you only preach verses 2–4.

Even for some of the longer openings, you still don't *have* to spend a whole sermon right there. When I preached through Galatians, my opening sermon covered verses 1–10, the first half of which consists of Paul's opening. My hope was to give the church a taste of Paul's apostolic defense and then show how that defense connected with the "problem" of the letter: the Galatians desertion of the true gospel. So I found it helpful not to say everything I could've said about verses 1–5 but instead to say a little less and incorporate verses 6–10, thereby actually saying a little more.

Wisdom must be applied here. What you do with the entrances will depend on what you do with the rest of the series. Some pastors have it in their minds that every sermon series needs to be six or eight weeks, no more. Often a church's small groups or Sunday school classes operate in these shorter cadences. Otherwise, so they erroneously think, people will get bored and lose interest. Tell that to every TV show ever. No one watches six episodes of *Stranger Things* and then decides to drop the series. Tell that to your sports season. No one follows six weeks of hockey and then says, "Eh, it's lost my attention." Soccer, maybe, but hockey . . . no way! Both your cultural/congregational context *and* the text itself should help determine how long your expository series should be.

By the way—all this advice also applies to exits. You probably won't preach Galatians 6:18 as an entire sermon.[13] If so, see chapter 4 of this book.

13. Galatians 6:18: "The grace of our Lord Jesus Christ be with your spirit, brothers. Amen."

The same goes for the short exit of Titus 3:15.[14] You'll probably end up lumping the Titus exit with the short people list of 3:12–14 (at least). The same goes for Colossians 4:18, which you will likely preach with the people list of 4:7–17. But Romans 16:25–27? Absolutely, spend a whole sermon right there! It's rich with theology and echoes the rest of the letter, making for a fine conclusion to a dynamic sermon series.

Here's the bottom line: Use your wisdom, planning, foresight, cultural/congregational context, and the letter itself to determine whether to move quickly through the entrance verses or to slow down and spend some time there.

Consider How Entrances Might Introduce the Themes of the Letter

We have already seen that some exits recapitulate themes and concerns within the letter. The same is sometimes true of the entrances. One way to spend an entire lesson in an entrance passage is to consider how those opening verses offer a glimpse ahead at the body of the letter.

If, in your studies, you detect some anticipation in these opening lines, lean into it. Use this to preview some of what will come in the sermon series. This assumes you've already done enough work in the rest of the text to have a reasonable knowledge of what's coming.[15]

Let's consider the entrance to 1 Corinthians. In the second verse, Paul talks about the Corinthians as "sanctified in Christ Jesus" and "called to be saints." Both "sanctified" and "saints" come from the same "holy" Greek root. The rest of the letter reveals that Paul uses words that characterize how

---

14. Titus 3:15: "All who are with me send greetings to you. Greet those who love us in the faith. Grace be with you all."

15. This is why it helps to begin some of your exegetical studies in a book well in advance and not rely only on a week-to-week study. I recognize some pastors find it difficult to work ahead, but if they were honest, most would admit this is probably due more to poor preparation, time management, and an unwillingness to rely on others to help in the pulpit than the constant demands of ministry. Lay teachers have their own unique challenges. I know one pastor who regularly takes several weeks out of the pulpit after a sermon series in order to spend time studying the next book. During those weeks, he fills the pulpit with other pastors, from both within the church and outside. He comes out of that time with a rough outline, a good grasp on the book's themes and topics, and a clear path ahead.

the Corinthians *should* act, not necessarily how they *are* acting. Just hearing these words might have had a convicting effect on the church, much like a teacher responding to a student caught cheating, "And this is my *honors* student!"

Even though Paul does not formally address the problems in the Corinthian church until 1:10, he sets the bar high at "sanctified saints" in the second verse. This invites the preacher to give the audience a glimpse of what is to come. What emotional appeal might have been behind that choice of words? Let your congregation know that this isn't the godliest church in the New Testament, to say the least. Perhaps offer them a preview of the topics to come (and why you chose to preach or teach this book). The Corinthian church struggled with unity (chapters 1–3), had problems dealing with gross sexual immorality (chapter 5), had believers suing each other (chapter 6), wrestled with questions of divorce and remarriage (chapter 7), and so on. Surely Paul knew what he was saying when he used the slightly ironic terms "sanctified" and "saints"!

All that being said, once again I urge caution. Sometimes an introduction is just an introduction and nothing more should be read into it. If that's the case, it's still okay to preview the book's themes and topics, but just make it clear to the church that this is what you're doing. At this point, you're not preaching the text; you're previewing the text. In most cases, this will not serve as the main focus of your sermon but as a tag at the end or a chunk in the middle. If your initial sermon takes the role of a nonfiction book introduction—surveying the chapters to come—then make it clear that you are *not* preaching the text itself. There is a place in the pulpit for such overview sermons (sparingly, in my humble opinion). These overviews generally work best when the text itself invites us to do so.

Dive Deep

When you spend half an hour preaching one or two verses in the pulpit, you can dive deep into each word and phrase. Preaching an entrance for an entire sermon often gives you the privilege of doing this deep dive.

When I started a series in 1 Peter at my current church, the first sermon was on Peter's entrance: "Peter, an apostle of Jesus Christ, To those who are elect exiles of the Dispersion in Pontus, Galatia, Cappadocia, Asia, and

Bithynia, according to the foreknowledge of God the Father, in the sanctification of the Spirit, for obedience to Jesus Christ and for sprinkling with his blood: May grace and peace be multiplied to you" (1 Pet 1:1–2).

I had no problem diving deep, since Peter had much to offer in these two short verses. Among a few other odds and ends, I spent time focusing on the following:

- The identity of Peter
- The meaning of "apostle"
- The location of Pontus, Galatia, Cappadocia, Asia, and Bithynia (using a map projected with PowerPoint)
- The historical background of the dispersion
- What it means to be an "elect exile" (with a special focus on the issue of predestination and foreknowledge and its relation to a believer's calling)
- The Holy Spirit's role in sanctification
- Jesus Christ's role in atonement

That may seem like a lot, and it is, but a careful read of the first two verses of Peter offered up these discussions on a silver platter.[16] Because I wasn't cramming 1 Peter 1:3–9 in the same sermon, I could take my time and elaborate on the coming themes of the letter. Though I didn't give a chapter-by-chapter breakdown of the epistle, I related some of these themes to Peter's main arguments in the body of the letter. By the end of the sermon, people knew that in the coming weeks, we would consider what it means to live holy lives in a hostile world.

When preaching entrances, "diving deep" means you take time to explain every nook and cranny of the verses in front of you. You can take a moment to explain what grace and peace actually mean—two words that we use frequently in church but don't often stop to relate their meaning.

This goes even for any name or place mentioned in the entrance text. Don't assume that your church members know all the names, even if they are familiar to you. Consider the entrance to Philemon (vv. 1–3). Not count-

---

16. For more on preaching 1 Peter, see Timothy E. Miller and Bryan Murawski, *1 Peter: A Commentary for Biblical Preaching and Teaching* (Grand Rapids: Kregel, 2022).

ing Jesus, it has five names in three verses (Paul, Timothy, Philemon, Apphia, and Archippus). Only two of them have direct relevance to the content of the letter, and a good sermon series will unpack Paul's relationship with Philemon. Timothy is well known elsewhere in the New Testament, but a new disciple or unbeliever may not know that. Sometimes, even for names that don't appear elsewhere in the Bible (like Apphia), it's even helpful to just give the briefest of statements—"We don't know who Apphia is. I'm sure Philemon did, though!"

One helpful question to ask yourself as you consider what to say: What would the original readers have immediately understood from hearing that word? When James opens by addressing "the twelve tribes in the Dispersion," this may not ring a bell for us, but it sure would for his original readers. Your job, preacher, is to help bridge the gap between their understanding and your church's understanding.

For example, if I said, "Philadelphia," a whole host of images and associations might run through your mind: Liberty Bell, Rocky Steps at the art museum, Ben Franklin, cheesesteaks (Pat's, not Geno's), rude sports teams. We have all these associations with Philadelphia, but if Paul's audience could be transported here, they would have none of that knowledge and would need to know what relevance this city had to the rest of the message. The reverse is also true. If Paul said, "Philadelphia," it should have a whole host of *different* meanings for the modern-day church: volcanoes, earthquakes, Dionysius, rude sports teams.

When Paul addresses his letter to "the church of God that is in Corinth," he is addressing a Philadelphia-level famous city in the ancient world (or perhaps Las Vegas is more apt). Dive deep by giving your audience a few insights into what ancient readers knew instinctively but modern readers need to have filled in.

Avoid the Temptation to Commentary-ize Your Sermon

One final caution is due: Avoid the temptation to dump data on your church while introducing a sermon series. Your introductory sermon is not a commentary. Commentaries sometimes have hundreds of pages of introductory material, covering issues like authorship, audience, historical setting, theological themes, text-critical issues, and so on.

Please, Preacher . . . *don't do this in your opening sermon*!

A sermon is not a running commentary. A sermon introducing the next ten to twenty weeks of your congregation's life *must* be more than a list of facts or critical issues in the book. If all you give the church is what you read in your commentaries during the week, why should your church listen to you instead of staying home to read their own commentaries?

There are a few people who might care that some scholars don't think Paul wrote Ephesians. But is that really the pressing issue of the day? How many people actually get stumped in their evangelism when someone brings up the claim that Ephesians isn't genuinely Pauline? Hardly any. Those who do will likely run back to you, Pastor, to seek help. At which point, you can blow the dust off those commentaries again and put your research to good use.

This is not to say that those discussions should *never* enter the pulpit. They might, sparingly (oh so sparingly!). But what does your audience need more when you introduce a series through an entrance text: a detailed discussion of the latest critical academic issues, or excitement about reading the book for themselves and looking forward to the coming weeks of study?

Again, there are times when the critical debates are directly relevant and have an actual impact, at which point you *should* find a way to address them in an appropriate, engaging manner. But clever preachers and teachers will recognize that these questions need not all be addressed at once, not even in the first sermon in the series.

When I preached Hebrews, obviously one of the biggest questions in academic debate was: Who wrote the book? I had to say *something* about the author throughout the sermon series. But the entrance text (Heb 1:1–4) was just so magisterial that I didn't want to break from the "hit-the-ground-running" style of the author to have a fifteen-minute lecture on who wrote the book! So I modeled my first sermon after the text and hit the ground running, preaching the first four verses without even a hint that more was coming. It worked. People were excited to come back, even if I didn't solve all the mysteries of the academic world.

Then, I really got them buzzing when I didn't address the authorship question in the second sermon, when I preached the rest of chapter 1. I didn't address the question *until the text itself brings it up*, with the first

first-person plural "we" in 2:1. Because the author naturally identifies himself in 2:1, that's where I brought that question into the pulpit.[17]

Be smart. It's not necessary to allow every academic debate into your pulpit. Consider what the audience *needs* to know to understand the context of the book and preach that.

Preaching Exits

Much of the advice for entrances also relates to exits, so this section will be considerably shorter than the previous. But some advice is worth reemphasizing, and I will highlight a few considerations that are unique to exits.

Consider How They Might Summarize the Themes of the Letter

At the risk of further beating a dead horse, sometimes exits provide great opportunities to recapitulate and reconsider the main themes of the epistle.

Consider again Galatians. Weima demonstrates that the Galatian letter closing purposefully expands on and adapts the closing conventions of Paul's day by setting out five sharp contrasts that recapitulate the key themes developed throughout the letter. He writes, "These contrasts involving the themes of persecution, boasting, circumcision, and new creation—as well as the implicit theme of 'the Israel of God'—serve to recapitulate the key themes developed throughout the Galatian letter."[18]

This, then, becomes a great opportunity to remind the church of many of the issues you preached about in the previous weeks and months. Though Weima's analysis considers Galatians 6:11–18, even if just the final verse is

17. For those itching to know, I discussed some of the historical debate, even quoting a few figures like Eusebius and Tertullian to highlight the difficulty of the issue. Then I did a "Top Four Countdown" to explain who I think is the most likely candidate for authorship. In order of least likely to most likely, I presented the possibility of Paul, Apollos, Luke, and Barnabas. I ultimately chose to call the author "The Preacher" throughout the sermon series due to the sermonic style of the book and the use of the "word of exhortation" that characterizes the letter in Hebrews 13:22.

18. Weima, *Neglected Endings*, 173.

preached as a stand-alone sermon, it still offers more than enough: "The grace of our Lord Jesus Christ be with your spirit, brothers. Amen."

The word "grace" should conjure up many fine memories and challenges from a series in Galatians. When I preached Galatians in late 2019, I adapted a Haddon W. Robinson "big idea" style for my sermons. At the end of the thirteen-week series, I collected all my big ideas and wrote a blog post for my church to help them reflect on the whole series. Here were my first few big ideas:

- Preach only the one true gospel of Jesus Christ (1:1–10)
- Good testimonies glorify God through the gospel (1:11–24)
- Preserve the truth of the gospel (2:1–14)
- Trust Christ's sufficiency for your salvation (2:15–21)
- Scripture is clear: Works never have—and never will—save (3:1–14)

Do you notice a theme? Grace! The gospel of grace is clear all throughout the letter. Just these first five sermons alone were enough to drive home the point. Preachers might find that the exit passage of a New Testament epistle will help generate this kind of reflection.

Explain the Value of a Benediction and a Doxology

Many exits give an explicit benediction or doxology. Those two words clearly fall into the category of "Christianese"—Bible words that we don't normally use outside the church.

A funny thing happened the other day. I was teaching a class called Introduction to Christian Theology. We were discussing ecclesiology—another Christianese term meaning "the doctrine of the church." One of the exercises I take my class through is to consider the "nonnegotiables" of a local church—things that must be in place for a church to be called a church.[19]

---

19. I encourage my students to answer the question, "Why isn't chapel church?" Cairn University, like many other Christian institutions, requires students to attend chapel several times a week. But chapel is not a substitute for church. Chapel doesn't have biblical leadership like elders and deacons; it does not model regular participation in the ordinances; it does not practice church discipline. Chapel is not church.

After students gave the normal answers—ordinances, worship, biblical leadership, etc.—one student raised his hand and said, "Benedictions and doxologies." About half the class looked at him with an expression that clearly said, "What in the world does that mean?"

I understand the feeling. I did not grow up in a church tradition that valued benedictions or doxologies. In my early years in the pastorate, I attended a pastor's conference at a local retreat center. I knew the director of the conference, and at the end of the session, he eyed me and asked me to "give the benediction" to close the service.

Frankly, I had no clue what he meant. I don't recall ever hearing that term in my childhood church. My current church never used that term either. I figured that no one would object to me closing in a word of prayer instead. After all—who would complain about prayer? Apparently, the answer is other pastors! The moment I said "Amen," I heard one grumpy old guy mutter loud enough to be heard by all, "*That* wasn't a benediction."

Thanks, buddy.

These two examples illustrate the point: Many in our churches do not know the value and place of a benediction or doxology. Many churches do not regularly incorporate such things at the close of their services.

- A benediction is a bestowal of blessing on the church at the close of a service.
- A doxology is a theological exclamation of praise glorifying God at the close of a service.
- Paul's typical closing, "The grace of the Lord Jesus be with you," is a benediction.
- Romans 16:25–27 is a doxology.

If your church does not regularly incorporate such endings into your service, maybe now is the time to explain their value and start doing them—at least for that particular Sunday. Instead of closing the service with a prayer, close with a blessing or close by singing the doxology. There's nothing like a group of believers singing the doxology *a cappella*!

If your church regularly practices benedictions and doxologies, allow the text to lead you to explain to them the biblical origin of such practices. It may be presumptuous of me, but I would venture to guess that many (often more liturgical) churches that practice such traditions often do so without explanation. Visitors or new believers might appreciate hearing why we follow these practices.

Preach It Like Any Other Text

To summarize most of the advice in this chapter, spend as much time in prep, in prayer, and in the pulpit for both entrances and exits as you would any other Sunday. Pour your heart into the text during the week. Allow the Holy Spirit to speak through the Scripture into your soul and you will know what to do with the text by Sunday morning.

Entrances and exits are part of "all Scripture" breathed out by God, useful for the sanctification of the believer, able to be preached (2 Tim 3:16–4:2). Don't rush past them in the beginning and don't ignore them in the end. Leverage them to enhance the sermon series. You may be surprised at how much a good appetizer and dessert can satisfy your church's appetite.

3

Preaching and Teaching Well-Worn Stories

It was my first Christmas sermon as a senior pastor, and I made the mistake of trying to do something *clever*.

The year was 2016 and Christmas fell on a Sunday. Because of this, and because the week before was the church's Christmas choir concert, the leaders decided not to have a traditional Christmas Eve candlelight service. All attention would be placed on Christmas morning.

A few months earlier, I began a long sermon series in Exodus. I had planned the series with Christmas in mind, ensuring that Exodus 3 fell on Christmas morning. The unburned burning bush. The revelation of YHWH—the Great I AM.

I could have done the rational thing and stopped the series for a few weeks to observe the first advent of Christ, then perhaps picked back up in Exodus in the new year. But I thought that people would appreciate my theologically brilliant idea to focus on Jesus through the lens of the I AM. Who is this baby Jesus? Why, none other than the fullness of *that God* in the form of a newborn baby!

I began the sermon by considering the parallels between the four hundred years of Israel's suffering in Egypt and the four hundred years of silence between the time of Malachi and the birth of the Messiah. I followed the text to the burning bush and then to the revelation of YHWH to Moses. I may have even used the word *tetragrammaton* at one point.

From the Great I AM, I connected the magnificent vastness of God with the beautiful fragility of the incarnation by landing the sermon in John 1, with a touch of John 8:57–58 for seasoning. Baby Jesus is YHWH! Good exegesis mixed with solid biblical theology, perfectly relevant for the season. Creative, engaging, rich! Isn't that exciting?

The answer, in case you were wondering, is no. No, it is not exciting.

I thought we could consider Christmas through the perspective of the revelation of YHWH at the unburned burning bush. This way, we didn't need to pause a perfectly good expository sermon series, allowing me to have my cake and eat it too.

I thought wrong.

The first hint of complaint came from a Facebook post by one of our members. "Is it so hard to ask for Baby Jesus on Christmas morning? Why can't we simply read the traditional Christmas story on Jesus's birthday?"

Similar complaints soon trickled in. To their credit, the other staff supported my sermon, as did the majority of people who attended the service. But the Facebook complaint—as annoying as the mode of communication was—stuck with me. My own mother has voiced similar complaints about her own church services to me. One year, I remember her venting about attending a Christmas sermon that focused on Jesus as the "Undercover Boss." It was more of a clever analogy than an expository sermon in Luke.

After an Easter service, she had similar complaints. Apparently, the pastor had the audacity to preach biblical theology—the Genesis 3 serpent included—leading up to the resurrection, rather than sticking with the more traditional texts. "I don't understand why Mary never gets to the tomb!" she mused.

I didn't tell her that it sounded like a great sermon to me.

Conversely, I can also recall the criticism I overheard by not a few church members as we walked out of a Christmas Eve sermon several years ago. "It's the same sermon every year," they balked. "I know it's Christmas and it has to be about the Christmas story, but isn't there a fresh way to deliver it?"

Therein lies the rub with preaching well-worn stories. We want the stories and the hymns and the traditions to stay the same because of our religious nostalgia, yet we expect preachers to deliver them in a creatively fresh and novel way. Give us the same exact thing, only completely different![1]

---

1. Churches have this problem in many different areas. We want to be cutting edge and innovative, all the while staying exactly the same as we are.

Well-Worn Stories

This chapter will deal with two types of well-worn stories.[2] Some Bible stories are well-worn because of how often they are preached and taught due to their connection with a religious holiday. The birth narratives in Luke and the death and resurrection narratives in the Gospels exemplify this category. Each year, they must be preached. People *expect* them to be preached. And not just people in your church. As pastors well know, the Chreasters show up on these special days.[3] Which means, even people who don't normally attend church come with certain expectations.

So those "holiday texts" end up as worn out as the carpet in the church sanctuary. We touch on the birth story on Christmas Eve, on the Sunday closest to Christmas Day, perhaps at the Christmas choir concert or the annual children's pageant. Easter is the same thing, only more challenging, since we have Good Friday, Easter Sunday, and sometimes other days depending on the church tradition. And the resurrection is a pretty big deal in Christianity, so we will probably find ourselves referring to it much more often than just during this holiest of weekends for the Christian church.

We might consider some of the traditional "communion" texts in this category: Matthew 26:26–28, Mark 14:22–24, Luke 22:14–23, 1 Corinthians 11:17–34. Even if your church observes the Lord's Supper only once a month, most pastors find themselves going back to the same texts to say the same old thing. It can get as stale as a communion wafer if we're not careful. Christmas and Easter texts might be preached once or twice a year, every year, year after year. Communion texts might be preached once to four times *a month*, year after year.

Other texts are worn and weathered for different reasons. Who hasn't heard the story of Jesus feeding the five thousand? It's one of the only non-passion texts that shows up in all four Gospels. It's a favorite for a reason.

And what about Jesus walking on water? Or the good Samaritan? Or John 3:16? We've heard these stories and read these passages time and time again. So how do we approach a text that is so familiar to our audience?

---

2. By "stories," I do not intend to imply that these are not historical or factual events. Some people use the word *story* as a functional synonym for "fairy tale"; this is not my intent in this chapter.

3. Chreasters: "Those who attend church only on Christmas and Easter."

Let's be honest: Even seasoned preachers may tire of preaching the same stories over and over. If we get tired of preaching these texts, or if we feel our well of creativity running dry, you can be sure your listeners will feel just as parched. This chapter gives several suggestions for keeping old things fresh in the pulpit, without selling our souls to the cultural pressure to bow to the idol of creativity and innovation.

Let's start with the Christmas and Easter sermons.

Christmas and Easter

First, don't feel pressured to produce something creative or clever. Clear and engaging? Yes. Rooted in the text? Always. An innovative Christmas sermon that no one has ever heard before? Not necessary.

We are not called to be clever. We do not measure our lesson's effectiveness by how cutting edge it was or how many pop culture references were peppered throughout. Believe it or not, we don't even measure a sermon's effectiveness by how many people came forward at the end or how many people were moved to action. We cannot control a person's reaction to the gospel.

From the beginning of their ministries, the prophets were informed that people would not listen to them.[4] Thus the measure of their effectiveness in ministry had little to do with how many people raised their hands for salvation; they were told up front that very few would. Rather, their measure of effectiveness was how faithfully they communicated God's message to the people. That's it. Were they faithful mouthpieces of YHWH?

Don't feel pressured to be the innovative church on Easter. Often, innovation distracts from the truth of God's word. There's no need to hike a Bible across the platform like a football or zipline onto the stage to show people the glory of a resurrected God.[5]

This brings us to our second point: Speak the truth in love. If your church is like mine, then a great number of people who show up on these religious holidays will never step foot in church any other time of year. This

4. E.g., Exod 3:19; 7:3–5; Isa 6:9–13; Jer 1:9–10, 18–19; Ezek 2:1–3:21.

5. Unfortunately, both of these are real news stories that broke the year of this writing.

leads me to believe that many people in church on those days do not have a relationship with Jesus Christ.

This means you are preaching to a people who are spiritually lost and eternally damned, should nothing change. They don't need cute platitudes or a cozy feel-good message. They need to be confronted with the reality of their sin and need for a Savior. They need someone to lovingly point them to the truth of the gospel.

Pastor, if an unbeliever walks out of your church on Christmas or Easter without having heard the gospel, you've done something wrong. Don't be afraid to talk about sin on Christmas. What good is a Savior if we don't know what we need to be saved from? Don't back down from calling out the sinfulness of hollow religion. You will have a contingent of people who think their twice-a-year attendance at church checks off a works-based box, ensuring their salvation. Smash that reality.

Yes, even on Christmas morning.

But do it with proper love and compassion. We are not called to bash people over the head with the gospel. If preached right, sinners will be lovingly confronted with the reality of their lifestyles.

Third, keep believers in mind as you prepare and as you preach. Often the overwhelming number of visitors on Christian holidays causes pastors to forget the primary purpose of church: the local gathering of *saints*. Though we should certainly keep the unbelieving crowd in our peripherals as we prepare, we need to maintain our focus on edifying the believers.

This means that at a bare minimum, at some point in your sermon, you should ask yourself, How does a *mature* believer apply this text? How should a Christian who has been in church for seventy years rightly think about the resurrection? Preach to your members just as much as you preach to your visitors.

Fourth, do your study. Treat whatever passage you're preaching like any other Sunday. You've heard the Easter story a thousand times, but that doesn't mean you shirk the hard work of exegesis during the week.

And preach the sermon like any other Sunday sermon. As the adage goes, what you win them with, you win them to.[6] This is probably more

6. I first heard this from my homiletics professor Don Cheyney, who admitted he heard the phrase elsewhere but did not know who coined it.

opinion than gospel truth, but I'm concerned about preachers who pare down their normal forty-minute feast for a twenty-minute feel-good sermonette for a holiday. As the other adage goes, sermonettes are for Christianettes.[7]

Catering to the "religious" crowd on a holiday does not help in the long run. If they return to church, what will they expect? More of the same. If you give them a twenty-minute sermon rife with cute illustrations and cheap platitudes and then deliver a sermon the next week that Spurgeon would've been proud of, it may be too much of a shock to the system.

To put it differently, I'd much rather visitors leave saying, "I've never heard preaching like *that*!" than saying, "My, that was a nice service!"

Finally, I encourage young preachers to make a list early in their ministry. The list should include the next ten years of Christmas and Easter texts (including Good Friday if your church has a sermon at that service), as well as a collection of other potential passages to preach.

This list is not: Here's what I will *definitely* preach for the next ten years of holidays. Instead, it is: Here's what I *could* preach for the next ten years of holidays.[8]

You have the flexibility to make different decisions. Generating a list like this could alleviate some of the pressure of worrying about what to preach on these special Sundays. You'll find many more texts to choose from than you previously thought.

I recommend—especially for Easter—choosing at least half of your texts from nontraditional passages. In other words, instead of just looking at the four Gospels for the resurrection, think of passages like 1 Corinthians 15. Because of the great focus on death and resurrection in the epistles, it will likely be easier to gather your list of resurrection passages than incarnation passages.

At the risk of doing it for you, here are two examples: one for Christmas, one for Easter. I've only done half, so as not to spoil your own fun in preparation. The Christmas Eve passages tend to be shorter due to the nature of

---

7. I also don't know where I originally heard this. Probably for the better.

8. Some people decry the use of such planning, thinking that it excludes the Holy Spirit's direction each year. But can a God who exists outside of time not work with such preparation? It's better to plan but do so with the "if the Lord wills" attitude seen in James 4:13–17.

the service. I also like to lean into either Old Testament or nontraditional passages for Christmas Eve, which is just my own preference.

Christmas Passages

Year	Christmas Eve	Christmas
2025	Isa 9:1–7	Luke 2:1–7
2026	Mic 5:2–5	Luke 2:8–21
2027	Matt 1:1–17	Matt 1:18–25
2028	Ps 98 (with Luke 1–2)	Luke 1:26–38
2029	Phil 2:5–11	John 1:1–18

Easter Passages

Year	Good Friday	Easter Sunday
2025	Luke 22:14–23	Luke 24:1–12
2026	The Seven Last Sayings of Jesus	Rom 5:6–10
2027	Luke 23:44–49	Luke 24:36–53
2028	Mark 15:42–47	Matt 28
2029	John 19:16–37	1 Cor 15:1–11

Communion

Once a month, typically on the first Sunday, our church celebrates the Lord's Supper together. We typically begin by "fencing the table," reminding people what communion is and is not. It is not a *means* of salvation; it is not for unbelievers or those under church discipline. It is for any confessing believer in the family of God; it is a reminder of Christ's death and a proclamation of his eventual return.

With only a few passages to choose from (Matt 26:26–28; Mark 14:22–24; Luke 22:14–23; 1 Cor 11:17–34) and little variation between these passages, how does one keep communion "fresh" when continually returning to the same thing month after month (and in some churches, week after week)?

Simply put, we do not.

That is, we do not attempt to keep communion "fresh." The whole nature of this observance is that it serves as a continual, repeated reminder of what Jesus has done for us. The repetition is purposeful; lean into it. It's not just a tradition; it's a *God-ordained* tradition that needs no variation to serve its purpose.

However, I understand the concern that rote repetition of tradition could lead to indifferent hearts. Leaders might want to consider varying the *method* by which they take communion. If your church has people come to the front to take the elements from a leader, consider having the leaders pass out the elements to the people. I saw one church put stations around the main auditorium for families to take communion together after a time of prayer. There are different methods for observing the Lord's Supper. Carefully observing it in a different way may give enough variation to help people see the elements anew.[9]

Regarding the homiletical aspect of communion, consider compiling a list of passages that are related to the Last Supper. Assuming people are quite familiar with the "typical" texts in the Synoptics and 1 Corinthians, you can allude to these while reading passages such as Isaiah 52:13–53:12, John 6:48–58, or Hebrews 8. Communion does not always have to be accompanied by reading the *same* passage of Scripture every Sunday it's observed. We can reflect on the death of Christ and the new covenant through many different passages.

Preaching Well-Worn Stories

Setting holidays and weekly/monthly texts aside, what happens when we face the feeding of the five thousand for the five-thousandth time? How do we engage an audience who thinks they already know everything there is to know about Peter walking on the water or the temptation of Jesus in the wilderness?

Just because a story has shown up on the flannelgraph countless times does not mean it cannot or should not be preached or taught again. In fact,

---

9. I do not mean to be ignorant or flippant toward traditions that believe in a particular method as the best method. Each church will need to develop and follow its convictions regarding these things.

you may even find that you can use an individual's knowledge of a text to leverage your sermon to a level more powerful than you previously thought.

Preach It Like They've Never Heard It

This is good advice for any text, but especially for those texts that grace the pages of every children's Bible ever printed. Let's face it: In our post-Christian climate in America, even the well-worn stories are not so well-worn anymore. There will likely be someone—maybe even a few people—in your church who has never heard the story you're teaching.

Or, more often, there are people there who have heard it but have never actually read it. There's a big difference.

Forgive me for injecting an Old Testament story into a New Testament book, but I recall that one time after preaching a sermon in Exodus, an older woman came up to me. Taking my arm, she said, "I have been a Christian all my life. I've heard the story you just preached. I even taught it in Sunday school to children. But until today, I'm not sure I ever *read* it!"

I could add dozens more stories like this. It's sad that a person who has been a believer for decades has not yet read through the entire Bible. But it proves my point: Even well-worn stories catch people afresh if you take the care to preach the text.

This is one of the reasons I recommend *inductive outlines* to my students when preaching narratives.[10] Instead of stating your "big idea" or main point at the beginning and letting people know where you're going, allow the tension of the text to do that for you. Narratives are stories.[11] How many people would enjoy a movie that begins with a summary of everything you're about to see, including the ending? (Warning! Spoiler alerts!) "In this thrilling follow-up to *Star Wars: A New Hope*, Luke Skywalker finds out that Darth Vader is his father. Over the next two hours, we'll learn about the problem of evil."

We would never do that with a movie. We would get angry if the back cover of a book did the same thing. "Harry Potter will find that he him-

---

10. See Robinson, *Biblical Preaching*, 77–96, for the different approaches to outlining a sermon.

11. For those interested in developing their skills in preaching and teaching biblical narratives, I highly recommend Mathewson's *The Art of Preaching Old Testament Narrative*. Though this resource focuses on the Old Testament, his principles and hermeneutical advice also relate to the New Testament narratives.

self is a horcrux and will come back from death in order to defeat Lord Voldemort."

If we wouldn't want a movie to summarize its plot and end in the opening credits; and if we wouldn't read a book that spoiled the entire narrative on the back cover, then why in the world do so many preachers do this with their narrative sermons?[12]

I believe the better way to approach a text is to allow the text to tell its own story. Even if the audience has heard it before, preach it like they haven't. Let the points of tension keep listeners on the edge of their seats.

My four-year-old son, Adam, loves the story of the three little pigs. He loves to tell it. He loves to act it out with his toys. He loves to watch the old cartoon version on YouTube. But most of all, he loves it when his parents or one of his older siblings tell it. Though he's heard and acted out and watched the story a thousand times, his eyes still get wide when that Big Bad Wolf comes up to the house of bricks and begins his huffing and puffing. Will the wolf succeed this time? Of course not, but a good telling of the story will make one wonder, nonetheless. When the Big Bad Wolf slides down the chimney, you should see Adam's face, smiling in anticipation for when the wolf burns his rear end on the fire the pigs have set for him.

Preach the text to make your church smile in anticipation at Christ reaching his hand out to Peter as the disciple sinks into the waves. Teach the text in such a way that your class will wonder whether that grave will be filled or empty. Preach the text in such a way that your congregation will weep alongside Christ, wondering if Lazarus will stay in the tomb. Don't grab the text's hand and lead it. Allow the text to lead *you* by the hand as you preach and teach. Make no apologies for preaching a well-worn story. When you preach it like they've never heard it, they experience a sermon they've never heard.

Preach and Teach the Text, Not the Story

This piece of advice flows from the last. When we preach the text, we preach *the text*, not the story in the text, but the text itself. The narrator

---

12. I feel the same way about church traditions that read the entire text before the preacher comes to preach. Though I appreciate the solemnity of the moment and the high value of reading Scripture, I prefer to read the text bit by bit throughout the sermon so as not to spoil the plot of the narrative.

told the story in that way for a reason—an *inspired* reason. Therefore, we would be wise to follow the contours of the text as closely as possible while preaching and teaching.[13]

When preaching John 2:1–12, the story where Jesus turns water into wine at the wedding in Cana, I was careful not to spoil the surprise miracle until the story revealed it (even though the majority of the audience probably knew where the story was heading). This kept the tension in the text. How will Jesus solve this disgraceful oversight? Why in the world would Jesus want more than one hundred gallons of water from unclean jars?

By preaching the text and allowing the text to unfold the story as it comes, you enable the audience to experience the text like a first-century original reader. Imagine hearing this for the first time and not knowing what's coming! The anticipation kills—but it also immerses the audience into the story and engages them on a deeper level than ever before. But my point is this: The punch of the whole narrative is weakened when we start by saying, "Now, I'm going to tell you the story of when Jesus turned water into wine."[14]

Teaching the text and not the story also means paying attention to and drawing out the various literary clues in the text for your audience. For ex-

---

13. I recognize that in some sermons of the New Testament—such as Peter's in Acts 3 or Stephen's in Acts 7—the speakers summarize parts of the Old Testament for particular purposes. Keep in mind that these individuals were not necessarily preaching expository sermons (though how they handle the Old Testament in their quotations can be quite instructive for us), and the recorded sermons were most likely not *exactly* what each individual said, but rather an accurate *summary* of what they said. You can read the Sermon on the Mount (Matt 5–7) out loud in about twenty minutes. Did Jesus really assemble everyone on the mountain for a twenty-minute sermon, or is the sermon recorded in Matthew an accurate depiction of the main points in Jesus's sermon? Lest you think this is heresy, consider Luke's version of the Sermon on the Mount in Luke 6:17–49. It contains many parallel elements to Matthew 5–7. Either we must conclude (1) they are not the same sermon (unlikely), (2) Jesus preached duplicate things in the same sermon with slightly different language (also unlikely), or (3) both versions accurately represent the same content of the same sermon (most likely).

14. The (editorial) headings of our Bibles do us no favors in this regard. Often the story is spoiled by the heading. "Jesus Cleanses the Temple" (John 2:13). "Jesus Feeds the Five Thousand" (John 6:1). I would hope that future editors of the Bible could be cleverer with titling these stories in such a way that captures the narrative's plot without giving away the punchline. "Jesus Visits the Temple." "Five Thousand Hungry Men."

ample, in the well-worn story of Philip and the Ethiopian eunuch, consider the way that Luke the narrator introduces the eunuch: "And there was an Ethiopian, a eunuch, a court official of Candace, queen of the Ethiopians, who was in charge of all her treasure. He had come to Jerusalem to worship" (Acts 8:27).[15]

Each of the five descriptions tells us something more about this man. He was an Ethiopian, possibly representing someone from "the ends of the earth," which is kind of a big deal in Acts.[16] He was a eunuch, which may echo Isaiah 56:1–8. Even in just these first two descriptions, Luke sets us up to think about the fulfillment of prophecies from both the Old and New Testaments.

He was a court official of Candace, queen of the Ethiopians, which means he served in a high official capacity. He oversaw all of Candace's treasure, something only a trustworthy servant could do. And he had come to Jerusalem to worship, meaning he was likely a proselyte.

By following the text's description, we progressively reveal more and more about this man whom Philip encounters. A man of high moral character whose location and lot in life hint toward greater fulfillment should he respond to the gospel.

Study Hard to Uncover Surprising Details

How many times have you read a well-worn passage of Scripture and suddenly thought, "I never realized *that* before!" That's the wonder of the Bible: We can read it a hundred times and every time come away with something new and fresh.

When preaching or teaching a well-worn story, invest the appropriate time into your studies during the week. Don't neglect the hard work just because the story is familiar to you.[17] If you're using quality commentaries and

---

15. Just a verse before this, the angel of the Lord says to Philip, "'*Rise* and *go* toward the south to the road that goes down from Jerusalem to Gaza.' . . . And he *rose* and *went*" (Acts 8:26–27). Notice how the narrator repeats the verbs of command from the angel. The way that Luke tells the story, Philip is perfectly and immediately obedient to God's prompting!

16. See Acts 1:8.

17. If you've taught the text before, find a fresh way to look at it again. You'll want to recontextualize your approach and applications for your new audience, but you may also want to pick up a new article, consult a newly published commentary, or read something you haven't read before on the text to look at it afresh.

resources—usually the kind you buy or borrow from a university library, not the free kind you find online—you are bound to come across some detail or tidbit that surprises you. And you can expect that if it surprises you, it'll surprise your church.

The goal is not to just preach something novel or surprising. Especially not for the purpose of wowing your church or flaunting how much you know. But sometimes these details can capture attention and give people a reason to listen to the same story for the thousandth time.

Like many in my generation, *The Office* is a show I have watched multiple times. To my great shame, I can probably quote nearly all of the main characters' lines for some episodes. As many times as I have watched it, I'm still a sucker for the YouTube clickbait "12 Fun Facts You Didn't Know about *The Office*" kind of videos. They always seem to point out at least one or two things I wasn't aware of, which makes me want to watch *The Office* again, this time with a more careful eye.

Of course, a sermon is more than just a list of "fun facts you didn't know." But seasoning your sermon early on with one or two of these "fun facts" might grip someone's attention and give them a good reason to listen to the rest of what you have to say.

Let's set aside Dwight Schrute for a moment and give a biblical example. I was preaching the triumphal entry from Matthew 21:1–11, a passage that many churches hear year after year on the Sunday before Easter. In my studies, I anticipated seeing the quote of Zechariah 9:9 in Matthew 21:5. I knew I'd see the link between "Hosanna" and texts such as Psalm 118:25–26. However, Matthew specifies the location as not only Bethphage near Jerusalem but also the Mount of Olives (Matt 21:1). I thought this may allude to the Zechariah 14:4 prophecy about the coming of the Lord to that mountain. Matthew sets up the triumphal entry to evoke Zechariah 14, but then he quickly pulls a switcheroo by showing that it's actually Zechariah 9:9 that Jesus fulfills. A humble king, not a conquering hero.

Following the text and letting the audience follow Matthew's surprise twist not only heightened the suspense of a familiar narrative, but it also gave the church something new to think about—some seasoning to start their meal.[18]

---

18. In addition to this initial surprise, I also found some of Matthew's language in 21:5 alludes not only to Zechariah 9:9 but also potentially to Isaiah 62:11. This

To my delight, I had one retired pastor come up to me after the sermon and tell me, "I've heard that preached many times in my lifetime, but never saw some of those things you talked about today!" To be sure, this kind of comment is not always a compliment or a surefire way of determining you were on the right track in the sermon. But in this case, after doing my own research, I found other commentators who detected the same allusions, so I don't think I was preaching heresy![19]

Play Off the Church's "Knowledge," Whether Real or Assumed

Sometimes you can use a church's "knowledge" of a passage against it. Two examples will help you understand what I'm getting at—one from Spider-Man, and one from the Bible.

It's well-known Spider-Man lore that Uncle Ben always dies. It is often said that in the comics, no one stays dead except Bucky (Captain America's BFF), Jason Todd (one of Batman's many "Robins"), and Uncle Ben. Uncle Ben always dies, usually after saying something to the effect of, "With great power comes great responsibility."

I'm going to spoil something for you now, so if you haven't watched *Spider-Man: No Way Home* (2021), the third movie in Marvel's rebooted Spider-Man trilogy, maybe you should skip the next paragraph.

In *No Way Home*, Spider-Man's Aunt May ends up on the receiving end of a villain's attack. Lying bleeding in the rubble, she tells Peter, "You have a gift. You have power, and with great power, there must also come great responsibility." Uh oh! We all know what happens when Uncle Ben says that line! Within moments, Aunt May is dead. This shocking turn of events messes with those who know Marvel's lore. The Bible can have a similar effect when people *think* they know where a story will go and why a story goes there.

I've often enjoyed preaching John 11, the story in which Jesus raises his friend Lazarus from the dead, but only after having a good cry with

---

is significant when we note that Isaiah 62:11 anticipates "your salvation comes," whereas Zechariah 9:9 anticipates "your king comes." See Craig L. Blomberg, *Matthew*, NAC 22 (Nashville: B&H, 1992), 311.

19. E.g., Blomberg, 311; and R. T. France, *The Gospel of Matthew*, NICOT (Grand Rapids: Eerdmans, 2007), 775.

Lazarus's sisters. He cries because he's human and that's what humans do when someone dies. Right?

I'm not so sure.

If I ask ten church members who know the story, "Why did Jesus cry in John 11?," nine out of ten will likely respond, "Jesus cried because he was sad that his friend died."

But a close read of the chapter points in another direction. Jesus announces from the get-go that Lazarus's illness would *not* lead to death (11:4). Then he purposefully waits two extra days before traveling to Jerusalem (11:6). Before getting to his location, Jesus tells his disciples, "Our friend Lazarus has fallen asleep, but I go to awaken him" (11:11). To make sure we all understand his metaphor, John tells us in no uncertain terms, "Now Jesus had spoken of his death" (11:13). Because of the way John narrates the story, right away we know what Jesus knows: Lazarus won't stay dead!

After a frustrating conversation with Lazarus's sister Martha, who doesn't seem to get the full picture, Jesus declares, "I am the resurrection and the life" (11:25). It's only after Jesus sees the people hopelessly weeping (11:33) that he becomes greatly indignant—this is the meaning of the word ἐμβριμάομαι, often erroneously translated "deeply moved." He's angry, not sad! He weeps only after finding out they've already buried Lazarus (11:34–35), and John follows this with a statement about how little the people believed in the resurrection power of Jesus (11:37).

It's almost absurd to think that Jesus was crying because he was sad his friend was dead. Multiple times the text tells us that Lazarus won't stay dead. Why weep over a temporary "sleep"? Rather, John gives many clues that link Christ's weeping with the people's lack of belief in his resurrection power. Even at the close of the story, John directly links this event with the Jewish leaders' plans to put Jesus to death (11:53).

When you preach John 11, preach it with the knowledge that most of your congregation probably has the wrong idea about Jesus here. You're not trying to "trick" them or "wow" them with your novel interpretation. Rather, you are preaching with the full awareness that they think they know where this story is going, *but for a totally different reason.*

Point out the clues along the way. If you're careful enough to do it, Jesus's indignation and subsequent weeping will click together for them. They're expecting Uncle Ben; surprise them with Aunt May.

There's Something to Say About Nostalgia

I don't care how many times I watch it, *Terminator 2: Judgment Day* will always be a great movie. Same goes with *National Lampoon's Christmas Vacation*. I can watch it every holiday season and still laugh and enjoy it just as much as the last time around.[20] Yet my repeated viewings of *Terminator 2* and *Christmas Vacation* have nothing on my children's fascination with *Sonic the Hedgehog 2*. When that movie came out on Amazon Prime, I'm pretty sure my youngest watched it on repeat every day for two months straight. At least, that's what it felt like from my perspective.

There's something comforting about an old movie you've watched fifty times. It's like sliding your bare feet into an old pair of slippers. Sometimes an oldie is a goodie for a reason.

This is just a simple reminder at the end of this chapter: Don't feel pressured to be clever. Or to pick a more obscure passage. Or to say something novel. Sometimes, it's worth preaching again, just like they know it. Not everyone grows bored with things they've already heard before. Many people get excited about the things they've already seen or read.

A few months ago, our family took a trip to Sight & Sound Theatres in Lancaster, Pennsylvania, to see its production of Daniel. It was a good production, but my nine-year-old son, Nathan, was a bit disappointed that no one died.[21]

"Dad," he whispered, leaning over to me as Shadrach, Meshach, and Abednego were thrown into the fiery furnace. "Didn't the guards die when they did that?"

Yes, yes they did (Dan 3:22). But not in this family-friendly theatrical production.

"Dad," he whispered again during the closing musical number. "Didn't they throw all the bad guys into the lion's den?"

Correct again—inclusive of the bad guys' family (6:24). But I guess it would break the PG flavor of the play if we heard the screams of the Persian children and women in the background of Daniel's big musical finale. What

---

20. I can also watch *Terminator 2: Judgment Day* every holiday season, but my wife isn't too keen on that one.

21. I have a feeling he will also share his father's taste in action movies one day.

my son really wanted was the story as he knew it, not some heavily edited, watered-down version. I couldn't blame him.

As I glanced at the past productions listed in the brochure, I noticed another pattern: People get excited about things they are familiar with. There's a reason the past plays focused on characters such as Moses, Noah, Samson, Jonah, and Jesus. These are the most familiar stories in the Bible. And they drew a crowd.

I doubt a play based on Euodia and Syntyche (Phil 4:2–3) would have sold out month after month.[22] But we understand why. These are not the most familiar, and familiarity can be comforting.

If *Terminator 2* and Sight & Sound do not prove my point, then consider how many times Paul's testimony appears in Scripture. Luke reports a lengthy story of Paul's conversion three times in Acts (chapters 9, 22, and 26). Paul tells a version of his testimony in Galatians 1:11–2:14, then a few times elsewhere in a much shorter form. Surely, there are theological reasons for this. But well-worn stories are worth telling again. Don't be afraid to preach them. Then, later on down the road, when the time is right, preach them again.

22. My letter requesting *Leviticus: The Musical* has been repeatedly ignored by the staff at Sight & Sound.

4

Preaching and Teaching the Nuggets

Readers will have to forgive me for starting this chapter in a book on preaching and teaching the New Testament with an illustration from the Old Testament.

Some time ago, I began preaching a brief seventy-five-week series through the book of Isaiah. I was averaging about a chapter a week, which was necessary if I wanted to finish preaching the book in this lifetime.[1] While preaching Isaiah's "Little Apocalypse" (chapters 24–27), I originally planned on preaching all of chapter 27 in a single sermon.

After my studies, as I sat down to write the manuscript, I found myself thirty minutes deep in the sermon and still on verse 1! It is an epic verse, one with swords and dragons and rich in biblical-theological allusions and typology.[2] Because of how much theology, challenging exegesis, and relevant application that verse offered, I switched gears and decided to spend the entire Sunday morning on that one line of Scripture.

In all my years of preaching Old Testament texts, I have come across this kind of "problem" just a handful of times. I have stopped a sermon series in an Old Testament book—where I typically average about a chapter or so a week—to do a deep dive into one or two verses on only a few occasions. Certainly, this kind of preaching *could* be done more often than I allowed

1. Sadly, I never finished the series, as I stepped down from that position after about thirty sermons in the book. Readers can consult my selective two-volume commentary if they want a taste of these sermons: *Preacher's Hebrew Companion to Isaiah 1–39* and *Preacher's Hebrew Companion to Isaiah 40–66*.

2. The verse reads, "In that day the Lord with his hard and great and strong sword will punish Leviathan the fleeing serpent, Leviathan the twisting serpent, and he will slay the dragon that is in the sea" (Isa 27:1).

it.[3] Part of the discipline of the preacher is to *not* say everything that *could* be said on any given Sunday. Restraint is needed in preparing every sermon.

In the New Testament, however, these theologically compact "nuggets" arise much more frequently than in the Old Testament. I call them "nuggets" because they pack a lot into a single bite of Scripture. One mouthful of text, yet a whole meal of flavor.

In my Old Testament volume on preaching, I dedicated a chapter to the challenge of preaching "Goliath" sermons: long pericopes that resist being separated into multiple sermons. I offered strategies for preaching longer texts such as these. Surely the New Testament has its fair share of Goliaths as well, and those principles shared in the first volume are also all relevant to New Testament texts.[4]

In this chapter, I'm seeking to help the preacher with the opposite kind of challenge: exegetical preaching or teaching when you have a very, very small amount of text—one or two verses—that offer so much that they can easily take up a whole sermon or lesson.[5] Allow me to share a half dozen examples with you, then explain why—if these kinds of texts offer up so much rich theology to be preached—they are still considered "difficult texts."

A Happy Meal of Nuggets

The book of Galatians is replete with pearls of theological wisdom, featuring statements like, "As we have said before, so now I say again: If anyone is preaching to you a gospel contrary to the one you received, let him be ac-

3. Some books offer more of an opportunity to do deeper reflection in single verses than other books. Many narratives require a broader view in order to understand the point of the author, whereas preachers might find it much easier and more appropriate to take a whole Sunday to reflect on a single wisdom saying (though they are rightly understood as "slices of truth" in need of a fuller picture; Gordon D. Fee and Douglas Stuart, *How to Read the Bible for All Its Worth* [Grand Rapids: Zondervan, 2003], 231–41).

4. Such as John 11:1–57; Acts 6:8–7:60; 10:1–48.

5. In this chapter, I'm avoiding using verses like 1 Corinthians 11:10 or 15:29. In this book, I call such verses "enigmas" since they seem to defy a clear, agreed-upon explanation. I will spend a later chapter on such difficult texts. These verses may indeed need their own Sunday sermon for a different reason, though the bulk of my advice in that chapter assumes you will *not* spend a whole sermon on these verses—in fact, that may be the wrong thing to do.

cursed" (Gal 1:9), and, "But I say, walk by the Spirit, and you will not gratify the desires of the flesh" (5:16).

But perhaps standing above them all is the classic verse, "I have been crucified with Christ. It is no longer I who live, but Christ who lives in me. And the life I now live in the flesh I live by faith in the Son of God, who loved me and gave himself for me" (2:20). Many a stained-glass window has portions of this verse etched below the artwork. Not a few young children have memorized the verse as part of their kid's Bible program. Ask one hundred adult Christians to quote their life verse and this one will surely be mentioned multiple times. Every phrase of this verse offers robust theology and challenging application. Galatians 2:20 can easily support an entire sermon, at the very least.

Romans 1:16–17 is another example: "For I am not ashamed of the gospel, for it is the power of God for salvation to everyone who believes, to the Jew first and also to the Greek. For in it the righteousness of God is revealed from faith for faith, as it is written, 'The righteous shall live by faith.' "[6]

Preachers can easily spend an entire Sunday meditating on the power of God in the gospel, along with thoughts on the priority of the gospel to the Jew and the revelation of God's righteousness. There is a lot here to work with.

We might add verses like 1 Peter 3:15 to this list: "But in your hearts honor Christ the Lord as holy, always being prepared to make a defense to anyone who asks you for a reason for the hope that is in you; yet do it with gentleness and respect." This is not even a full sentence, but it's enough of a nugget to chew on for an entire morning.

Or perhaps Philippians 4:8: "Finally, brothers, whatever is true, whatever is honorable, whatever is just, whatever is pure, whatever is lovely, whatever is commendable, if there is any excellence, if there is anything worthy of praise, think about these things." Six adjectives, two nominative nouns, followed by an imperative. That's enough for a sermon indeed![7]

These are the kinds of verses where a church would expect a pastor to come to a screeching halt and *preach*. You could be tarred and feathered if you breeze past such texts or if the congregation feels like you've buried them

---

6. Romans has its fair share of nuggets, another memorable one being 12:1–2.

7. I am trying to avoid examples like John 3:16. Yes, it can be developed into a sermon. Many fine evangelists have done so. But because it's embedded in a narrative, and the narrative genre almost always requires the broader pericope to understand the author's point, I am avoiding such examples in this chapter.

with other "lesser" verses.[8] Why do these verses present such a challenge to preach and teach properly? Let's use Hebrews 13:2 to illustrate the problem.

Entertaining Angels

Hebrews 13:2 says, "Do not neglect to show hospitality to strangers, for thereby some have entertained angels unawares." This verse is a nugget. You could easily build a whole sermon around it. It's short and packs a punch. Here's what a typical sermon might look like if you were to camp out in this verse for an entire morning.

You open with an illustration about the value of showing hospitality to people. Perhaps a celebrity who was *not* shown hospitality when the host did not recognize him or her. You connect that with the verse in Hebrews, explaining the sometimes sneaky nature of angels appearing as human beings for a time. This leads to a few scriptural examples of angels doing such a thing—such as with Abram in Genesis 18 or Lot in Genesis 19. You spend a few more minutes giving a brief theological overview of the nature of angels and their ministerial service to humankind. Pepper in some pithy principles ("Angels minister to humans"; "Show hospitality to all, whether they have wings or not") and a few applications. Wrap it up with a positive story contrasting your opening illustration.

And there you have it: a sermon on Hebrews 13:2.

Except, it's not.

At least, it's not an *expository* sermon on Hebrews 13:2. It's a sermon about angels. More specifically, it's a topical sermon on a theology of angels that uses Hebrews 13:2 as a springboard rather than actually exegeting the text itself. And therein lies the challenge of preaching and teaching nuggets. When faced with a nugget, the temptation is almost always to preach a *topical theological sermon* rather than an *expository sermon*. Verses are not springboards for launching into a theological topic to preach at will. Preaching a verse means you preach its meaning, including drawing application from it and wrestling with its implications.

In the sermon I just described, the preacher might devote five minutes to the verse under consideration. But the majority of the sermon would be

---

8. Please understand, I am not saying the other verses actually *are* lesser! I am trying to empathize with the mindset of the congregation.

jumping around to other Scriptures and having a theological discussion about angelology.

Now, there's nothing wrong with theological discussions about angelology! In fact, when I teach my Introduction to Christian Theology class to incoming first-year students every semester, the angelology section is typically the one with the most discussion and most interaction, oftentimes from students who won't participate in any other topic. People love to talk about angels. Angels are a big part of Scripture and an essential part of a Christian's understanding of the unseen spiritual world around them. So, a theological discussion on angels has its place in a church. Maybe even in a pulpit. But this is not the same thing as an expository sermon on a verse.

What *would* an expository sermon on Hebrews 13:2 look like? Maybe something like this.

Start with the same opening—a celebrity gets snubbed when she's not recognized by a host. Use this as a means of getting to the verse at hand. After reading the verse, remind your congregation of its context: Hebrews 13:1 commands believers to show brotherly love. What does that love look like? Verse 2 gives us an illustration. So the command to "show hospitality to strangers" is a means of showing brotherly love.

For the bulk of the sermon, since you're only dealing with a verse consisting of a few words,[9] you spend most of your time diving into the meaning of those words, illustrating them, and applying them where appropriate. What does it mean to "neglect" something? And what is the force of the present middle imperative?[10] What did "hospitality" look like for the author of Hebrews and his audience?[11] You might use "entertained" to further illuminate what that hospitality looked like. You use a few scriptural examples of the "some" who entertained angels unawares, giving a *brief* summary of these stories. You say a word or two about the nature and ministry of angels, but only enough to help your church understand the text at hand. You talk about whether or not "angel" has the supernatural meaning or the common mean-

---

9. Eleven words in Greek, between thirteen and twenty-two in most English versions.

10. I am not suggesting you use these words, but these are some of the questions you might wrestle with in a more layperson-friendly way.

11. You may want to bring out the ξενία part of φιλοξενία, the word translated "hospitality." It literally means "love of strangers."

ing of "messenger." After carefully exegeting the verse, you consider some applications in the end that derive from the command to "show hospitality to strangers." What does that look like for the modern church?

Do you see the difference? In the first example I gave, the sermon veered into a topical discussion on angels, merely launching from the verse in Hebrews. In the second example, the sermon rooted itself in the verse and sought to derive application directly from it. In the former, the verse was the dressing and the topic of angelology was the main course. In the latter, the verse was the main course, with a little seasoning of angelology as needed to bring out the dish's flavor.

Before you start writing your angry emails, allow me to restate: I'm *not* saying topical sermons are inherently wrong or unbiblical or that the first sermon example I gave was a bad sermon. I *am* saying that it's not an *expository* sermon, and expository sermons and lessons are what this book focuses on.

How to Preach and Teach the Nuggets

How do we preach and teach the nuggets? The last few illustrations have already provided you with a few clues but allow me to make it concrete.

Study Deep

I know I already gave this advice in the previous chapter, but it's worth repeating. If you're going to say something with substance, you'll have to have something with substance to say. This means you'll have to read something with substance and stretch yourself in your studies.

If you're trained to do so, translate your passage before preaching it.[12] With such a small passage, there is really no excuse not to at least wrestle with the Greek a little bit.

You'll also want to invest in a good commentary or two. A *good* commentary or two. Not the kind you can find for free on the internet. Not the kind that comes in paperback and can just as easily be read by someone without seminary training. Find something to challenge you.

---

12. This is good advice for *any* passage you preach, even the longer ones. I start every Monday morning by translating whatever I'm preaching next. I recognize that this isn't always possible for every pastor or Bible teacher, due to education, time constraints, etc. But for those who have the tools to do so, it's an indispensable part of study.

When I candidated at my first church for the position of youth/young adult pastor, I preached on Ephesians 5:1–2. I took two years of Greek as an undergraduate, so I started my message prep by translating my passage. In our Greek class, we used Harold W. Hoehner's commentary on Ephesians.[13] Until then, I had never experienced such depth in biblical scholarship. I never even knew something like that existed! Hoehner spent nearly two decades studying and writing on those six chapters of Scripture. It shows. He provides a word study for every Greek term, extensively discusses the grammar and syntax, methodically presents each option and its pros and cons for any exegetical debate in the text, and even suggests some theological and practical application in each unit. It's more than nine hundred pages. It's magisterial. You probably need a good year or two of Greek before it's really accessible to you.

Preacher, there's a Hoehner for every New Testament book.

Romans has Moo and Cranfield—not to mention Schreiner, Longenecker, and many others.[14]

For 1 Corinthians, check out Fee or Thiselton or Garland.[15]

Philippians has Fee, the Pastoral Epistles have Mounce, Revelation has Beale and Aune and many others.[16] You can even find specialized

---

13. Harold W. Hoehner, *Ephesians: An Exegetical Commentary* (Grand Rapids: Baker Academic, 2002).

14. Moo, *Romans*; C. E. B. Cranfield, *A Critical and Exegetical Commentary on the Epistle to the Romans*, 2 vols., ICC (New York: T&T Clark, 1975, 1979); Thomas R. Schreiner, *Romans*, 2nd ed., BECNT (Grand Rapids: Baker Academic, 2018); Richard N. Longenecker, *The Epistle to the Romans: A Commentary on the Greek Text*, NIGTC (Grand Rapids: Eerdmans, 2016).

15. Gordon D. Fee, *The First Epistle to the Corinthians*, NICNT (Grand Rapids: Eerdmans, 1987); Thiselton, *1 Corinthians*; Garland, *1 Corinthians*.

16. Gordon D. Fee, *Paul's Letter to the Philippians*, NICNT (Grand Rapids: Eerdmans, 1995); William D. Mounce, *Pastoral Epistles*, WBC 46 (Grand Rapids: Zondervan, 2016); G. K. Beale, *The Book of Revelation: A Commentary on the Greek Text*, NIGTC (Grand Rapids: Eerdmans, 1999); David E. Aune, *Revelation 1–5*, WBC 52A (Grand Rapids: Zondervan, 1997); David E. Aune, *Revelation 6–16*, WBC 52B (Grand Rapids: Zondervan, 1998); David E. Aune, *Revelation 17–22*, WBC 52C (Grand Rapids: Zondervan, 1998). Also worthy of mention is Robert L. Thomas, *Revelation 1–7: An Exegetical Commentary* (Chicago: Moody, 1992); Robert L. Thomas, *Revelation 8–22: An Exegetical Commentary* (Chicago: Moody, 1995).

commentaries, like Keener's four-volume, 4,500-plus-page social-historical work on Acts.[17]

This list is by no means exhaustive and is probably more preferential than representative of the most comprehensive or longest works out there. I should also mention the plethora of specialized articles in academic journals that are readily available through every college library. Chances are, something has been written about your verse in a highly focused way.

This is not to say that you will have the time to read every Hoehner available. Nor should you spend your time like that as a pastor, neglecting your other shepherding responsibilities.[18]

If you're unsure where to begin with good commentaries, I'd recommend checking out D. A. Carson's *New Testament Commentary Survey*, now in its seventh edition.[19] I've also found the website bestcommentaries.com quite helpful. It does for Bible commentaries what sites like IMDb or Rotten Tomatoes do for movies and TV shows.

I would contend that any preacher who does not have enough to say about any single verse in the New Testament has simply not studied hard enough. When entire dissertations can be written around a single verse, certainly thirty-minute lessons can likewise be produced.

So preacher, study hard. Study deep. You'll have more than enough to say.

Preach and Teach It in Context

Even when your sermon focuses on a single verse, no verse in the Bible actually stands alone. Every verse should be preached within its surrounding context, not divorced from the overall argument of the letter or book. Its meaning derives from that context.

---

17. Craig S. Keener, *Acts: An Exegetical Commentary*, 4 vols. (Grand Rapids: Baker Academic, 2012–2015). The four volumes are titled "exegetical" commentaries, but Keener himself admits that it has a "social-historical" focus (6).

18. Nor am I saying you should preach every sermon on just a verse or two. I'm not convinced that spending twenty years in a single New Testament book in the pulpit is the best legacy for a pastor.

19. D. A. Carson, *New Testament Commentary Survey*, 7th ed. (Grand Rapids: Baker Academic, 2013). There's a similar volume by Tremper Longman III for the Old Testament: *Old Testament Commentary Survey*, 5th ed. (Grand Rapids: Baker Academic, 2013).

Therefore, even if you choose to focus your entire lesson on a verse or two, it's always appropriate to bring into the discussion some measure of what's happening around the verse. What led to Paul saying, "I have been crucified with Christ" (Gal 2:20)? The apostle Paul doesn't just write a postcard with those words plastered across the front. He writes a *letter*, and those words are nestled about a third of the way into it. There's a lot that came before. There's a whole lot more after.

How do Galatians 1 and 2 set up the statement in 2:20? What parts of Paul's arguments are necessary to help us understand 2:20 better? How does the text that follows continue to develop the verse? You might save the latter question for next week's sermon, but it won't hurt to give the church a brief glimpse ahead or a teaser of what's to come.

It's helpful, then, to inform (or remind) the audience of the verse's context. You can be creative about how you approach this. Here's a hint: You don't need to tell the church what you're doing. Just *do* it. Share with them the context without using the word *context*. It'll sound less stiff and less academic and hopefully be much more engaging.

When sharing the context, don't feel pressured to say everything. When I preached through Galatians, it was a thirteen-week series. By the time I got to 2:20, I was on week four. I didn't try to set the context by cramming three weeks of preaching into a two-minute review. I simply summarized some of the main thoughts that were necessary to get us back into the apostle's thinking.

If you're jumping into your text without having built up to it in an expository series, my advice remains the same: Set the context. It might take a bit more work since the church hasn't had the privilege to work through it to that point. But you can briefly summarize what needs to be known in just a few minutes in order to illuminate the verse even more.

Save the Topical-Theological Discussion for Another Day (or Another Venue)

Let's go back to the Hebrews 13:2 angelology discussion. It's not wrong to have an extended teaching time for your church on angels and their role in the lives of believers. In fact, many would argue that churches spend too little time in this area, especially in light of the widespread confusion that pervades our culture's idea of angels and demons.

But sometimes, we need to make a difficult decision: Do I want to preach an expository message on a verse, or do I want to do a topical survey on a topic related to this verse? I'll say it again—it's fine for preachers to pause an expository series once in a while for something topical. Topical sermons can be biblical sermons. In my experience, they take proportionately *more* time to prepare than a "normal" expository message, assuming you prepare them correctly.[20]

One way to handle this difficult decision is to offer the systematic or topical study in another venue or on another Sunday.

When I was teaching a young adult Bible study some years ago, we were working through 1 Corinthians. This book has an enormous amount of theological and textual controversy in its sixteen chapters, perhaps more than any other New Testament book besides Revelation. When we got to chapter 13 (the so-called love chapter), I knew we would need an extended discussion on the issue of tongues. But I didn't want to distract from the main point of the author, which has much more to do with love in the church than it does a theological discussion on cessationism. So I took a week to exegete and apply 1 Corinthians 13, working through it verse by verse. I let the students know that I was saving the tongues discussion for the next week. We were able to focus on the passage instead of the topic.

And the next week, I kept my word. We had an in-depth discussion on the nature and purpose and modern use of tongues. We looked at Acts, 1 Corinthians, and a few other passages elsewhere that were relevant to the topic. I didn't pretend I was doing the same thing we normally did on a Sunday night. It was a systematic study of tongues, not an exegetical/expository study of 1 Corinthians 13.

---

20. By "correctly," I mean you let the text control and dictate what you'll say in your sermon. The improper way to preach topically is to decide what you want to say about a topic, perhaps five principles about angels and demons, then find Scripture that supports each point. That's improper because it puts the cart before the horse, so to speak. A better way to approach topical sermons is to decide your topic, determine everything Scripture (or a book or area of the Bible) has to say about that topic, study those passages individually, *and then* construct your principles and sermons based on your research. It's a lot more work to preach topical sermons well. This has proven true in my own preaching. I've never worked harder at sermon prep than when I did eight weeks of topical sermons in Proverbs.

You can do this in the pulpit too. Perhaps you preach on Hebrews 13:2, maybe on its own as a nugget or maybe with some of the surrounding text. You know the issue of angels will be on people's minds, so you invite them back later that night for an extended discussion on angelology. Or you devote your normal Wednesday night Bible study to the topic. You might even set aside the next Sunday's sermon to preach topically on angels.

This kind of approach will (1) generate interest in the follow-up discussion or sermon and (2) demonstrate to the church the difference between preaching the text and preaching a topic in the text. But you should relieve your self-imposed responsibility to say everything there is to say on every word or topic that arises in Scripture. Preach the word.

Add Topical-Theological Details Only as They Explain the Nugget

I've already covered this advice to some degree, so a brief note will be sufficient here. It's not wrong to say a few things about angels (Heb 13:2), or about the flesh (Gal 2:20), or about ecclesiology in relation to Jews and Greeks (Rom 1:16). It would be difficult not to say anything about some of these larger areas of theology when preaching a nugget.

The principle is simple: Say only what needs to be said to explain and illustrate the verse at hand. Again, your verse is not a springboard into a topic. Your goal is not to offer a comprehensive word study or systematic survey of everything in your verse. Just preach the text.

At times, you may need to say a few extra things to help people understand the text. For Hebrews 13:2, it will help to briefly remind people what Hebrews said earlier about angels (they are ministering spirits sent to serve the elect—1:14; Jesus is far superior to them in every way—Heb 1–2; etc.). When preaching Galatians 2:20, your audience will need a short theological explanation of how Paul uses "flesh." This will require a cross-reference or two.

But the thesis of this chapter is that these sidebars are just that: sidebars, not the main point of the sermon. They are seasoning to your main course. They help illuminate the text at hand; they do not replace preaching the text at hand.

So ask yourself: What *needs* to be said about angels in order for my audience to understand what the author is saying in Hebrews 13:2? What must my church members know for them to grasp Paul's meaning of "flesh" in Galatians 2:20? These kinds of questions will help keep you on track as you prepare your sermon.

Memorize It

I once heard a woman on the radio who had memorized multiple books of the Bible. She explained her methodology. I was impressed, encouraged, and motivated by her discipline. But then she stated, "No pastor should preach any sermon without first having memorized the text he's preaching." I'm guessing this woman does not preach very often—certainly not on a week-to-week basis with different texts each week, and most definitely not with larger narrative pericopes!

However, her advice holds true for certain sermons, such as when you're preaching a nugget. Discipline yourself to memorize your text before preaching it if the text is small enough to do so in the time you have to prepare. If somebody shakes you awake on Saturday night and asks, "What are you preaching on tomorrow?" you should be able to repeat the verse, word for word.[21]

By the time you're ready to preach a nugget—because it's so bite-sized and you've (ideally) spent the time translating it, studying each word, examining its grammar and syntax and context, writing a sermon on it, and so on—you should have that verse embedded in your heart.

Challenge your congregation to memorize it as well. You may find yourself repeating the verse or its parts enough times in the sermon that someone could walk out of the building at the end of the service having already committed it to memory. If you encourage the people to put it to heart, it may serve as a good opener for next week's sermon to have those who memorized it stand and recite it together. Because the text is short enough, do things with it that you cannot necessarily do in other sermons.

Potential Outline

Let's bring all this together with an example outline of a sermon on Philippians 4:8, which says, "Finally, brothers, whatever is true, whatever is

21. I recall reading something similar to this sentiment related to the "big idea," perhaps in Robinson's *Biblical Preaching*, but I was not successful in tracking down the reference.

honorable, whatever is just, whatever is pure, whatever is lovely, whatever is commendable, if there is any excellence, if there is anything worthy of praise, think about these things."

Here's a thirty-minute sermon outline using that nugget:

1. Intro: What do you think about? (2 minutes)
2. "Finally, brothers": Context of Phil 1–3 (3 minutes)
3. "Whatever is . . .": Explain and illustrate each word (2 minutes each = 16 minutes)
    a. True
    b. Honorable
    c. Just
    d. Pure
    e. Lovely
    f. Commendable
    g. Any excellence
    h. Anything praiseworthy
4. "Think about these things": Briefly discuss λογίζομαι ("dwell/think on") (4 minutes)
5. Conclusion: What are you thinking about? (5 minutes)

Notice how the outline stays rooted in the text. It does not embark on long explanations on "what is truth?" or "reasons why we praise God." It gives equal proportion in the sermon to the elements in the verse. It pays attention to the surrounding context. It draws application from the text itself.

Of course, this isn't the only way to handle this verse. It might not even serve as a stand-alone sermon in your exposition of Philippians. But at least it gives you an idea of how to treat these texts without losing the focus.

5

Preaching and Teaching Textual Nightmares

Many lifetimes ago, I was a youth pastor. For a long season of life, I served full-time in ministry while also working through my MDiv at Cairn University.[1] The university was about an hour and a half from where I lived (or an hour and fifteen if I drove like I was from New Jersey). The church was quite supportive of my educational endeavors, not only supplying me with a yearly stipend toward costs but also providing me with a vehicle and gas to drive back and forth to the university while I took classes, sometimes several times a week.

Unfortunately, the vehicle was a fifteen-passenger van with the church's logo plastered on the side. There's nothing sexier than rolling around town in a nineteen-foot-long white van with five rows of seating.

One day, I pulled up the van to a Wawa to grab some dinner between classes.[2] I purchased a sandwich and a Coke—along with a cookie for a snack—and sat in the van to do some reading and eat my meal in peace. It was a nice day, and I had the window down.

Not two bites in, a man strolled up to my open window and pointed to the lettering on the side of the van. "That your church?" he asked.

"Yes," I said, chasing down a bite of turkey, ham, and cheese with a swallow of soda.

"What kind of church is it?" he asked.

---

1. At that time, Philadelphia Biblical University.

2. For those who didn't grow up on the East Coast, Wawa is a convenience store/gas station that is infinitely superior to Sheetz, 7-Eleven, Speedway, or any other similar establishments. I'm pretty sure there will be Wawas in heaven, right next to the Chick-fil-As.

My red flags started to wave in the wind. I explained to him we were an independent Baptist church in New Jersey.

He nodded approvingly and then asked the question he had come over to ask: "What version of the Bible do you use?"

I immediately saw where this conversation was going. I suppressed the urge to get snarky and tell the guy we preached from *The Message* right after the lead drummer finished his interpretive dance on stage while wearing ripped blue jeans and sneakers. Instead, I told him I usually translate right from the Greek and Hebrew.

The guy hardly heard a word I said. He launched into a diatribe about how so many churches were using liberal translations that cut verses out of Scripture and changed the Bible and how we needed to get back to the *Authorized Version*, which was the only true, inspired version and . . .

It's only fair to say that I hardly heard a word he said either. I was glad that I was sitting in an elevated vehicle, high enough so that he couldn't see the book open on my lap—*Harry Potter*.[3] The man—whose name I never received—came to pick a fight.

Now, there's nothing wrong with those who prefer King Jimmy's translation. It's a fine translation, one that I grew up memorizing in my conservative Baptist church. It boasts literary excellence and a very "literal" translation. I'm not looking to pick a fight over your preferred translation. But my conversation with Wawa Man in the parking lot revealed to me that some people are very, *very* passionate about translation issues in the Bible. What else would cause a complete stranger to walk up to someone with the sole intent of arguing about what Bible translation their church uses?

Defining a Textual Nightmare

At some point, this issue will impact your pulpit, no matter which side of the debate you're on. And no, I'm not talking about the issue of which translation to preach from (though that issue will likely impact you too). I'm talking about one of the issues *behind* translations—the issue of textual criticism.

Wawa Man didn't know it, but he was touching on this very topic when he complained about churches cutting verses out of the Bible and changing

3. For research purposes only, of course. I was a youth pastor, after all.

Scripture. The vast majority of your sermons will probably never have to bring up the issue because most text-critical issues are easily resolved and widely agreed upon.

But every now and then you come across an Acts 8:37.

Sometime during those same youth pastor years when I encountered Wawa Man, I was teaching the book of Acts to a youth group Sunday school class. We were in Acts 8, which was going well until we hit verse 37.

There is no verse 37.

At least, there isn't in the ESV. The text runs from verse 36 to verse 38. Somehow, I had missed this in my studies during the week, but one of my astute students noticed.

"Pastor Bryan—my Bible is missing verse 37!"

A little note at the bottom of the page reads, "Some manuscripts add all or most of verse 37: *And Philip said, 'If you believe with all your heart, you may.' And he replied, 'I believe that Jesus Christ is the Son of God.'*"

That's a lot of text to "cut out" of the Bible.

It launched us into a healthy conversation about manuscript transmission and text-critical issues, which I'm sure each of those teens still remembers to this day as one of their favorite youth group discussions.[4]

What do you do when you're teaching Acts 8 and need to explain why a verse is absent from your church's translation? Or what about when your translation says one thing and other favored translations say something radically different? Or what happens when you're preaching Mark 16 or John 8—two of the biggest offenders of all—where a massive chunk of text may or may not be the inspired original? How do you handle *that* from the pulpit?

Those kinds of things are what I'm defining as "textual nightmares." If you don't handle them carefully, you may end up angering the Wawa Men of your congregation (though let's be honest, Wawa Men typically find reasons to get angry no matter what!). If you ignore the problem, you may get away with it—sometimes. But eventually, if your ministry should so tarry, you'll have to decide how to end the Gospel of Mark or what to do about Jesus and the adulterous woman.

4. In case you missed it, this sentence uses the theological strategy known as "sarcasm."

If you explain yourself poorly, some in your church will likely consider you a heretic. "Pastor is cutting verses out of the Bible!"

If you ignore the problem, then your congregants won't know what to do when they're reading the Bible and their favorite translation appears to be "missing" a verse. They also won't know how to respond if they're engaged in an apologetic debate with someone who claims the Bible has been twisted and argues that these textual issues prove Scripture is not trustworthy.

If you get too academic with the issue, you'll lose people. If you don't get academic enough, you may not win over the true skeptic.

Do you see what I mean? It can be a nightmare preaching and teaching these passages. This chapter will begin by offering general homiletical advice on handling textual nightmares. Then, it will break those nightmares into four primary categories that cover most of what you'll encounter in the New Testament: (1) missing verses (like Acts 8:37); (2) John 8; (3) Mark 16; and (4) other textual difficulties. Under each category, I will offer specific advice on how to handle these issues from the pulpit.

Preaching and Teaching the Nightmares: General Advice

Before working through the four specific categories, let's begin with some general advice on how to tackle these nightmare textual issues.[5]

---

5. I consciously decided not to include an extended discussion on textual criticism in this chapter. This is not the place for that sort of thing, and careful readers will see where I fall on the issue in the following pages anyway. For preachers who need to touch up on textual theory, they can find helpful discussions in Bruce M. Metzger, *A Textual Commentary on the Greek New Testament* (New York: United Bible Societies, 1971), xiii–xxxi; Paul D. Wegner, *The Journey from Texts to Translations: The Origin and Development of the Bible* (Grand Rapids: Baker Academic, 1999), 165–240; and Gordon D. Fee and Mark L. Strauss, *How to Choose a Translation for All Its Worth* (Grand Rapids: Zondervan, 2007). For those wishing to dive deep into Hebrew textual criticism, see Emanuel Tov, *Textual Criticism of the Hebrew Bible*, 3rd ed. (Minneapolis: Fortress, 2012). I have also found the book *Myths and Mistakes in New Testament Textual Criticism*, ed. Elijah Hixson and Peter J. Gurry (Downers Grove, IL: IVP Academic, 2019), to be a helpful presentation of text-critical issues.

Gauge How Much Your Church Will Care

Start with a brief assessment of how much your church cares about this issue. If you've been in your church for several years, you will probably have a good feeling for this already. If you're new to your position, take a few seasoned elders or longtime church members out to breakfast to explore this area to get a sense of it.

One of the prime considerations will be your church's history. Does it have roots in a conservative Baptist, King James-only tradition? If so, there will likely be people lingering from that tradition who are particularly sensitive to your conclusions. Generally speaking, due to the dominance of a single translation fifty years ago, the older the church, the more people it will have who were raised in a particular tradition.

If you've recently switched from one translation to another, some people could be unfamiliar with and even suspicious of that new translation. They may have already disliked the change—it messed with all the verses they memorized as children. Now you're giving them even more ammunition against the new version because it appears to *leave out* beloved verses.[6]

You should also consider how many people have come from such a church tradition. Even if your church isn't very old, it may still have many people who migrated there, bringing their opinions with them.

If you think that your argument for the exclusion of a Bible verse due to manuscript evidence will ruffle quite a few feathers, then you will need to take even more care (and prayer!) to explain yourself and defend your position. Some churches, though, won't worry about it.

The week I wrote this chapter, I preached Acts 8:26–40. I gave a brief, two-minute explanation of the "missing verse" in Acts 8:37. I didn't get into manuscript theory. I didn't quote Metzger. I mentioned why it's footnoted in the ESV (our church's current version of choice) and then moved on. As far as I can tell, no one cared. Out of the more than six hundred people who attended and watched online, I had *one guy* come up to me

---

6. The Lord's Prayer is one of the prime "offenders" in this regard. Older English translations finish with the phrase, "For thine is the kingdom, and the power, and the glory, for ever. Amen" (KJV). Though most manuscripts have the phrase, what most scholars believe are the more reliable manuscripts leave out this last line. But to heck with the evidence: You try getting an older congregant to stop the Lord's Prayer one line earlier and see what happens!

afterward and say, "Thanks for that explanation! I was wondering about that." Otherwise, not a peep. But I remember preaching a similar passage years before at a church with conservative Baptist roots. The reaction was quite different!

Be Humble and Don't Vilify the Other Side

I poked fun at Wawa Man earlier in this chapter. And let's be honest: His arrogance needs some rebuke. But when we deal with these things in real life, we must approach the issue with great care and humility. You may be 100 percent convinced that this particular verse isn't what Luke originally wrote. Guess what? You'll probably have a church member who is just as convinced that it is original.

And you'll both be sharing space for all eternity. Best to get along now.

What you do with the ending of Mark isn't an issue of eternal salvation.[7] I'm sure there will be people on both sides of the debate in heaven. When we get there, we can ask Mark how he ended his Gospel. Someone will be right; someone will be wrong. We'll all have a good laugh about it and then go talk to John and see who is right about that one.

We must approach our opinions with a great deal more humility. Preachers who think the verse shouldn't be there must keep in mind that those who think it's original (1) believe that you may be committing a heinous sin by tearing a precious verse out of the Bible and (2) have the majority of manuscripts on their side. This calls for a humble approach.

Conversely, preachers who think the verse should be there must remember that people who don't think it's original (1) have just as much concern that you're *adding* something to Scripture as you have of them *subtracting* something from the original text and (2) have the majority of academics and the older manuscripts on their side. This also calls for a humble approach.

We must not make villains of other evangelicals over this issue. I come from a conservative Baptist background, and such individuals have a great passion for the word and place a high value on Scripture. I may not always agree with their views on certain Bible translations or textual issues, but I

---

7. I recognize some might disagree, perhaps on the basis of Revelation 22:18–19. But the issue is not someone knowingly, hard-heartedly removing a passage from Scripture. Rather, the issue is whether or not that passage was there to begin with.

can appreciate their perspectives and show them the appropriate amount of love, even in our disagreements. We can agree to disagree agreeably.

Consider the Various "Categories" of Belief

That said, there comes a time when Wawa Man needs a loving rebuke. Also, whoever represents the opposite of Wawa Man needs correction from time to time.[8]

The majority of those with strong convictions on textual issues generally fall into one of two categories: ignorant or arrogant. Some people have strong convictions due to their tradition's values, but they are uninformed about the real issues. They don't understand textual criticism or translation theory. They are ignorant. The remedy for ignorance is education, which can come from the pulpit.

Other people have strong convictions due to a belief that their position makes them "better" or more Christian than those who hold to an eclectic text (or conversely, those who hold to the *Authorized Version*). I can count on one hand the number of times I've met a humble KJV-only proponent. But again, how many times have I encountered academics on the other side with similarly arrogant perspectives? Such hubris should be rebuked.

One's opinion on these textual matters should not be the litmus test to determine what keeps someone in or out of church membership or under the "evangelical" label. It is neither a measure of faith nor a standard of orthodoxy.

You may think this discussion has gotten a little off track of homiletics. It hasn't. Take all this and apply it to the pulpit or classroom. If your church is full of Pharisaical hotheads who have no regard for other opinions, feel free to bring some heat from the pulpit. If you sense that your church is simply misinformed or uninformed, approach it with more gentleness.

Either way, present it with love.

---

8. Perhaps this could be represented by a certain college Bible professor my friend had, who arrogantly showed the class how he blacked out the ending of Mark and the early part of John 8 with permanent marker, so confident he was that these passages did not belong in the Bible. Surely the arrogance is seen on both sides. However, D. A. Carson's words ring true: "I know of no local church that excludes users of the KJV; I know of quite a few that exclude, or try to exclude, users of anything else." *The King James Version Debate: A Plea for Realism* (Grand Rapids: Baker, 1979), 78.

Uphold the Authority and Trustworthiness of Scripture

Preachers who bring up textual issues must be aware that the discussion itself has the potential to throw a believer's trust in Scripture into question. How can we know if *other* verses might have been added or removed by mistake? What confidence can I have in the Bible?

A great deal, actually.

If your sermon warrants any kind of extended discussion on a textual issue, make sure you spend enough time to assure your congregants of both the authority and trustworthiness of Scripture. When I preached John 8a (more on that below), I spent a few minutes comparing the "embarrassment of riches" (to borrow a phrase from Daniel B. Wallace)[9] of New Testament manuscripts with surviving manuscripts of other works in that time.[10] I even put a quote from Wallace on the screen at one point to show people, from a New Testament authority, the scope of the issue and the reliability of the text we have.[11]

After a long discussion on the issue, my "big idea" for the sermon was "God has faithfully preserved his word." Even though an old, much-beloved, and possibly true story about Jesus was added to John's Gospel more than one thousand years ago, *we are aware that it's not original!* Therefore, we have great reason to rely on God's word, even when we face difficult textual issues.

---

9. Darrell L. Bock and Mikel Del Rosario, "The Table Briefing: Engaging Challenges to the Reliability of the New Testament Text," *BSac* 175 (2018): 99. Although the article is attributed to Bock and Del Rosario, it is an interview with Daniel B. Wallace to whom the quoted phrase is attributed.

10. The chart was adapted from Josh McDowell and Sean McDowell, *Evidence That Demands a Verdict* (Nashville: Thomas Nelson, 2017), 56.

11. The quote came from the article by Bock and Del Rosario, "Table Briefing," 98: "I'd say over 99%, in fact well over 99%, of all our textual variants are either not meaningful, that is, they don't affect the meaning of the text, or not viable, that is, they don't have any likelihood of going back to the original, or both." I then explained, "What he means is that of all the verses with textual issues in the New Testament, less than 1 percent are truly questionable. When we compare all these manuscripts, they give us a great deal of confidence that we know exactly what those original authors wrote, even if we don't have the original documents in front of us."

Four Kinds of Nightmares

Now that I've offered some general advice on how to deal with these kinds of texts, let's look at four specific kinds of nightmares that you will encounter in the New Testament.

1. John 8

The ESV puts the text of John 7:53–8:11 in brackets and has a note preceding the section that reads, "The earliest manuscripts do not include 7:53–8:11." This note has its own footnote, which elaborates, "Some manuscripts do not include 7:53–8:11; others add the passage here or after 7:36 or after 21:25 or after Luke 21:38, with variations in the text." Other modern translations treat this text similarly, some choosing to put brackets around it (NASB), and others adding a note before it (NLT).

There are many ways to handle this from the pulpit. First, preachers must decide what they believe about John 8. Do your research. Pick up a copy of Metzger. Dust off your Greek apparatus. Grab a few *good* commentaries and consider how they weigh the evidence.[12]

It's not imperative to make a firm decision. But it *is* important that you at least know how you'll handle the text when it comes time to teach. Some of you might walk away with the strong opinion that this text is not original to John and thus not inspired. This will color the way you handle it. Some will walk away with the opposite conclusion. If so, you'll preach it like any other text of Scripture. Most of the advice in this chapter is for those who question the passage's authenticity and inspiration.

A few honest preachers may conclude that they just aren't sure. That's okay. God does not call everyone to be a textual critic, despite what your second-year Greek professor in seminary led you to believe. If that's the case, it may help to reveal that hesitancy from the pulpit. It will showcase your humility: "After studying this issue, I'm still not sure where I fall on it. Because of my own hesitancy, I'm going to preach it like I would any

---

12. I read more than a dozen commentaries on John while preaching through the book. The best ones I found were D. A. Carson, *The Gospel According to John* (Grand Rapids: Eerdmans, 1991); and Leon Morris, *The Gospel According to John*, rev. ed., NICNT (Grand Rapids: Eerdmans, 1995). Carson's was especially helpful with the textual issue in John 8.

other text." Or "After studying this issue, I'm still not sure where I fall on it. Because of my own hesitancy, we will move ahead to John 8:12. Maybe we'll revisit this story another day if my studies lead me to the conviction that it's inspired."

If you go with the latter approach, lean into the context of the story. Preach what surrounds it, read 7:53–8:11, and then move on to verse 12.[13] That way, for those who believe this is inspired Scripture, they at least heard it read aloud in church.

You may even want to consider inviting a guest preacher to deal with the text, someone with a firmer commitment that the text is inspired.[14] It's fine to acknowledge when you're over your head or when the issue in the text extends beyond your seminary training.

Here's my sermon outline, which will reveal how I handled the text:[15]

1. *Introduction to 7:53–8:11* (I introduced the problem by pointing out the ESV note.)
2. *Explanation of Biblical Inspiration/Canonicity* (I briefly surveyed some indicators that a text is inspired and canonical, along with an explanation of how textual criticism shapes that debate.)
3. *Explanation of the Textual Problem in John 8a* (I outlined both external and internal evidence that demonstrates why this passage is questioned; though my evidence largely favored my own opinion on the matter, I addressed some of the counterarguments to avoid demonizing the opposing viewpoint.)
4. *Conclusion and Application* (My sermon's "big idea" was "God has faithfully preserved his word." Since I believed this text is not original to John, I didn't draw application from it. Instead, I drew application from God's sovereign preservation of his word and the trustworthiness of the inspired Scriptures in our hands.)

---

13. One of the reasons some scholars believe John 7:53–8:11 is unoriginal is because 7:52 and 8:12 appear to connect seamlessly without the intervening material. The pronouns of 8:12 match 7:52 but not 8:11.

14. If the latter, they should not be obnoxiously arrogant about their position. You will need someone with the right sensitivity to address the topic.

15. Strangely enough, I preached the text on Mother's Day. This was not the original plan, but due to a few weather-related cancellations earlier in the year, my original sermon schedule was delayed. Nothing like a good Mother's Day sermon on the woman caught in adultery!

It was a strange sermon. By that I mean, it was by no means an expository sermon. But my convictions about the text—stemming from careful research—led me to preach it that way. I ended the sermon with a quote from *Bibliotheca Sacra* (not my usual practice!), which is worth reproducing here in full:

> In the end, Christians can be confident that most English translations of the Bible are fair representations of what the biblical authors wrote. A vast number of textual variants exist only because a vast number of ancient, hand-copied manuscripts exist. No textual variant anywhere calls any essential Christian doctrine into question or indicates completely different, competing theologies among the New Testament authors. We have not lost the message of the text. God has preserved his Word, and the text's wording is trustworthy.[16]

2. Mark 16

It is incorrect to think that the Gospel of Mark has two endings. It is more accurate to say that it has *multiple* endings, at least five:

1. 16:8
2. 16:8 + long ending
3. 16:8 + short ending + long ending
4. 16:8 + alternate short ending
5. 16:8 + long ending with extra addition after v. 14[17]

Just like the John passage, modern translations do various things with the ending of Mark. Some bracket the material after verse 8; others put it in italics; some make it look like the surrounding text and add a hearty footnote.

I confess I have yet to preach through Mark's Gospel, though I have taught through it on several occasions. But I recognize the oddity of closing a sermon series with an ending that may not be the original ending.

---

16. Bock and Del Rosario, "Table Briefing," 104–5.

17. Much of my understanding of Mark 16 has been informed by James R. Edwards, *The Gospel According to Mark* (Grand Rapids: Eerdmans, 2002), 497–504; and Mark L. Strauss, *Four Portraits, One Jesus: A Survey of Jesus and the Gospels*, 2nd ed. (Grand Rapids: Zondervan, 2020), 239, along with a few other sources.

Again, your approach must begin with a careful study of the issue. If you believe it's original and inspired, then preach it. At some point in the sermon, you may want to mention why some people believe it's not inspired. Remember: Be humble in your approach, charitable in your words, and don't vilify the other side. But go ahead and preach the text.

If you have the opposite conviction—that this is *not* the ending Mark intended, for whatever reason—then it may be more challenging to figure out how to approach the text from the pulpit.[18] The way I see it, a preacher has several options:

(1) Treat the text in a similar way to the way I treated John 8. Preach Mark 16:1–8 as one sermon. Then, assuming you don't think the rest of the text is inspired, don't preach it as such. Instead, in another sermon, offer a reasonable explanation for your informed opinion and help your church find assurance in the trustworthiness of Scripture through the art and science of textual criticism. When I preached John 8, I relied on passages like Matthew 24:35, Psalm 119:89, and Isaiah 40:8 toward the end of the sermon.

This approach gives you a way to deal with Mark 16 without preaching verses 9–20. The drawback is the awkwardness that comes from finishing a sermon series and then adding a bonus sermon about a presumably uninspired text.

(2) If the bonus sermon idea does not fit your preaching schedule, then condense it into a few minutes of explanation at the end of your Mark 16:1–8 sermon. In other words, treat 16:9–20 like any other textual issue by saying, "The best manuscripts don't support this. Let's move on." It doesn't need a whole sermon. A few minutes of explanation will suffice before cycling back to the *real* ending in verse 8. After the text-critical explanation, you have

18. Those who believe Mark 16:9–20 is not original debate the Gospel's original intent. John D. Grassmick, "Mark," *The Bible Knowledge Commentary: New Testament*, ed. John F. Walvoord and Roy B. Zuck (Colorado Springs: Cook Communications Ministries, 2000), 194, provides a helpful summary of the most common theories about Mark's ending: (1) Mark finished his Gospel well past verse 8, but the original ending was lost/destroyed in some way before it was widely copied; (2) Mark finished his Gospel well past verse 8, but it was intentionally omitted for some unknown reason; (3) Mark was prevented from finishing his Gospel for some unknown reason, such as his death; and (4) verse 8 is the intentional ending. These are all, at best, conjecture.

a perfect opportunity to segue with the question, "If 16:9–20 isn't original, then what in the world was Mark thinking by ending his Gospel in such a dreary way?" There are good explanations for this;[19] now you have a way to address the issue and close the series in one shot.

(3) End the sermon series in 16:8 and then point the congregation toward other helpful resources for those interested in the textual issue. This avoids long explanations in the pulpit and keeps the inspired text the focus of the sermon.

You can provide a summary handout at the back door when the sermon ends. If you blog, perhaps designate the week's entry to the issue, providing space to explore it thoroughly. You may want to stock your church library with a resource or two that you find helpful for this issue. Even making yourself available after the service for a light brunch (Wawa subs?) or coffee could also do the trick.[20]

This latter method scratches the itch of those more academically minded who want a more detailed explanation, whereas those who would be bored to tears in a talk on textual criticism can enjoy a good sermon without all that.

3. Missing Verses

As I sat down to write this section, I quickly checked my email and found one from a pastor who will preach Saul's conversion in Acts 9 this coming Sunday. The email asks, "Have any idea why Acts 9:5 *in KJV only* includes the quote inserted from Acts 26:14, 'it is hard for thee to kick against the pricks/goads'?"

The problem extends into verse 6 as well. Compare the KJV of Acts 9:5–6 with the ESV:

> And he said, Who art thou, Lord? And the Lord said, I am Jesus whom thou persecutest: **it is hard for thee to kick against the pricks. And he trembling and astonished said, Lord, what wilt thou have me to do? And the Lord said unto him,** Arise, and go into the city, and it shall be told thee what thou must do. (KJV)

---

19. I have found Edwards, *Mark*, 495–96, most helpful.

20. It could also attract those with an unhealthy attention to such things, so apply wisdom to this advice and use it cautiously.

> And he said, "Who are you, Lord?" And he said, "I am Jesus, whom you are persecuting. But rise and enter the city, and you will be told what you are to do." (ESV)

The bold text is unique to the KJV. These lines are not found in any Greek text but first appear in Jerome's Latin Vulgate, which Erasmus later translated into Greek for the Textus Receptus.[21] The added verses seem to have been borrowed from Acts 26:14 and 22:10, respectively.

Technically, there are no verses *missing* between Acts 9:5–6. If you were preaching this, the only people who would notice would be those who grew up memorizing the KJV or who still use it. But I've already mentioned the missing Acts 8:37, which might be more of an issue since there's a gap between verses 36 and 38.

I ran into a similar problem years ago while preaching the Gospel of John. There is no John 5:4. Instead, the ESV has a footnote that reads:

> Some manuscripts insert, wholly or in part, *waiting for the moving of the water; for an angel of the Lord went down at certain seasons into the pool, and stirred the water: whoever stepped in first after the stirring of the water was healed of whatever disease he had.*

This is a case where no manuscript before AD 400 has this verse. To make matters worse, later manuscripts that do have the verse often mark it with the ancient version of an asterisk to indicate the copyist wasn't certain it should be there.[22]

In other words, these three examples—Acts 8:37; 9:5b–6a; John 5:4—all seem to be cases where the omitted verses are omitted for good reason: They were not original to the text and thus are not inspired Scripture.

How do we deal with this sort of thing from the pulpit?

Simply put, you have two options: Draw attention to it or don't. For all three of these examples, I could make a reasonable case that attention should be drawn to them. When a verse seems to be *missing* in Scripture, it's hard to pass over it without saying anything. Acts 9:5b–6a is a well-known passage that might raise questions for that reason. I suppose if I were preaching in a church with shallow historical roots, I might pass over

21. Metzger, *Textual Commentary*, 362.
22. Metzger, *Textual Commentary*, 209.

it without a word. Just be prepared to answer a question or two after church from any eagle-eyed observers.

If you do say something about the missing verse, I recommend limiting your explanation in proportion to the size of the gap in the text. When I was preaching John 5, my explanation of the missing verse was two pages long in a 12.5-page manuscript. That's about 15 percent of the sermon given to the textual issue. While that may seem like too much, I was purposefully preparing the congregation for the much lengthier discussion on John 8 just around the corner. When preaching Acts 8:26–40, I had half a page (out of eleven) dealing with the textual issue, about 5 percent of the sermon. This was directly proportional to the size of the verse, which was less than 7 percent of the text.

The bigger the verse and the greater the potential impact, the more you should say about it in the sermon or lesson. But sometimes, it's best to keep moving and follow up with questions after the service for those who might've noticed something was missing.

4. Other Textual Difficulties

Other textual difficulties have the potential to invade a perfectly good sermon. At times, there are questions about what Greek word was original or what tense or form the word should be. Ninety-nine percent of the time, these issues go unnoticed by most readers and often by many Bible teachers. But sometimes, they are too big to ignore.

One notorious issue comes at the end of John 20. Verses 30–31 read, "Now Jesus did many other signs in the presence of the disciples, which are not written in this book; but these are written so that *you may believe* that Jesus is the Christ, the Son of God, and that by believing you may have life in his name" (emphasis mine).

Unlike the "missing" verses in Acts 8:37, 9:5b–6a, and John 5:4, the manuscript evidence is evenly split regarding the verb "believe" in John 20:31. About half of the surviving Johannine manuscripts have πιστεύητε, a present subjunctive. The other half have πιστεύσητε, an aorist subjunctive. It's the difference of one little sigma![23]

---

23. Metzger, *Textual Commentary*, 256.

Many Bible teachers have argued that the present subjunctive carries the nuance "that you may *continue* to believe" whereas the aorist subjunctive should read "that you may *come* to believe." The former would indicate John's Gospel is aimed at believers, while the latter, unbelievers.

That's a big deal.

What helps is that there may not be much difference in meaning between these two verb forms. Largely following Carson, many modern commentators recognize that John tends to use both verbal forms interchangeably when talking about believers or unbelievers.[24] When I studied the passage, my own exegesis led me—from the immediately surrounding context—to lean toward an unbelieving audience in John's Gospel.

Do you need to draw attention to this from the pulpit? By now, the answer might infuriate you: *maybe*. It depends on a lot of things—primarily, which translation you usually preach from and what your conclusions are about John's audience.

Let's say you preach from the ESV. The ESV reads like the purpose of John's Gospel is so that *unbelievers* might come to salvation. If your studies have led you to conclude that John writes to unbelievers, then you might not need to say anything. The text is translated just like you think it should be; therefore, just preach it!

Maybe you think the text should have been translated from the present subjunctive or that John's Gospel is written primarily for believers. If so, and you're preaching from a version like ESV that seems to lean toward the unbeliever, then you might need to say a few words about it. The driving question in a preacher's mind should be this: Does this discussion *add* anything to the sermon or *clarify* something that would otherwise be unclear?

One more example might help. The letter to the Ephesians opens with the words, "Paul, an apostle of Christ Jesus by the will of God, To the saints who are in Ephesus, and are faithful in Christ Jesus" (Eph 1:1).

Or does it open with those words? The phrase "in Ephesus" (ἐν Ἐφέσῳ) is missing from some of the earliest and best manuscripts. It is also missing from several early translations and quotations from church fathers.[25] To

24. Carson, *John*, 661–62.

25. Along with Metzger's brief explanation (*Textual Commentary*, 601), Hoehner, *Ephesians*, 144–48, does a thorough job examining the evidence.

further muddy the waters, at least one early writer (Marcion) referred to it as the letter to the Laodiceans. This has led many scholars to believe that the letter was originally meant to be cyclical. The gap where "in Ephesus" should be in some manuscripts acts as a "fill in the blank" for whatever church the letter was passed to next.

It's possible. You'll find evangelicals on both sides of the issue.

Is it something your church *needs* to know in order to better understand Ephesians? Probably not. It might color how you talk about the recipients of the letter, but the vast majority of Ephesians is fairly general, not nearly as specific as other letters like 1 Corinthians, Galatians, or Philemon. Therefore, many pastors have preached this book as a letter "to the Ephesians" with no ill effects.

A more pertinent question might be: Do you want to start your sermon series with a discussion on whether "Ephesus" or "Laodicea" or "fill in the blank" is the original recipient of the letter, or is it better to excite the church about the rich theology in the book? If it were me, I would choose the latter.

Final Thoughts

Much of the advice in this chapter depends on your church context and what you believe about the passage at hand. You must apply wisdom to your situation. Consider how much potential impact the textual alternative has on the meaning of the text. Some textual issues you can't ignore; some you must treat with care and humility, not to mention charity toward those with opposing viewpoints.

6

Preaching and Teaching the Old Testament in the New Testament

Making a reference in a sermon or lesson is always risky business. It does not matter what you reference or its purpose—whether to illustrate something in the text, provide a supporting anecdote, or simply add some needed seasoning in your talk—references are risky.

There's a risk that people will miss the reference. One time I thought I was being clever by adding a Bruce Buffer "It's tiiiiiiiime!" into the sermon, complete with the dramatic voice and all. In case you missed the reference like 95 percent of my audience did, Buffer is the famed announcer for all UFC fights.[1] The ten young adults who watched UFC instantly lit up, but the rest of the crowd looked at me like I was nuts.

Sometimes, you risk offending people. In another sermon, I referenced Katy Perry lyrics. It was for the purpose of illustrating the sinful junk that was infiltrating our teenage culture. A family with young kids promptly got up and made a show of leaving the auditorium. An angry email followed the next morning. Another time I referenced the movie *Braveheart*. I received a call from a concerned parent the next morning wondering whether R-rated movie references were a norm for my preaching. Their daughter was in a perilous state in her Christian walk, and they wanted to make sure the preacher was influencing her in the right direction.[2] I don't blame them for calling.

---

1. Bruce is half-brother to Michael Buffer, the guy who uses the patented catchphrase "Let's get ready to rumble!" for boxing and pro wrestling events.

2. I was sure glad this couple didn't catch my *The Silence of the Lambs* reference a few months earlier while preaching Leviticus; otherwise, they would've cooked my liver with some fava beans and a nice Chianti.

When dropping a reference in the sermon, you also risk distraction. People may become so focused on your reference that they miss what you say next, or they might start scrolling on their phones to find the meme you just displayed on the screen. What you hoped would illustrate your point has instead diverted attention away from it. References can be risky. Yet good sermons make references, whether to pop culture, movie quotes, books, other preachers, and so on.

The most pervasive references in the writings of the New Testament are the writings of the Old Testament. While we do find references in the New Testament to current events, "pop culture" (contemporary to the New Testament writers), historical figures, and various other things that traditionally pepper modern sermons, we most often hear the New Testament authors referencing their ancient prophetic counterparts.

This chapter will provide an overview of the methodology and practical strategies that preachers can use when encountering a New Testament reference to the Old Testament in their text.[3] Though many researchers regularly publish academic-level material in this field[4]—including overviews on the topic and sometimes dissertation-level monographs on single verses—very few, if any, *homiletical* resources are available to guide preachers and teachers in processing such material into a preachable format for the masses. How can a preacher help modern audiences know what to do when encountering

---

3. In my *Preaching Difficult Texts*, I have a chapter dealing with "parallel texts" in the Old Testament (147–63). This is not quite the same concept that I am describing here. The Old Testament use of the Old Testament is a large part of Scripture's use of Scripture, but it is distinct enough to warrant a separate category from the New Testament's use of the Old Testament.

4. Some of the most influential and lasting resources on the New Testament's use of the Old Testament include C. H. Dodd, *According to the Scriptures: The Substructure of New Testament Theology* (New York: Fontana Books, 1953); R. T. France, *Jesus and the Old Testament: His Application of Old Testament Passages to Himself and His Mission* (Vancouver: Regent College Publishing, 1998); and Richard B. Hays, *Echoes of Scripture in the Letters of Paul* (New Haven: Yale University Press, 1989).

For readers who want a helpful starting point on this topic, see especially G. K. Beale, *Handbook on the New Testament Use of the Old Testament* (Grand Rapids: Baker Academic, 2012); and Gary Edward Schnittjer and Matthew S. Harmon, *How to Study the Bible's Use of the Bible: Seven Hermeneutical Choices for the Old and New Testaments* (Grand Rapids: Zondervan, 2024).

a quotation or an allusion that requires knowledge of the Old Testament? There are easy steps preachers and teachers can take to help an audience understand the hermeneutics of allusions and quotations without making them feel like they're sitting through a seminary class.

Before we get into the how-to, let's survey a few definitions and one "typical" example of methodology regarding the New Testament's use of the Old Testament. This chapter will have more material on methodology than most chapters since the homiletical advice will depend on what is discussed. While this section is slightly more technical than most sections of this book, I think it will be necessary and helpful to demonstrate some of the difficulties in this field of study.

A Few Terms and Definitions[5]

We can rightly say, without exaggeration, that the New Testament is soaked in the Old Testament. To understand the New Testament, we must have a better understanding of the Old Testament.[6] One of the challenges with studying this field is that there is little agreement on terminology and definitions. Scholars can't even agree on what to call this field of work: intertextuality? inner-biblical exegesis? inner-biblical interpretation?[7] Scholars squabble over terms. Quotation, allusion, and echo seem to be the most commonly used terms to describe inner-biblical references.

---

5. Much of the following discussion is adapted from my dissertation, "'To Study the Law of the Lord': The Use of Deuteronomy in Ezra–Nehemiah" (PhD diss., Westminster Theological Seminary, 2020), 45–47.

6. I once told my congregation that the next book we were preaching would be Hebrews. They cheered. I then told them we would first do a thirty-week extensive introduction to Hebrews in the book of Leviticus. They stared at me. They thought I was joking. I was not. To this day, I still get regular texts, emails, and calls about that Leviticus series, with people grateful we took the time to work through that book.

7. "Intertextuality" is probably still the most common way for people to talk about the phenomenon of one text's use of another, though many scholars today eschew the term based on some of its presuppositions in connection to its relation to diverse literary theories. See Jonathan Gibson, *Covenant Continuity and Fidelity: A Study of Inner-Biblical Allusion and Exegesis in Malachi*, LHBOTS (New York: Bloomsbury T&T Clark, 2016), 31–32. The term "intertextuality" was coined by Julia Kristeva, *Desire in Language: A Semiotic Approach to Literature and Art* (New York: Columbia University Press, 1980).

G. K. Beale defines a quotation as "a direct citation of an Old Testament passage that is easily recognizable by its clear and unique verbal parallelism."[8] Richard L. Schultz notes that a quotation is also sensitive to and aware of its source context.[9] His criteria to identify a quotation is twofold: It must have (1) verbal and syntactical correspondence (including a determined direction of borrowing and a conscious, purposeful reuse) and (2) contextual awareness, which includes interpretive use.[10] To combine these two criteria, along with Beale's definition, we may arrive at a working definition: *A quotation is a literary phenomenon in which one text uses the exact language of another in a contextually sensitive and interpretive manner.* The phrase "exact language" does not preclude some minor grammatical or interpretive changes to the text, as most of the time some modification is necessary to fit a quoted text into a new context. However, the less the later text resembles the earlier text, the more likely that it is *not* a quotation.[11]

Defining allusions and echoes is even more difficult than defining quotations. Scholars can't agree on how to differentiate an allusion from an echo and both from a quotation. The areas of disagreement include how explicit or implicit each term is in relation to the reference,[12] the amount of intentionality to assign to each,[13] and how much of the original passage

---

8. Beale, *Handbook*, 29.

9. Richard L. Schultz, *The Search for Quotation: Verbal Parallels in the Prophets*, JSOTSup 180 (Sheffield: Sheffield Academic, 1999), 224–27. G. K. Beale, "The Cognitive Peripheral Vision of Biblical Authors," *WTJ* 76 (2014): 263–93, also argues for the contextual awareness of biblical authors quoting biblical sources.

10. Schultz, *Search for Quotation*, 222–24.

11. Some prefer to distinguish between a citation (a reference with an attributing formula explicitly acknowledging the source) and a quotation, which uses the source in the same or similar manner without an explicit attribution; e.g., Gibson, *Covenant Continuity*, 41.

12. For example, Gibson sees an allusion as "an intentional, implicit reuse of keywords or a phrase from an earlier work, which begins to exert interpretive significance in the alluding text." *Covenant Continuity*, 41. Gibson later notes that "the line between quotation and allusion is admittedly porous, but the qualitative difference between them is the element of reworking" (41–42). Hays, *Echoes of Scripture*, 23, argues, "Quotations, allusion, and echo may be seen as points along a spectrum of intertextual references, moving from the explicit to the subliminal."

13. Beale, *Handbook*, 31, includes in his definition of an allusion that it is "consciously intended by an author." It is noteworthy that he does not propose

was altered in an interpretive fashion. Coming to specific definitions for these terms is difficult enough; determining a passage's intentionality and coming to an agreement regarding whether it represents an allusion, an echo, or something else is even more difficult.

Many recognize that when biblical texts cite other biblical texts, they commonly do so with a broader contextual awareness.[14] This might be the best approach to the question of intentionality. If there is a clear awareness of the broader context of the referenced text, there is a higher likelihood that the author was intentionally making a reference.[15] Generally, the closer one gets to a quotation on the spectrum between quotation and allusion/echo, the more certain one must be of the author's intentionality in making the reference.

This will also help to distinguish between stock biblical vocabulary and an intentional quotation. An exact phrase might be used without respect to the original source context simply because it has become part of the everyday language of God's people and not because the author is making an explicit reference to the source.

Clear as mud, right? This conversation reveals just how much consternation and argumentation surrounds this topic. And if terms and definitions are challenging, then figuring out *how* to study the Old Testament in the New Testament is even more of a challenge.

---

criteria for discerning the difference between an allusion and an echo. Yet Gibson, *Covenant Continuity*, 41–43, differentiates an allusion from an echo by its intentionality.

14. Dodd, *According to the Scriptures*, 99–102; Beale, "Cognitive Peripheral Vision," 263–93; Hays, *Echoes of Scripture*, 100–101; Ian Turner, "Going Beyond What Is Written or Learning to Read? Discovering OT/NT Broad Reference," *JETS* 61 (2018): 577–94. Hays leans more toward a reader-focused approach in regard to the broader context, whereas Beale, Turner, and Dodd lean more toward an author-focused approach.

15. Determining the amount of intentionality in a quoted or referenced text should be approached on a sliding scale of probability. In many cases—especially in texts that lack a clear quotation formula—absolute certainty of intentionality is impossible. This is even more true when attempting to determine whether an author *unintentionally* referenced another biblical text. Subtle references with few lexemes could be intentional, whereas exact language might simply reflect biblical stock vocabulary with no reference to the original context. Preachers must proceed with caution in this area.

"Typical" Methodology

I placed the word "typical" in quotes because anyone who has done any research in this field will tell you—as the previous section demonstrated—there is no "typical" anything. Just as there is little agreement on terminology and definitions, there is even more disagreement on methodology—*how* we should study the Old Testament in the New Testament. There are arguments about how many references truly exist in any given text, to what extent they reveal intentionality, and how much context of the source text is to be considered relevant.

One of the most helpful recent resources on this topic is Beale's *Handbook on the New Testament Use of the Old Testament.*[16] The handbook walks through some of the challenges associated with this field of study, provides a few definitions and criteria used to discern quotes and allusions, and recommends a nine-step approach to interpretation. Here is a summary of that approach (though I urge you to pick up the book and work through the steps in more detail):[17]

1. Identify the Old Testament reference (is it a quotation or an allusion?).
2. Analyze the New Testament context.
3. Analyze the Old Testament context.
4. Survey the use of the Old Testament text in early and late Judaism.
5. Compare the texts in different translations and languages (e.g., New Testament Greek, Old Testament LXX Greek, Masoretic Text, Targums, etc.).
6. Analyze the New Testament author's textual use of the Old Testament (is he using his own translation or adapting the LXX?).
7. Analyze the author's interpretive/hermeneutical use of the Old Testament.
8. Analyze the author's theological use of the Old Testament.
9. Analyze the author's rhetorical use of the Old Testament.

---

16. Beale, *Handbook*. Another helpful resource is Schnittjer and Harmon, *How to Study the Bible's Use*. It discusses many of the topics already mentioned in this chapter as well as typology. It has many helpful case studies that demonstrate the methodology in action used throughout the rest of the book.

17. Beale, *Handbook*, 42–43, with elaboration on these steps in 43–54.

There is much about this methodology that is helpful, but there is also much that is too academic and impractical for a busy preacher or volunteer teacher.[18] A student with an entire semester to study a single New Testament quotation of the Old Testament has the time to dig into Judaic and patristic uses of the Old Testament text, as well as multiple translations.

Busy pastors are lucky if they can remember how to translate Greek. They are even luckier if they have easy access to some of the expensive academic resources needed to survey the Targums and other Jewish writings, not to mention having the time to do so.

However, pastors can use helpful "shortcuts" in these areas. Nearly two decades ago, Beale and Carson published their *Commentary on the New Testament Use of the Old Testament*, a monumental resource that discusses every New Testament quotation.[19] It modifies the nine-step methodology that Beale later lays out in his handbook with six sections per reference: (1) New Testament context, (2) Old Testament context, (3) use in Jewish sources, (4) textual background, (5) hermeneutic employed, and (6) theological use. The authors of each book were asked to study the New Testament quotations by following this methodology, allowing busy preachers and teachers to flip to a page in the commentary and quickly read a summary of how Jewish and patristic writers used that particular Old Testament text. It saves time and effort, though you skip the "fun" of doing the hard work yourself!

Preachers and teachers should also consider consulting an academic article or two on an quotation or allusion. By now, nearly every New Testament quotation has an article published somewhere on it.[20] You may not have time to translate the Masoretic Text, the Septuagint, and New Testament, do a comparative study on the differences in the translation, and

18. To be fair, Beale's book was not written primarily with lay teachers in mind.

19. G. K. Beale and D. A. Carson, eds., *Commentary on the New Testament Use of the Old Testament* (Grand Rapids: Baker Academic, 2007). For the Old Testament use of the Old Testament, no resource comes close to Gary Edward Schnittjer, *Old Testament Use of Old Testament: A Book-by-Book Guide* (Grand Rapids: Zondervan, 2021).

20. Don't skip past your commentary's footnotes. They often contain references to these more specific articles.

think deeply about the hermeneutical and theological significance of any changes, but surely someone has already done so. You probably have time to read their five-thousand-word article. It will stretch you, but it will also edify you and enrich your pulpit.

How to Preach and Teach the Old Testament in the New Testament

How a preacher approaches an Old Testament reference in a New Testament text will depend on a number of variables:

- How much time do you have to preach and how much other text do you have to preach?
- How significant is the quotation or allusion to the main point of your passage?
- How much was changed from the Old Testament source material, and how significant are those changes?
- What background knowledge is necessary to understand the original Old Testament context?

There are a whole host of other relevant questions too. But these may be the most important to discern how to approach the text. If you have a lot of time and a little bit of text, you can spend more time working through the Old Testament background. If some of the changes from the Old Testament to New Testament significantly impact the meaning of the text or relate directly to the author's point, then focus on that in the sermon or lesson.

Apply these questions and your own wisdom to the following advice.

Always Demonstrate Proper Hermeneutics

Every time you preach and teach, you should demonstrate proper hermeneutics in your methodology. Show *and* tell people what it looks like to study a passage. When you teach, you model what your small group members should do in the Bible during their own times of reading and study. Monkey see, monkey do; well, church see, church do. What pastors do with the Bible will directly impact what their congregants do with their Bibles.

Therefore, when it comes to difficult texts like the Old Testament references in the New Testament, preachers and teachers should take extra care to model proper hermeneutics and sometimes even spell it out for the congregation.

When I preached Hebrews 1:5–14, it didn't take me long to realize I was facing a text immersed in the Old Testament, with no less than seven Old Testament quotes in just ten verses. In what became one of my most notorious analogies, I likened the text to the dirty habit of chain smoking. Chain smokers smoke one cigarette after the other. They smoke one, and before that one's even completely finished, they light up another right away—one after the other. Often, they use the embers of the still-burning cigarette to light the next cigarette to smoke. Similarly, Hebrews 1 chain smokes the Old Testament! It goes from one Old Testament Scripture to another, often using the embers of the last one to stoke the fire of the next. The analogy isn't exactly prim and proper, but it's accurate and it helped my people see what the text was doing.

This was the second week in a thirty-week series focused on a book that heavily uses the Old Testament in nearly every paragraph, more than most other New Testament letters.[21] My congregation needed a crash course on understanding the New Testament's use of the Old Testament.

So, before we looked at the text itself, I gave them a hermeneutical overview in three simplified steps.[22]

Step 1: Study the Old Testament passage first. Figure out what Scripture the New Testament quotes and go there. Preacher, put yourself into the shoes of a new believer who has never read the Bible or a young teen who is just starting out. They don't know an Old Testament quote from a New

---

21. One of the fun things I did in my Hebrews series was to have my two assistant pastors focus on the original contexts of some of the most-used Old Testament passages in Hebrews when their time came to preach. So, while I preached the New Testament, they preached sermons on Psalms 2, 95, 110, and Jeremiah 31, which complemented the main series.

22. Beale has nine steps in his handbook. Beale and Carson have a more simplified six steps in their commentary. I've further modified this to three steps for the layperson.

Testament quote, and they don't always recognize when the latter quotes the former. You need to tell them how to recognize such things.

Let the church know: Many of your Bibles will have a cross-reference system or footnotes indicating which passages are being quoted. Most versions put quotations—get this—in quotation marks! Surprising, right? Other Bible translations do something special to let you know you're looking at quotations. The NASB puts the quoted material IN ALL CAPITAL LETTERS, LIKE THE TEXT IS YELLING AT YOU! The CSB puts the quoted material **in bold, so you know it's a quote**. Help your church know what your church's translation of choice typically does.

Once you've discerned a quotation or allusion, turn there and study it. What's the author saying? What was the original context? That might give you a clue why the verse is being quoted.

Step 2: Determine how and if the verse has changed from one context to the other. Does the New Testament writer modify the original verse? Leave out part of it? Add something to it? This happens a lot because sometimes the authors of the New Testament emphasize something special or highlight something in particular.

Sometimes the authors don't quote an entire verse. Sometimes they combine verses. All sorts of fun things can happen from one part of the Bible to another. Think about what has happened and consider why the author did what he did.

Step 3: Study the New Testament context and how it uses the quotation. Now that you know the Old Testament context and have seen how the quotation has changed, ask: What does the New Testament do with this passage? What was the point in quoting it? What's the author trying to say? How does this quotation enhance his argument?

As we've already seen, there are other steps you can engage in, like translating the Hebrew and the Septuagint or searching the intertestamental literature for other uses of the passage. But realistically, most pastors will not have time for this kind of intensive study during the week, and nearly all volunteer teachers will not only lack the time for in-depth study but also not know where to begin. Many have minimal training in the Bible, much less in extrabiblical literature.

When I preached Hebrews 1:5–14, I reviewed these three steps with the goal of revisiting them every couple weeks throughout the series. After this review, I demonstrated the steps seven times while preaching through the passage. My hope was that my church would not only know better by the end of the series, but they would also know how to read other New Testament books. I don't want to just preach the Bible; I want to teach people how to *study* the Bible better so that they're not dependent on me for spiritual insight.

It's like that old saying: You can give a man a fish and feed him for a day. Or you can teach a man to fish and feed him for a lifetime.

In the book of Hebrews, I could have just fed people a fish every week. Instead, I taught them how to fish . . . for Old Testament quotes. I was focused on the long game: My people, I hope, would read Matthew, Romans, and Revelation and discover that the New Testament uses the Old Testament constantly. If we want to be better readers of Scripture, we need to be dual testament readers.

At the end of this chapter, I'll reproduce an excerpt from my Hebrews 1:5–14 sermon that shows exactly how I dealt with the two Old Testament quotes in Hebrews 1:5.

Do It with Them

Sometimes, your church benefits more from you walking them through your process step by step rather than simply summarizing the results of your research. If you're teaching in a classroom setting, you can even give them time to do this themselves. We might call this process "guided self-discovery."[23] You know what you want them to learn; guide their steps to get there.

This is why many kids love science class. Science is often hands-on, experiential, interactive learning. The best science teachers do not just stand at the front of the room and lecture about chemical reactions; rather, they take their students outside and make elephant toothpaste with them.

Take a page out of your favorite science teacher's methodology. Walk your church through, step by step, how to study the New Testament's use of the Old Testament, gradually revealing what you want them to know.

---

23. One of my favorite resources to hone your skills in this area is James C. Wilhoit and Leland Ryken, *Effective Bible Teaching* (Grand Rapids: Baker Academic, 2012). It offers practical advice for teachers as it walks you through a helpful methodology for pedagogy in the church.

Hebrews 1:6 offered me a great opportunity to do just that. I had a hard time skimming past this verse, partly because I had written a thirty-page term paper on it for one of my doctoral classes, and partly because of its christological significance in the argument of Hebrews 1. When I came to this text, I invited the church to walk with me through the hermeneutical steps of discerning how the author was using the quotation.

I showed them how to look at their Bible's footnotes to figure out where the quotation was from.[24] Then we all turned in our Bibles to Deuteronomy 32:43. I showed them how the quotation in Hebrews 1:6 combines two lines of Deuteronomy 32:43 as a way of referencing the entire verse. I pointed out how that verse comes at the end of the Song of Moses, and we looked at a few significant verses in the Song of Moses to understand its context and focus.

After helping the church understand the original context of the quotation, we then turned back to Hebrews, and I asked them a few simple, leading questions:

> When Deuteronomy 32:43 commanded the Israelites to "worship him," who was the "him"?
>
> (The answer: YHWH God.)
>
> When Hebrews 1:6 applies that verse, who does it say to worship?
>
> (The answer: Jesus!)
>
> What, then, does the author of Hebrews imply about Jesus?
>
> (Jesus is YHWH God!)

I could have just said, "Hebrews 1:6 commands angels to worship Jesus because Jesus is God." Instead, I felt it was more important, more meaningful, and potentially more impactful to walk the congregation through the methodology to reach that point. This approach concretizes the steps of hermeneutics and shows the church what good Bible study looks like in action.

The other benefit of this method is that it tends to lend greater authority to the preacher or teacher. The church does not just have to take your

24. The quotation in Hebrews 1:6 is a bit more complicated than most because it possibly comes from Psalm 97:7 or Deuteronomy 32:43. I argued it came from the latter, based on a version found in the Dead Sea Scrolls, which predates the Masoretic Text. I'm sure my church members were grateful that I at least summarized *that* part of the methodology for them!

word. By leading the church on a guided *self*-discovery, they come to the same conclusion as you did, but the authoritative, inspired text of Scripture gets the "credit" for the conclusions.

It's great when we can take audiences on a journey through the text and teach them hermeneutics along the way. One warning, though: Remember that your church won't necessarily be able to or want to replicate everything you're doing from the pulpit.

If you do not have access to resources or the ability to translate the Septuagint, the average Joe in the pew likely will not either. If your congregants can't replicate what you're doing from the pulpit without an advanced Bible degree, whatever you're doing may be counterproductive.

There are certainly times when you'll do something from the pulpit that they cannot or are not expected to do from home. You know Greek. You know Hebrew. You've spent years studying this stuff, learning from experts. You *should* say profound things from time to time that your congregants may not necessarily arrive at on their own.

But if you regularly feed your people something they can't make at home, it can breed frustration or an unhealthy dependency on your interpretation or even smack of arrogance on your part.

So, do it with them. But do it in such a way that they can not only follow along with you on Sunday morning but on Monday morning as well.

Do It for Them

Sometimes, due to time constraints or other factors, preachers will find it best to simply do the work *for* the congregation and report the results.

Let's use another example from Hebrews 1:8–9, which quotes Psalm 45:6–7. When I was preaching this passage, by the time I got to this quotation, I had already summarized many others. The significance of the quotation was easily seen, and I didn't believe the full details of the psalm required a long explanation for the church to catch the meaning and purpose of the reference.

So, instead of going back to Psalm 45 and studying it with the church, I simply said,

> This quotation comes from Psalm 45:6–7. That psalm speaks of God's righteous reign. Hebrews reproduces the text of the original exactly, with just one minor change:

> Psalm 45:6 reads, "The scepter of your kingdom is *a* scepter of uprightness."
>
> Hebrews 1:8 reads, "The scepter of your kingdom is *the* scepter of uprightness."[25]

In other words, Hebrews makes it more definite. The Son of God rules with *the* scepter of righteousness, par excellence! Jesus rules as the prime and ultimate example of what it means to rule with justice and integrity!

In fewer than one hundred words, I summarized (1) the original context of Psalm 45, (2) the significant textual change between the passages, and (3) the significance of the quotation in context with Hebrews 1.

Do a detailed textual comparison from the pulpit *only when necessary.* Painstakingly going through every hermeneutical step may have some value, but it's not always needed. After all, you don't share the results of every word study you do from the pulpit, do you? You don't say everything you could say every time (I hope!). Sermons are not commentaries. Sermons are not dissertations.

Sometimes, the result of your careful study is to confirm what is already obvious in the text. Or to craft the way you will say a line or two in the sermon. You don't need to air out from the pulpit everything you've done in the office each week.

Again, use discernment. Sometimes the church needs to work through the steps themselves (with you). Sometimes you can use a shortcut to get them to the results faster. Different sermons and lessons require different strategies.

Use Visuals When Making Detailed Comparisons

Preachers too often forget that their churches have not spent ten or more hours studying the passage throughout the week. If we're lucky, a small number in our churches have *read* the passage ahead of time. Even fewer have given it any thought and prayed over it.

Therefore, we can't expect them to follow every word without giving them some serious help, especially if our texts are difficult and rely on complicated intertextual comparisons.

---

25. I intentionally modified the order of the text in order to draw out the parallelism between the verses.

So, use visuals whenever possible. The more complicated the quotation (and thus, the more you have to discuss it), the more necessary the visual.

For example, not too long ago I was preaching on Acts 7—Stephen's sermon before he was martyred. Talk about a sermon *soaked* in the Old Testament! Nearly every line of his message quotes or alludes to other Scripture. Because of the amount of text I had to preach, I had to be selective in which allusions to spend extra time on. One of the references I zeroed in on was Acts 7:7, which reads, "'But I will judge the nation that they serve,' said God, 'and after that they shall come out and worship me in this place.'"

After studying the passage, I was convinced Stephen was pulling his quotation from two sources: Genesis 15:14 and Exodus 3:12. Because the quotation combined the purpose of worship with the exodus from Egypt and introduced significant theological themes in Stephen's sermon, I felt it was helpful to demonstrate the multiple sources of the quotation and explain why Stephen chose to spice up Genesis with Exodus. I used a simple PowerPoint slide to show the relationship between the texts and where each part of the quotation came from:

> "*But I will judge the nation that they serve*," said God, "*and after that they shall come out* and **worship me in this place**." (Acts 7:7)
>
> *But I will bring judgment on the nation that they serve, and afterward they shall come out* with great possessions. (Gen 15:14)
>
> He said, "But I will be with you, and this shall be the sign for you, that I have sent you: when you have brought the people out of Egypt, **you shall serve God on this mountain**." (Exod 3:12)

Notice how the italics in Acts 7:7 correspond to the italics in Genesis 15:14, while bold text matches the bold text in Exodus 3:12.[26]

I did something similar when preaching Acts 2. Notably, Peter quotes Joel 2:28–32 [3:1–5 LXX] in Acts 2:17–21. There are a few significant changes between the two texts. For the first major change, which I felt was significant enough to draw attention to, I put this on the screen:

26. I noted in my sermon that the bold portions of the two texts in New Testament Greek and the Septuagint correspond even more closely in Greek than in English.

> "*And it shall come to pass afterward*, that I will pour out my Spirit on all flesh." (Joel 2:28)
>
> "*And in the last days it shall be*, God declares, that I will pour out my Spirit on all flesh." (Acts 2:17)

The italicized text emphasizes what was changed. This was a simple way for people to visualize what Peter did in his quotation. By changing the opening phrase of the prophecy to "in the last days," Peter was effectively correlating the events of Pentecost with the events of Joel 2 and also characterizing his time as "the last days." This is a radical shift in perspective, one worthy of highlighting on the big screen.

Visuals don't have to be only about individual verses. Going back to Stephen's sermon in Acts 7, he borrows from a number of Old Testament sources throughout Scripture to make his case before the Sanhedrin. To help people follow the many textual shifts, I displayed this slide on several occasions (the sections of Stephen's sermon also corresponded with my sermon outline):

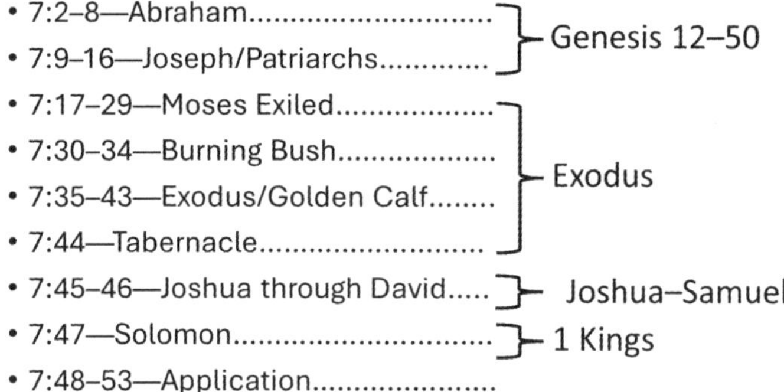

Whenever possible, using graphics not only aids the visual learners in the church but also helps people keep track of the sometimes complicated data that characterizes much of intertextual exegesis.

You don't need to be an expert on intertextuality to successfully preach the Old Testament in the New Testament. Though these texts offer unique challenges, a few simple strategies will help you guide your church through your passage.

Excurses: Manuscript for Hebrews 1:5
(Part of My Hebrews 1:5–14 Sermon)[27]

> For to which of the angels did God ever say, "You are my Son, today I have begotten you"? Or again, "I will be to him a father, and he shall be to me a son"? (Heb 1:5)

Notice the opening word "For." When you're studying Scripture, it's always good to ask, "What is the *for* there for?" It connects one thought to the next.

Here, the "for" proves the point. The author of Hebrews just finished showing how Jesus is greater, having inherited a name more excellent than the angels. That name, we saw, was the "Son" of God. To prove his point, he quotes the Old Testament twice and says, "God never said *this* about angels. But God said it about his Son." The first quote comes from Psalm 2:7, which is in an important messianic psalm. This psalm has historical relevance for the people of Israel, but it ultimately points to fulfillment in the Messiah, in Jesus Christ.

To summarize the psalm, the nations and kings are plotting against God and God's king. They want to overthrow the throne of Israel, and God sits up in heaven and laughs at their plans. God set his king in Israel, and he isn't moving until God decides he's moving. There's nothing the nations can do about it! Then God shows the reason for his certainty that the king of Israel won't be moved. Psalm 2:7 says: "I will tell of the decree: The Lord

---

27. Note that this is not the full sermon. The full sermon is available online on YouTube. This excerpt is intended to illustrate how proper hermeneutics *can* be demonstrated in a sermon that deals with the Old Testament in the New Testament. Before getting to this point in the sermon, I reviewed last week's sermon, and I walked through the three steps to interpreting the Old Testament in the New Testament, as explained above. This is not the only way, or even the best way, to preach this text, but this was my way, for better or worse. I pray preachers and teachers might learn something from it. I edited portions of this sermon for readability in a book.

said to me, 'You are my Son; today I have begotten you.'" Hebrews quotes Psalm 2:7 exactly, or at least the last half of the verse. It doesn't change or modify anything.

God is the speaker in the beginning of this verse. He says, "I will tell of the decree." He's referring here to what we call the "Davidic covenant"—the promise that there will always be a son of David on the throne of Israel. That one day, a descendent of David will sit and reign on Israel's throne forever and ever.

Psalm 2:7 summarizes that covenant by picturing the Lord saying to this future Davidic king, "You are my Son; today I have begotten you." The early church and even the Jewish people interpreted this psalm messianically. They said, "This psalm is looking at more than just David, more than Solomon, more than any earthly king of Israel. It looks forward to the Messiah." God sits in heaven and laughs at earthly rulers, because he knows that the Messiah will inherit the earth as eternal, sovereign king. And God in this psalm calls the Messiah "Son." You are my Son.

The second quote in Hebrews 1:5 comes from 2 Samuel 7:14, which is situated within the context of the covenant that God made with King David. This *is* the Davidic covenant chapter! So these two quotes go together. They were interpreted in light of each other.

In 2 Samuel 7, David asks God if he can build a house for God, a temple. And God says, "I'll do you one better. I'll build *your* house, your dynasty. Your offspring will build a house for me, and then I'll establish the throne of his kingdom forever." Ultimately, God's not just talking about King Solomon here. He's talking about the Messiah. That prophecy—the Davidic covenant—is fulfilled in the Messiah, in Jesus. It's in that context that God says, "I will be to him a father, and he shall be to me a son."

So Hebrews 1:5 quotes from two passages—one speaks of the Messiah as sovereign king who will rule over all the earth one day, while the other speaks of God's covenant with King David, promising that the Messiah will one day rule on David's throne forever. In both passages, God calls the Messiah "Son." The point that the author of Hebrews makes is that God *never* called the angels "Son." They don't share that special relationship with God.

Now, we do see places in the Bible where the angels *collectively* are called the "sons of God." In Job 1 and 2, the "sons of God" come with Satan to present themselves before God. Genesis 6 *might* refer to angels as "sons of God."

So the Bible does use "*sons* of God" to refer to angels sometimes. But no single angel is ever called "the *Son* of God." And especially not in the sense that it's used here: the Davidic ruler, the sovereign king, *that* Son of God!

Sometimes my kids think they're funny and they call me "Pastor Bryan" around the house. Little comedians. I tell them, "Hundreds of people call me pastor. But only *you*, Son, only *you*, Daughter, have the privilege of calling me 'Dad.'" That makes them special in relationship to me. God says, "I might call the angels 'sons of God,' but there is only one true Son of God, and that's Jesus." And that relationship makes Jesus most special.

So this is the author's first point: Jesus is greater than angels because he is the Son of God, the Davidic king. Jesus is the fulfillment of the Old Testament Davidic covenant. The angels are not.

7

Preaching and Teaching the Apocrypha

Many legends are born from some degree of truth. Sometimes, the further down the line the legend passes, the more the story obscures the core truth and enhances the fanciful details.

Legend has it in my family that my great Uncle Eddy—known as "Fast Eddy" by the Jersey City mafia—once got so drunk that he stole an airplane and drove it around in circles on the runway of Allaire Airport until it ran out of fuel.[1] How much of that legend contains truth?

Knowing my late uncle's reputation, probably too much.

Separating truth from apocrypha can be tricky enough in life. It is even trickier in the Bible. Many Christians are quite disturbed to hear that the Bible sometimes references noninspired texts, like Jude's and 2 Peter's references to Enoch or Hebrews 11's possible allusion to 2 Maccabees. How does a preacher treat these allusions appropriately without elevating a noncanonical text too highly while still helping the audience understand the value of such ancient documents?

Furthermore, if these biblical authors quote or reference nonbiblical texts, what exactly does that say about the historicity and veracity of those sources? If part of 1 Enoch represents truth, does that mean the rest of the book follows suit?

Exacerbating the problem is most people's ignorance and confusion about these noncanonical books. Years ago, I was teaching a class in church on the doctrine of the word of God. After an opening discussion on the

---

1. Allaire Airport in Wall Township, New Jersey, is now known as Monmouth Executive Airport.

doctrines of inspiration and inerrancy, we talked about how the church came to recognize the inspired canon of Scripture.

I summarized a few "tests of canonicity." Adapted from Norman L. Geisler and William E. Nix's excellent book *From God to Us: How We Got Our Bible*, we can consider the following questions to determine whether a book is from God.[2]

(1) *Is it inspired by God*? This may seem a bit circular, but we must remember that the books of Scripture were inspired immediately upon writing.[3] Perhaps it is more accurate to say that the books of Scripture were inspired upon their final form, but this nuance extends beyond the scope of this present work. Inspiration was not something conferred on a book decades or centuries later by some church council. We *recognize* inspiration, but we do not *decide on* inspiration.

(2) *Is it written by a spokesperson of God*? Prophets and apostles were spokespersons of God. They represented God in his authority and word and communicated his word to others. At times, God inspired them to write his words, which would be recognized as authoritative Scripture for all times (2 Pet 1:21).

Normally, spokespersons of God were prophets and apostles. There are a few exceptions, though most, if not all, of these exceptions seemed to have a direct connection with the prophets and apostles. Some of these non-apostolic writers include Mark, Luke, possibly the author of Hebrews, James, and others.

(3) *Was the book collected and preserved by the people of God*? The community of faith must have recognized its authority and preserved it. I'm sure some of the apostles wrote grocery lists at times when running to the market for their wives. That doesn't mean those lists were inspired Scripture. We

---

2. Norman L. Geisler and William E. Nix, *From God to Us: How We Got Our Bible* (Chicago: Moody, 2012), 93–96. Note that I have modified their five steps. Their five "principles for discovering canonicity" include (1) Was it written by a prophet of God? (2) Did the writer have credentials from God? (3) Did it tell the truth about God, man, etc.? (4) Did it possess the life-transforming power of God? (5) Was it received or accepted by the people of God for whom it was written? My fourth question is an addition to Geisler and Nix's principles.

3. By "upon writing," I am not meaning to disregard "inspired updates" to texts, such as the ending of Deuteronomy or alleged anachronisms in Genesis (e.g., 36:31).

know Paul wrote letters that were not preserved as canon.[4] There is good evidence throughout both the Old and New Testaments that immediately upon being written, Scripture was accepted and viewed as Scripture.[5] If a book was not recognized as inspired by the community of faith, that may indicate it was not inspired!

(4) *Does the work accord with other known inspired books*? God is true in all he says. Truth does not contradict other truths. Therefore, the Bible will not contradict itself. If a text contradicts another text, then either one of the texts is wrong (and thus not inspired) or both are wrong (and neither are inspired). But both cannot be true and inspired while contradicting.[6]

Going back to my church Bible class—after reviewing these "tests of canonicity," we then worked through a few books of the Bible as examples. Along the way, several questions arose about noncanonical books. What about those books that didn't make the cut? Why didn't they? And why do some religions and denominations accept them into their canon and others do not?

Because of these questions, we spent a week talking about the Apocrypha (since that was most relevant to our cultural context, considering the

4. Such as the letter to Corinth that preceded 1 Corinthians (1 Cor 5:9). This test of canonicity helps answer the question, "What would happen if we discovered one of Paul's lost letters?" The answer is that it would still not be included as Scripture. The early church had the letter and did not preserve it, which indicates that they did not recognize it as inspired. Just because an apostle wrote it does not mean it is inspired.

5. There is a great deal of evidence within the canon of Scripture that the community of believers recognized Scripture as Scripture soon after it was written. For some Old Testament examples, 1 Kings 16:34 recognizes Joshua 6:26 as "the word of the Lord"; Daniel considered Jeremiah to be prophetic Scripture (Dan 9:2; Jer 25:11–12); the people in Zerubbabel's day recognized the law of Moses as Scripture (Ezra 3:1–4). In the New Testament, many writers claimed that their works came from God (1 Thess 4:15; 2 Pet 3:2). Some even recognized other contemporary New Testament letters and works as inspired Scripture (1 Tim 5:18; 2 Pet 3:15–16). These texts demonstrate that it didn't take several centuries and many church councils to determine what was in Scripture and what was not, but the inspired texts were recognized as such upon their completion.

6. To avoid getting too distracted by the topics of canon and inspiration, I would refer readers to the Chicago Statement of Biblical Inerrancy for an articulation of the theological and practical applications of this doctrine. Several works have been written to help evangelicals deal with supposed contradictions in known inspired writings, such as Norman L. Geisler and Thomas Howe, *The Big Book of Bible Difficulties* (Grand Rapids: Baker, 1992).

many Catholic churches in the area). As we discussed the Apocrypha and I drew a few conclusions about their noninclusion in Protestant Bibles, a woman raised her hand and asked, "If the Apocrypha is not inspired Scripture, why then did Jude quote it?"

It felt to me like an "Aha! Gotcha!" moment. She thought she had pinned me, or at least that she had some knowledge I had missed in my preparation and presentation.

My answer to her was simple: "Jude did not quote the Apocrypha."

She, of course, was quick to rebut, "Jude quotes 1 Enoch! He quotes the Apocrypha!"

"First Enoch is not part of the Apocrypha," I explained.

What followed was a good discussion about the differences between the Apocrypha, the Pseudepigrapha, and other texts that surround the two Testaments. Because many Christians and—unfortunately—many Bible teachers and pastors do not know the difference between these extrabiblical works, I will provide a brief overview of them so that we know what we're talking about in this chapter.

Overview of Noncanonical Works

The following is designed to provide a brief description of the noncanonical texts and offer preachers and teachers a useful starting point for finding more information. Readers should consult other books for a more comprehensive list of such works.[7]

The Apocrypha

The Apocrypha are the books most Christians are semi-familiar with, as they appear in the canon of the Roman Catholic Church. These books are found in the Septuagint (the Greek translation of the Hebrew Old Testa-

---

7. The most helpful lists I've found are in Geisler and Nix, *From God to Us*, 115–29 (Old Testament noncanonical texts) and 143–60 (New Testament noncanonical texts), which detail the reasons for acceptance or rejection by certain traditions. Cf. J. Julius Scott Jr., *Jewish Backgrounds of the New Testament* (Grand Rapids: Baker Academic, 1995), 29–39, 357–63. The list in this book features only a few of many possible extrabiblical texts. Readers may also want to consider other texts such as the Nag Hammadi Scriptures, Josephus, and Philo.

ment), and most were written during the years between the Old Testament and New Testament.[8] These books include Wisdom of Solomon, Sirach (Ecclesiasticus), Tobit, Judith, 1–2 Esdras, 1–2 Maccabees, Baruch, Epistle of Jeremiah (not the same as the biblical book of Jeremiah), Additions to Esther, Prayer of Azariah, Susanna, Bel and the Dragon, and the Prayer of Manasseh.

Some of these books detail the history of intertestamental Judaism (e.g., 1–2 Maccabees). Others are stories of Jewish heroes (e.g., Tobit and Judith) or additions to or expansions of biblical books (e.g., Additions to Esther and Prayer of Manasseh). Some sound like Hebrew poetry and wisdom literature (Sirach and Wisdom of Solomon).

Though these books are accepted as canonical by the Roman Catholic Church and a few others, both Judaism and Protestant Christianity never accepted them as inspired Scripture.[9]

The Old Testament Pseudepigrapha

"Pseudepigrapha" means "false writings." These books were written by Jews between roughly 200 BC to AD 200. Their diverse literary forms—including history, legends, prayers, psalms, wisdom literature, and apocalyptic literature—are matched only by their range of theological viewpoints.[10] The number of works included in this list fluctuates depending on who's counting, but the classic two-volume edition edited by James H. Charlesworth contains more than sixty texts.[11] Some of the more familiar ones include 1–4 Enoch, Testament of Job, Jubilees, and Jannes and Jambres.

These books were *not* written by the authors to whom they are attributed. Enoch did not write 1 Enoch. It is debated to what extent these books reflect the original teachings of their eponymous authors, but each case

---

8. The exception is 2 Esdras, written c. AD 100.

9. See Geisler and Nix, *From God to Us*, 120–28, for a helpful list of apocryphal texts, as well as some discussion on why certain groups accept these books while others don't.

10. I am indebted to Scott, *Jewish Backgrounds*, 30, for this description of these works.

11. James H. Charlesworth, ed., *The Old Testament Pseudepigrapha*, 2 vols. (Peabody, MA: Hendrickson, 1983). Additional texts have been published in *Old Testament Pseudepigrapha: More Noncanonical Scriptures*, ed. Richard Bauckham, James R. Davila, and Alexander Panayotov (Grand Rapids: Eerdmans, 2013).

must be decided with care and extreme caution. Most, if not all, of these works have clear historical errors coupled with outright heresy and unbiblical, fanciful teaching.[12] Like the Apocrypha, these works were never accepted as canonical by either Jews or Protestant Christians.

The New Testament Pseudepigrapha

Much like their Old Testament counterparts, these books were not written by those whose names are on the cover, so to speak. There are three hundred or so of these works spanning several centuries *after* the time of Christ, so their actual bearing on New Testament interpretation is limited. Some of the more notorious texts include the Gospel of Thomas (first-century gnostic text about the miracles of Christ), the Gospel of Judas (second-century gnostic text making Judas a hero), and the Epistle to the Laodiceans (a clear forgery).[13] Others, such as the Barnabas (c. AD 70s), the Shepherd of Hermas (c. AD 115–140), and the Didache (c. AD 100–120) were held in high regard by the early church but ultimately rejected as noncanonical.[14]

Geisler and Nix list about half a dozen reasons these books were virtually unanimously rejected, including their obvious false authorship, false claims about biblical events, false teachings, denial of the deity of Christ, and rejection by both early church fathers and modern experts.[15]

The Dead Sea Scrolls

The Dead Sea Scrolls, accidentally discovered in 1947 by a shepherd looking in Qumran for his lost flock, remain the most significant biblical archaeological discovery of the last several centuries. The scrolls include hundreds of Old Testament texts, providing a wealth of text-critical resources for scholars. Additionally, they include many apocryphal and pseudepigraphic texts, as well as documents outlining the community beliefs of the Essenes, including eschatological speculations and biblical interpretations.[16] They even include a copper treasure map!

---

12. See a list in Geisler and Nix, *From God to Us*, 117.

13. See Geisler and Nix, 144–47, for a more complete—though not exhaustive—list.

14. Dates from Geisler and Nix, 154–56.

15. Geisler and Nix, 147–49.

16. List from Scott, *Jewish Backgrounds*, 31–32.

Although the scrolls represent material completed before the time of Christ, they provide invaluable information about the community of faith leading up to the apostolic era.

The Mishnah, Talmud, and Other Jewish Writings

The Jews wrote a lot. Much like modern-day Christians, they loved arguing and codifying interpretations and opinions on the Bible. Several significant texts provide insights not only into their theological interpretations of the Old Testament but also into the cultural and historical background of the New Testament.[17]

The Mishnah is written documentation of the oral tradition of the Jewish people. Although it was eventually codified in written form around AD 200, the traditions it records date back to the time of Christ and earlier.

The Talmud comes in two editions: the Jerusalem Talmud, completed in the late fourth or early fifth century AD, and the much longer (thirty-five-volume) Babylonian Talmud dating to the late fifth century AD. The Talmud contains legal rulings and interpretations (*halakah*) and nonlegal legends and narratives (*haggadah*). Strauss summarizes some difficulties with using these texts to study the New Testament:

> The greatest problem with using the Talmud to study the background to the New Testament is the difficulty in dating its material to the first century. Even when rabbis from the first century are quoted, it is not certain that material attributed to them is authentic. At the same time, the many agreements between the New Testament gospels and the Talmud with reference to Jewish culture, customs, and theology confirm that the Talmud, and especially the earliest part of the Mishnah, provides valuable information for first-century Jewish background.[18]

Other Jewish writings include the Targums (Aramaic expanded paraphrases of and additions to the Old Testament), Midrash (Jewish commentaries on the Old Testament), the Tosefta (oral traditions written several hundred years after the time of Christ), and the writings of Josephus and Philo.

---

17. The following list relies heavily on Strauss's overview and charts in *Four Portraits, One Jesus*, 182–84.

18. Strauss, *Four Portraits, One Jesus*, 182.

Why Do New Testament Authors Quote or Allude to Non-Inspired Texts?

The challenge with studying and preaching these texts in the New Testament is their different purposes and functions within their respective contexts. They may even represent different levels of truth. This is why I've included a brief overview of many major biblical texts that quote these extrabiblical sources at the end of the chapter to aid preachers.

However, we can still discern some major trends within this wide variety of texts.

Sometimes, noninspired texts have nuggets of truth in them. This may be the case with Hebrews 11:35, which possibly alludes to 2 Maccabees 7. Hebrews 11:35 reads, "Women received back their dead by resurrection. Some were tortured, refusing to accept release, so that they might rise again to a better life." In a list of other factual, historical examples from the Old Testament of men and women who had faith, suffered, and did not receive earthly rewards, there seems to be an allusion to an event outside the Old Testament.

If this is indeed the case, then it may reflect an account that actually happened. This does not mean that the entire book of 2 Maccabees should be considered either inspired or entirely factual. Surely it got a few things wrong, which would remove it from both the inspired and entirely factual categories![19] But this particular story, at least in some form, probably did happen—assuming this is indeed what Hebrews 11:35 refers to.

Jude 14–15 is a more challenging example. Here, Jude quotes 1 Enoch 1:9. Jude writes, "It was also about these that Enoch, the seventh from Adam, prophesied, saying, 'Behold, the Lord comes with ten thousands of his holy ones, to execute judgment on all and to convict all the ungodly of all their deeds of ungodliness that they have committed in such an ungodly way, and of all the harsh things that ungodly sinners have spoken against him' " (14–15).

Scholars agree that Jude is quoting some form of 1 Enoch 1:9. He introduces the quote with the verb "prophesied," a term often associated with inspired texts of Scripture elsewhere (e.g., Matt 11:13). What do we do with this?

---

19. Wegner, *Journey from Texts*, 125, has a chart listing many of the inaccuracies of the apocryphal books, including errors of chronology, geography, and theology.

Opinions have ranged from including 1 Enoch as Scripture to excluding Jude as Scripture, with a host of positions in between. It could be that Jude is quoting a passage from 1 Enoch that *was* an actual prophecy—either prophecy passed down (orally?) from Enoch's generation (unlikely) or prophecy written by the author of 1 Enoch, who was most certainly not Enoch himself. Could it be that, amid all the other wacky statements and prophecies in 1 Enoch, the author actually got something correct? After all, if you throw enough spaghetti against the wall, something's bound to stick, right? And in 1 Enoch, there's a *lot* of spaghetti being thrown.

Or could Jude be referencing the story in 1 Enoch without necessarily saying it is inspired or truthful? He's using "prophesied" from his audience's perspective. Many of his contemporary readers valued 1 Enoch to some degree, and he quoted a familiar prophecy from it to make his point.[20]

It would be like me saying from the pulpit, "In the movie *The Matrix*, the Oracle prophesied that the coming of the One would herald the destruction of the Matrix." In giving this illustration, I'm not saying that *The Matrix* is inspired Scripture, nor that the Oracle is a real historical figure,[21] nor that the Oracle is accurate in anything she says. I'm drawing an analogy from pop culture.

Let's take a breath and summarize.

Sometimes noninspired texts have a nugget of truth in them. Other times they don't, and the authors reference them simply to represent commonly known stories that their contemporary readers would have been familiar with. You, preacher, will have the difficult task of discerning which is which as you wrestle through these quotes.

Keep in mind, *you don't always need to have an opinion on how much "truth" is assumed in the noninspired text.* It's not always necessary to determine this in order to understand, preach, and apply the biblical author's point.

Because every quote or allusion to a noninspired text comes in a context of inspired biblical truth, your main task is to discern the point of the biblical author, not how much weight to give the noncanonical source. Jude uses 1 Enoch to make the point that ungodly sinners will be decisively and righ-

---

20. Carson, "Jude," pages 1074–75 in *Commentary on the New Testament Use of the Old Testament* (Grand Rapids: Baker Academic, 2007), has a helpful, albeit brief, discussion on the matter.

21. Though Enoch is, which is where the analogy breaks down.

teously judged. You don't need to know how much of 1 Enoch represents the facts about angelology and eschatology in order to follow Jude's argument.

Make sure, then, that you stay focused on the overall argument of the biblical author and stay grounded in the inspired context.

Preaching and Teaching the Noninspired Texts

Much of your homiletical work will resolve itself as you study these noninspired references individually in the context of your passage. But some specific advice for preaching and teaching will help you maintain perspective as you wrestle with these difficult texts.[22]

Don't Be Afraid to Handle the Texts

Any other Sunday, it would be exceedingly strange to open the Mishnah and begin reading from a noninspired oral tradition written several centuries after Jesus. Yet when the text of Scripture explicitly touches on such tradition, it invites the preacher to do something that he wouldn't otherwise do from the pulpit. Don't be afraid to interact with these noninspired texts. It's okay to quote them and even to open your physical copy and read from them (assuming you have a physical copy—some of these books can be quite expensive!).

The truth is, we read and quote and reference noninspired texts all the time from the pulpit, don't we? How many preachers have embellished stories from the New Testament, whether through dramatic retellings or simply by adding details the text does not provide? Whether through talking vegetable cartoons for children or uber-popular TV shows like *The Chosen* for adults, many of us have sanctioned fanciful "additions" to the biblical text for years.

Old-school pastors seem to delight in using apocryphal stories as illustrations—like the father who works as a drawbridge keeper who makes the choice to crush his son to death to save a train full of passengers.[23] Or

22. Much of the following advice is also relevant for several Old Testament books, like Chronicles and Ezra-Nehemiah, which rely heavily on outside sources and sometimes even reference noncanonical texts (e.g., 1 Chr 29:29; 2 Chr 12:15; 33:19).

23. Snopes rates this story as "legend" and traces it to a 1967 short story written by Dennis E. Hensley in the *Michigan Baptist Bulletin*, which itself may have roots in another story from the late 1800s. Barbara Mikkelson, "Did a Father Sacrifice

the little girl who needs a blood transfusion to save her life, and her younger brother volunteers. Right before the doctors begin the transfusion, the boy asks in a trembling voice, "How long will it take for me to die?" Clearly, the boy misunderstood what was happening. He thought he was giving *all* his blood to his sister. What sacrifice!

And what apocryphal rubbish! This one was popularized by the widely read *Chicken Soup for the Soul*.[24] I would encourage preachers to stay clear of these kinds of apocryphal illustrations, as they only tend to cause congregants to groan inwardly. We've heard them all one hundred times, and we know they're not true. It only makes you sound like you believe every email forward you read.

But these aren't the only kinds of noninspired texts that preachers reference from the pulpit. What pastor hasn't referenced *The Hobbit* or taken his congregation through a brief trip to Narnia via a magical wardrobe? Just as with the noninspired texts used by scriptural authors, we reference these classics not because we believe they're true but because they've become part of the cultural *zeitgeist* we grew up reading.

You wouldn't hesitate to make a reference to Tolkien or Lewis. Likewise, don't be afraid to reference Enoch or Maccabees.

Handle—with Care!

Don't be afraid to handle these texts . . . but handle them with care!

The Lewis/Tolkien analogy may help, but there are some major differences. Few Christians hold Narnia or Middle Earth as *actual* inspired texts (though some cosplayers and super nerds get pretty close). But because there are some traditions within Christianity that hold some of the apocryphal or pseudepigraphic texts as canonical, we must take extra care to

---

His Son for a Train Full of Passengers?," *Snopes*, 16 March 2001, https://www.snopes.com/fact-check/father-sacrifice-son-train-bridge/.

24. Dan Millman, "On Courage," in *Chicken Soup for the Soul: 101 Stories to Open the Heart and Rekindle the Spirit*, ed. Jack Canfield and Mark Victor Hansen (New York: Guideposts, 1993), 27–28. This story later found life again as it circulated in various forms on the Internet. Snopes also rates this story a "legend," and it may have roots going back to the early 1900s. Barbara Mikkelson, "Transfusion Confusion," *Snopes*, 24 November 2000, https://www.snopes.com/fact-check/transfusion-confusion/.

explain to our church how and why we're using these texts, as well as what their value is for an evangelical Christian.

Be honest and clear with your congregation. These texts are not inspired. They are not canonical. They *may* have some historical value. Some have motivational value, on the same level as a popular devotional. The biblical authors may be using them as illustrations or as cultural connecting points.

When I preached Hebrews 11:35, I spent several minutes carefully explaining and reading a large portion of text from 2 Maccabees 7 to help listeners understand what the author of Hebrews was referencing.[25] After reading Hebrews 11:35 and explaining that it was probably a reference to 2 Maccabees 7, I said, "Now, I want to read for you a selection from 2 Maccabees 7. Maccabees is a book that tells the story of the Jewish people between the time of Malachi (the last book of the Old Testament) and the time of Christ. Maccabees is not part of Scripture. It's not inspired by God. Why? The short answer is that Maccabees doesn't claim inspiration for itself. In fact, 1 Maccabees even says that the time of the prophets has ceased. The Jews themselves never accepted these books as part of their Scripture.

"But Maccabees does record a great deal of *historically true* data, even if it's not *inspired*. Something can be *true but not inspired*. Gretchen Whitmer is the governor of Michigan.[26] That's a true statement. But that true statement is not inspired Scripture. Do you see the difference?

"It shouldn't surprise us that the Bible would reference other true stories written during this time. As the Bible shows, even donkeys, demons, and false prophets occasionally speak the truth, sometimes even carrying messages from God himself! So let me read you part of a story from 2 Maccabees that is probably *true*, but not on the same level as *inspired* Scripture."

I proceeded to read and explain nearly a dozen selected verses from 2 Maccabees 7. It would have been dangerous and inappropriate for me to open Maccabees and just start reading without this kind of lead-in. No one needs to be told Narnia doesn't exist (I think). But because of Roman

---

25. The actual boundaries of the sermon focused on Hebrews 11:32–12:2. In my preaching calendar, it was the fourth sermon in the "Hall of Faith" section of Hebrews.

26. This was true and relevant at the time of my sermon, preached in Belleville, Michigan, on March 28, 2021.

Catholic or Greek Orthodox influences, they probably need help putting 2 Maccabees in its proper place within the evangelical worldview.

Build Discernment Between Inspired Truth, General Truth, and Incorrect Worldview

As we have seen, sometimes a biblical author may reference a nonbiblical text because that text contains some kernel of truth, such as Jude's quote of 1 Enoch or Hebrews' reference to 2 Maccabees. Other times, an author references a noninspired source for the opposite reason: The cultural understanding of the "truth" is incorrect.

This is the case for the reference to rabbinic tradition in Matthew 19:3–9. In this passage, the Pharisees test Jesus by asking him about an age-old crux in the interpretation of the Torah. They ask, "Is it lawful to divorce one's wife for any cause?" (v. 3). They want to know the legal grounds for biblical divorce.

Without getting lost in the mire of healthy (and unhealthy) debate over this issue, I'll offer the briefest sketch of what's happening here. The Old Testament law permits divorce for several reasons.[27] Deuteronomy 24:1 permits divorce when a man finds "some indecency" in his wife. Some 1,500 years after Moses wrote these words, the rabbis in Jesus's day were still debating the meaning of "some indecency."

The Mishnah (recorded c. AD 200, but the oral tradition predates Jesus) records the debate between rabbinic schools on this passage (m. Gittin 9:10):

> The School of Shammai say: A man may not divorce his wife unless he has found unchastity in her, for it is written, *Because he hath found in her* indecency *in anything.*
>
> And the School of Hillel say: [He may divorce her] even if she spoiled a dish for him, for it is written, *Because he hath found in her indecency in* anything.
>
> R. Akiba says: "Even if he found another fairer than she, for it is written, *And it shall be if she find no favour in his eyes.*"[28]

---

27. Cf. Exodus 21:7–11; Deuteronomy 24:1–4. See my *Preaching Difficult Texts*, 68–86, for tips on interpreting and preaching the Old Testament law.

28. Translation from Herbert Danby, *The Mishnah* (Peabody, MA: Hendrickson, 2011), 321.

So those who followed Rabbi Shammai's teachings believed that "some indecency" refers to immorality or adultery. Rabbis Hillel and Akiba both had a more male-centered interpretation: Even a spoiled dish or finding a hotter wife would give allowance for divorce.

Even though the Mishnah was not written until several hundred years *after* the time of Christ, it reflects the oral tradition that existed *during* the time of Christ, from rabbis who lived *before* the time of Christ. When the Pharisees ask Jesus in Matthew 19, "Is it lawful to divorce one's wife for any cause?" the phrase "any cause" is a reference to the classic rabbinical debate over Deuteronomy 24.[29] They are asking Jesus, "Who do you agree with? Shammai or Hillel and Akiba?"

Jesus's response clearly rejects Hillel and Akiba's interpretations, which allowed a Jew to divorce his wife if she overcooked his lamb steak. The point here is not to get lost in the debate over the permissibility of divorce for today's Christians or even to offer my own thoughts on the matter. The point instead is to illustrate that Matthew shows the Pharisees referencing a cultural debate, later reflected in the writings of the Mishnah, to uphold one teaching and reject another.

Again, it may help your congregation for you to illustrate why this is "allowed" by biblical writers. Preachers do this more often than they realize. Pastors might reference a teaching in the Quran to contrast Christianity with Islam. They might quote a politician or a line from a movie, not to uphold its truthfulness but to reject a cultural norm or popular teaching.

Biblical writers did this too. In fact, they did this first.

Remember, when you preach, you teach proper hermeneutics. Carefully help your congregation discern the difference between what is true and what is inspired. Use it as an opportunity to strengthen their understanding of the concepts of canon and inspiration. Help them understand that "all truth is God's truth" but not all truth is inspired.

When we help the church discern how to evaluate a cultural "truth," this also helps them formulate their worldview and understand how to filter all they experience and hear through the word of God. The apostle Paul models this well. In 1 Corinthians 15:33, Paul quotes a line from Menander

---

29. For more on the Jewish background of the divorce debate, see David Instone-Brewer, *Divorce and Remarriage in the Church: Biblical Solutions for Pastoral Realities* (Downers Grove, IL: InterVarsity Press, 2003).

(a Greek playwright three hundred years before Christ) that had, by Paul's time, become a popular catchphrase: "Bad company ruins good morals."

By quoting this popular phrase, Paul acknowledges the truth in the maxim and applies it to a biblical worldview. Preachers do the same when they filter cultural memes and proverbs through a biblical grid.

I once heard a preacher begin a sermon in 1 Corinthians 13—the "love chapter"—by referencing the movie quote, "Love means never having to say you're sorry."[30] Setting aside the dated nature of the opening illustration, the preacher was effectively testing a common thought in pop culture and showing how the Bible's definition of love is often at odds with some of our cultural definitions.

To summarize, preachers and teachers need to discern between multiple levels of text:

1. Inspired and canonical: The text comes from God through its human author(s) and was received by God's people as holy Scripture.
2. Noninspired but truthful: The text reflects actual truth but is not inspired Scripture.[31]
3. Noninspired and false: The text does not reflect true biblical principles and most certainly is not part of the Bible.[32]

Preachers not only have to discern these differences in the cited texts but also assist the church in recognizing those differences.

---

30. The quote was popularized from the 1970 movie *Love Story*, which is an adaptation of the Erich Segal novel by the same name.

31. Churches and denominations are more used to this category than they are comfortable admitting. Baptists regularly refer to their church constitutions during leadership or congregational meetings, sometimes on a nearly equal playing field as Scripture itself. A Presbyterian's relationship with the Westminster Confession of Faith is somewhat similar. Neither group would affirm that these documents are inspired, but both can develop the habit of treating them as near-absolute truths in practice.

32. Somewhere between these two we might want to add a category (2.5) Noninspired and reflecting cultural norms. By referencing these works (like Matthew's description of the rabbinical debate on divorce), the biblical author is not necessarily speaking to the truthfulness of the reference but instead borrowing a cultural meme to make a point.

Don't Get Lost in the Non-Inspired Texts

The apocryphal and pseudepigraphic texts are interesting. They are of great value to believers, helping us understand the theology, *mythos*, and history of our ancestors. But they are, ultimately, not the point of your sermon.

It may be fun to read a few chapters of 1 Enoch in your personal study. It may give you some insight into the beliefs and legends of the early church. But don't get so caught up talking about 1 Enoch that you forget to talk about Jude. Jude quotes 1 Enoch not to encourage you to play around with it in the pulpit but to support the argument he is making.

Here's a general rule of thumb: If you spend more than ten minutes on a noninspired text, you've done your congregation a disservice.[33] Jude may be an exception since the pseudepigraphic texts are so prevalent in it, but even that depends on how much of Jude you are preaching or teaching on a given Sunday.

At the end of the day, if the church leaves without understanding the historical value of 2 Maccabees or the theological value of 1 Enoch, that's okay. But it's *not* okay if they leave without understanding the value of Hebrews 11 or Jude 14–15. Don't forget what you're doing behind the pulpit, no matter how excited you are to talk about some of the strange and foreign texts.

Overview of Major Texts

Paul quotes Greek plays (1 Cor 15:33), poets (Acts 17:28), prophets (Titus 1:12), and philosophers (Acts 17:24). It's clear that Paul was well read. You should be too.

The following is meant only to help you get on the right track. It is by no means exhaustive, but it is intended to cover the most notorious and explicit quotations and references of extrabiblical literature in the New Testament.[34]

---

33. By the way, I would apply the same advice to other illustrations and analogies too. There is such a thing as spending too much time on examples and stories. Stick to the text.

34. I leave out many references and possible references. For example, some believe James 5:11 refers to the Testament of Job (not the same as the biblical book).

Pay attention to the footnotes, for I've tried to provide helpful starting points in the conversation with these challenging passages. But don't neglect your own research. Visit a library; buy a book; read a few articles. These are difficult texts for a reason.

Gospels

The Gospels' use of the Mishnah (or, less anachronistically, use of oral tradition that later developed into the Mishnah) could fill its own chapter, indeed its own book. I am convinced that all pastors should have a copy of the Mishnah on their shelf. It's worth reading cover to cover, if only for the historical Jewish background information.

My first read-through of the Mishnah, I did so with pen in hand (as with most books I read). I used one of the mostly blank pages after the table of contents and kept a running list of passages in the Mishnah that related to passages in Scripture. It has become a kind of quick reference guide for me.

Beyond the passage already mentioned (m. Gittin 9:10 on the different rabbinic views of divorce; cf. Matt 19:1–12), many other significant passages reflect the oral traditions that were influential during the time of Christ and the apostles. For example, m. Shabbat 7:2 lists thirty-nine activities that count as "work" to be avoided on the Sabbath. One of them is "taking out aught from one domain into another," where "aught" refers to anything you possess.[35] This may explain why the Jews were so upset that Jesus commanded a crippled man to "take up your bed" on the Sabbath, claiming "it is not lawful for you to take up your bed" on such a day (John 5:8, 10). What law did the man break? Not one in the Torah, but rather, the *oral* tradition of the religious rulers, later written in the Mishnah.

Peter H. Davids, *The Epistle of James: A Commentary on the Greek Text*, NIGTC (Grand Rapids: Eerdmans, 1982), 187, notes a few terms that link the works and argues that since Job was less than patient in the canonical work, the reference is likely to the Testament of Job, not the canonical book. This, of course, is far from certain, hence its omission in this list.

I also avoid any possible apocalyptic references in Revelation, as I have a separate chapter that deals with eschatological texts. I find Beale's commentary *The Book of Revelation* especially helpful for intertestamental influences on Revelation.

35. Danby, *Mishnah*, 106.

You can find information in the Mishnah regarding Jewish teaching on the forty lashes minus one (m. Makkot 3:10–14; cf. 2 Cor 11:24), cultural opinion on the significance of a woman with her hair unbound (m. Ketubbot 7:6; cf. John 12:3), and details on the Feast of Tabernacles, which illuminate (quite literally) some of Jesus's teachings in John 7–8 (m. Sukkah). It's not that these teachings represent the views of all Jews at that time. We can't even say that these traditions had the same impact on each of the passages cited. But nearly all Bible teachers agree that the traditions found in the Mishnah represent at least *some* of the influences on the Jewish people during the time of Christ, many quite significantly. Therefore, it's worth it for a Bible teacher to get acquainted with these writings.

Acts

Much of Acts consists of speeches within the narrative, accounting for nearly a third of the overall book.[36] The speakers drop several references within their speeches to outside writings and popular sayings. The following will survey the more overt sayings.

Some scholars have suggested that Peter and John's words in Acts 4—"Whether it is right in the sight of God to listen to you rather than to God, you must judge, for we cannot but speak of what we have seen and heard" (vv. 19–20)—intentionally reflect the words of Socrates as recorded in the writings of Plato.[37] It's possible that the saying became proverbial by this time and the apostles were not directly referencing but simply alluding to a well-known phrase of the day.[38] A similar phrase is used in 5:29, with much the same analysis of its source.[39]

This is similar to when a pastor uses a well-known phrase without necessarily needing the audience to know the original source, though knowing the source wouldn't hurt. Saying "Toto, I've a feeling we're not in Kansas

---

36. Darrell L. Bock, *Acts*, BECNT (Grand Rapids: Baker Academic, 2007), 80.

37. The reference comes from Plato, *Apol.* 29D. See Craig S. Keener, *Acts: An Exegetical Commentary*, vol. 2 (Grand Rapids: Baker Academic, 2013), 1161.

38. John B. Polhill, *Acts*, NAC 26 (Nashville: B&H, 1992), 146; cf. F. F. Bruce, *The Book of the Acts*, rev. ed., NICNT (Grand Rapids: Eerdmans, 1988), 96.

39. "But Peter and the apostles answered, 'We must obey God rather than men.'" (Acts 5:29). See Keener, *Acts*, 2:1218. Keener, 2:1976, also notes a "fairly strong allusion to Socrates" in 17:18–19.

anymore" communicates that you're lost or that something in your environment has gone awry. One does not necessarily need to know this comes from *The Wizard of Oz* to follow the meaning.

In Paul's sermon in Athens in Acts 17, he makes several references to pagan philosophers and pagan sayings. Many scholars recognize allusions to the teaching of the Stoic philosopher Seneca (17:24) and two notable quotations in 17:28: "For 'In him we live and move and have our being'; as even some of your own poets have said, 'For we are indeed his offspring.'" The first of those quotes is more contentious, with some scholars suggesting its origin in a poem addressed to Zeus, attributed by later writers to Epimenides of Crete (sixth c. BC).[40] Because we only have this quote from Epimenides from other sources, and because similar assertions were made by other Greek writers, one cannot be dogmatic about the exact source of the quote.[41]

The second quotation in 17:28 can be more confidently attributed to Aratus of Cilicia (third c. BC), a philosopher/poet writing about Zeus.[42] Paul's reference to "*some* of your poets" (emphasis mine) may indicate that Aratus was not the originator or the only one to say such things.[43]

Whether we're looking at one quotation or two, and whether we know the source of either, it's clear what Paul is doing: He's referencing popular and well-accepted ideas from the pagan culture that agree with Christian truths, at least to a degree. The quotes were originally attributed to Greek gods such as Zeus, but the theology behind the quotes—we exist and continue to exist due to a divine being, and as his creations, we are all his children in some sense of the term—was common ground for Paul and his audience. It may be similar to a preacher saying, "There was a big bang," to refer to the origin of the universe and then proceeding to detail what that "big bang" consisted of—God's words speaking creation into existence.

Finally, in 26:14, Jesus (through Paul's testimony) uses the phrase, "It is hard for you to kick against the goads." This has become a phrase many are familiar with today, and it was a common phrase back then as well, appear-

40. Bruce, *Acts*, 338–39; David G. Peterson, *The Acts of the Apostles*, PNTC (Grand Rapids: Eerdmans, 2009), 499.

41. Peterson, *Acts*, 499. Polhill, *Acts*, 375, contends the first "quote" is a common Greek triadic formula.

42. Polhill, *Acts*, 376. The quotation comes from Aratus, *Phaenomena* 5.

43. Polhill, *Acts*, 376.

ing as a proverb in a number of ancient accounts.[44] Because of how prolific this phrase was in ancient times, it is difficult to identify whether Jesus was referring to a specific usage outside Luke's writings. More likely, Jesus appropriated a common catchphrase in his rebuke of Paul.

These references—which are certainly not exhaustive—show that the writers and speakers in the New Testament were not afraid to borrow and appropriate popular cultural lingo, some even from pagan sources. These phrases are all set within the context of a Christian worldview, with some being affirmed and some being adapted. Pastors who pepper their sermons with modern pop culture references should take heart: They are in good company.

1 Corinthians

In 1 Corinthians 15:33, Paul writes, "Do not be deceived: 'Bad company ruins good morals.'"[45] Here, Paul references a popular cliché that—as far as we can tell—originated with a Greek playwright named Menander (c. 340–290 BC) in his lost comedy *Thais*. By the time of Paul, this phrase had become a popular maxim, given its frequent use in other texts outside its original source. There is also the possibility that Menander himself may have adapted a proverb that was already around in his time.[46]

David E. Garland writes, "This may be a quotation from Menander's (died 292 B.C.) lost comedy, *Thais* (fragment 187 [218]), but one cannot assume that Paul was familiar with Menander any more than one can assume that a person who cites a famous line from a Shakespeare play has read Shakespeare. It had become a cliché, perhaps even before Menander."[47]

---

44. Polhill, *Acts*, 502, has a helpful footnote with several sources.

45. Some think 1 Corinthians 15:32 comes from an Epicurean slogan. It may also come from Isaiah 22:13. In his excellent commentary on the epistle, Thiselton, *1 Corinthians*, 1252–53, writes, "Is he quoting from Isa 22:13, or from an Epicurean slogan, or from an anti-Epicurean slogan which offers an ironic overstatement of Epicurean philosophy? . . . In practice virtually all major commentators assume or argue that Paul quotes from this passage. The question which arises is simply whether this quotation *also* coincides with a quotation from hellenistic philosophical or ethical controversy."

46. Mark Taylor, *1 Corinthians*, NAC 28 (Nashville: B&H, 2014), 398.

47. Garland, *1 Corinthians*, 722. Thiselton, *1 Corinthians*, 1254, writes, "Jerome seems first to have attributed the quotation to Menander's comedy, but

This seems to be a case where Paul uses a slogan made popular from a line in a comedy to illustrate a common truth that backs up his point. As far as we know, no knowledge of the context of the play is needed to agree with the quote (if so, we've all missed the joke!). It is not unlike a preacher dropping a line from *Seinfeld* or *The Office* that most people would recognize, even if they hadn't watched the source episode.

2 Timothy

In 2 Timothy 3, Paul warns his young protégé of the dangerous and evil people who will creep into the church in the last days (vv. 1–9). After a slew of unflattering descriptions, Paul adds, "Just as Jannes and Jambres opposed Moses, so these men also oppose the truth, men corrupted in mind and disqualified regarding the faith. But they will not get very far, for their folly will be plain to all, as was that of those two men" (vv. 8–9). One can scour the pages of the Old Testament and never find mention of either Jannes or Jambres. However, these figures show up in Jewish legends and writings and were supposedly the Egyptian magicians who replicated Moses's sign by turning their own staffs into serpents.

These magicians were named in the Exodus 7:11 text in Targum Pseudo-Jonathan (an Aramaic expansive "translation" of the Hebrew text). They were subsequently referred to by Origen and many other early Jewish, Christian, and even pagan writers. A translation of some fragments from one of the works bearing their names appears in Charlesworth's second volume.[48]

Paul's mention of these two individuals, in line with Jewish tradition, should not be understood to mean that he affirms all things about that tradition, nor that the unnamed individuals in the Hebrew text of Exodus are actually named Jannes and Jambres. Rather, Paul is borrowing from Jewish-Christian "pop culture" (so to speak) to make a rhetorically powerful analogy, comparing these two notorious legends with men who oppose God's truth and reveal their own folly.

---

there is clear evidence that it had also become a popular maxim. . . . We may infer neither knowledge nor ignorance of Greek literature on Paul's part from this quotation."

48. Charlesworth, *Pseudepigrapha*, 2:427–42.

Titus

After giving a list of qualifications for the church office of elder/overseer (Titus 1:5–9), Paul contrasts these men of integrity with some of the divisive, insubordinate rabble-rousers in the church (1:10–16). Describing these opponents of the faith, he writes, "One of the Cretans, a prophet of their own, said, 'Cretans are always liars, evil beasts, lazy gluttons.' This testimony is true" (1:12–13).

Though scholars have posited several possible sources for this quote,[49] most agree that Paul is quoting Epimenides of Crete, a sixth-century BC prophet/poet.[50] The apostle makes the point that even among their own people, these Cretans are known as treacherous people. It would be like a preacher referencing Las Vegas as "Sin City" and saying, "Even they know their reputation!"

This quotation comes with a special challenge, though. Paul calls the source of this quote "a prophet of their own" and then adds, "This testimony is true." The latter phrase is not so difficult, as we have seen in this chapter. Even broken clocks are right twice a day; even unbelievers stumble on the truth at times.

Calling the source of the quote a "prophet" is more challenging. Mounce clarifies the difficulties and summarizes the issue well when he writes, "Paul's use of the citation here, of course, does not mean that Paul accepts everything Epimenides taught, and the additional affirmation that 'the testimony is true' is what gives the statement authority; the designation προφήτης, 'prophet,' is merely the common title given him."[51]

So even from this quote, we don't need to assume that Epimenides *was* actually a prophet, no more than calling Daniel Radcliffe a wizard assumes the *Harry Potter* actor is actually a wizard. It merely hijacks a popular title given to him for the purpose of illustration.

---

49. Craig A. Evans, *Ancient Texts for New Testament Studies: A Guide to the Background Literature* (Peabody, MA: Hendrickson, 2005), 395, lists four possible background sources: Callimachus, Epimenides, Leonidas, and Polybius. Jerome D. Quinn, *The Letter to Titus*, AB 35 (New York: Doubleday, 1990), 107–12, lists even more. Cf. Robert W. Yarbrough, *The Letters to Timothy and Titus*, PNTC (Grand Rapids: Eerdmans, 2018), 495.

50. Mounce, *Pastoral Epistles*, 397–98, has a wealth of excellent information on Epimenides.

51. Mounce, *Pastoral Epistles*, 399.

Hebrews 11:35

We have already discussed Hebrews 11:35's use of the story in 2 Maccabees 7 at length above, so I'll offer only a brief summary here. Hebrews 11:35 reads, "Women received back their dead by resurrection. Some were tortured, refusing to accept release, so that they might rise again to a better life." This probably alludes to a historical account in 2 Maccabees that tells of King Antiochus who arrests seven brothers and their mother and tries to torture them into repudiating the Jewish law by eating pork. One by one the brothers refuse, even under torture, and are murdered.

Finally, only the youngest son and the mother remain alive. Antiochus pleads with the mother to convince her son to abandon his faith and live. The mother boldly turns to her son and says, "Do not fear this butcher, but prove worthy of your brothers. Accept death, so that in God's mercy I may get you back again along with your brothers" (2 Macc 7:29 NRSV). Eventually, both the remaining son and his mother are martyred.

Maccabees records much that is historically true, though it may suffer some exaggeration of details. It is not inspired though. We might liken it to *Foxe's Book of Martyrs* or *The Diary of Anne Frank* in terms of historical-motivational value without being inspired Scripture.

Jude

The most contentious and challenging extrabiblical references in the New Testament come from Jude. Since we already dealt with this at length above, a summary will suffice.

Some believe Jude's noncanonical references begin in verses 5–7, before his more explicit allusions. Most recognize that Jude alludes to the events in Genesis 6:1–4 in step with the predominant Jewish interpretation of that passage, which understands the "sons of God" as fallen angels intermixing with the "daughters of men" (human women).[52] Though many scholars agree that Jude 6–7 refers generally to the events in Genesis 6, some argue that his reference leans on the stories of the fallen angels in books like 1 Enoch rather than the Hebrew Scriptures.[53] If, like most Bible teachers,

---

52. For an excellent summary of how Jewish traditions interpreted the Genesis 6 Nephilim passage, see Schreiner, *1, 2 Peter, Jude*, 448–52.

53. Gene L. Green, *Jude and 2 Peter*, BECNT (Grand Rapids: Baker Academic, 2008), 66.

you see Jude's allusion in these verses primarily or strictly as a reference to Genesis 6, then you will not need to pull in any pseudepigraphic works (at this point in the text, at least).

The first of the two more explicit references to nonbiblical sources appears in Jude 9: "But when the archangel Michael, contending with the devil, was disputing about the body of Moses, he did not presume to pronounce a blasphemous judgment, but said, 'The Lord rebuke you.' "

Deuteronomy 34:1–8 is the only detailed passage in the Old Testament that refers to the death of Moses, and it mentions nothing of a dispute between Michael and Satan. The phrase "The Lord rebuke you" may allude to Zechariah 3:2, a scene that includes "the angel of the Lord," Satan, YHWH, and the prophet Zechariah.

Most likely, Jude 9 alludes to a work called the Assumption of Moses, which may share roots with what is known as the Testament of Moses.[54] Unfortunately, we no longer have complete copies of the Assumption of Moses, but we have a decent idea that its ending included this story about Moses, based on the number of other sources that attest to it.[55]

As noted above, Bible teachers face the challenge of figuring out if Jude's reference indicates that the event is historically accurate, or if he was alluding to a popular belief. Neither conclusion warrants adding material to the canon of Scripture.

Finally, in verses 14–15, Jude also makes a clear reference to 1 Enoch 1:9. Jude 14–15 states: "It was also about these that Enoch, the seventh from Adam, prophesied, saying, "Behold, the Lord comes with ten thousands of his holy ones, to execute judgment on all and to convict all the ungodly of all their deeds of ungodliness that they have committed in such an ungodly way, and of all the harsh things that ungodly sinners have spoken against him."

First Enoch 1:9 reads, "Behold, he will arrive with ten million of the holy ones in order to execute judgment upon all. He will destroy the wicked ones and censure all flesh on account of everything that they have done, that which the sinners and the wicked ones committed against him."[56]

---

54. Charlesworth, *Pseudepigrapha*, 1:924–25; J. Daryl Charles, "Jude's Use of Pseudepigraphical Source-Material as Part of a Literary Strategy," *NTS* 37 (1991): 130–45.

55. See Richard J. Bauckham, *2 Peter and Jude*, WBC 50 (Waco, TX: Word, 1983), 65–76, for an excellent excursus on these sources.

56. Charlesworth, *Pseudepigrapha*, 1:13–14.

Charlesworth argues that 1 Enoch is a composite, representing numerous periods and writers from the early pre-Maccabean era to the late pre-Christian time.[57] Very few religious groups consider 1 Enoch canonical Scripture.[58] The challenge lies in the way Jude cites the book, as if it were Scripture (see the discussion above). On Jude's use of "prophesied" to refer to this text in Enoch, Bauckham argues that Jude regarded the prophecies in 1 Enoch as inspired by God but not canonical. Bauckham references literature from Qumran that similarly holds Enoch literature in high value without including it in the canon.[59] It may go too far to refer to all of Enoch's prophesies as "inspired," but due to Jude's use of 1 Enoch, we should recognize that the pseudepigraphic book has something of value to say.

Perhaps we can summarize much of our argument in this chapter using the words of Geisler and Nix: "Truth is truth no matter where it is found, whether it is uttered by a heathen poet [Acts 17:24, 28], a pagan prophet (Num 24:17), a dumb animal (Num 22:28), or even a demon (Acts 16:17)."[60]

---

57. Charlesworth, *Pseudepigrapha*, 1:6–7.

58. Schreiner, *1, 2 Peter, Jude*, 468, notes that 1 Enoch is not considered canonical by Judaism, Roman Catholicism, Greek or Russian Orthodoxy, or Protestantism.

59. Bauckham, *2 Peter and Jude*, 96.

60. Geisler and Nix, *From God to Us*, 116. Mounce, *Pastoral Epistles*, 399, also notes that the words of Caiaphas, a Jewish high priest, were also regarded as prophetic in John 11:51.

8

Preaching and Teaching Enigmas

As a young pastor, I made many mistakes.

There was the great goldfish incident that almost killed my brother.[1] There was the impromptu swim down the treacherous James River, which nearly drowned half a dozen students. There was the time we crammed thirty-seven people in an elevator and had to call the fire department when it got stuck between two floors.[2]

When young pastors think about their young pastor mistakes, those mistakes often fall into the categories of poor event planning or inexperience. But when I consider the mistakes I made in ministry in my early twenties, unfortunately, the way I approached and handled the Bible also comes to mind.

I thought I knew a thing or two coming out of Bible college. After a long study in the book of Ephesians, I arrogantly thought I could handle teaching through 1 Corinthians. After all, one of my undergraduate Bible classes covered the book! I knew all there was to know about Paul's letter to the troubled church.

I quickly discovered that this epistle had no shortage of difficult texts. It seemed that for every problem, there were multiple plausible solutions. I began to realize my error in thinking that enough study would always lead me to a certain conclusion. Divorce and remarriage, head coverings, angels watching women while they worship, prophecy, tongues, baptizing on behalf of the dead . . . what did I get myself into?

---

1. To my credit, this actually happened while I was an intern. Plus, my brother Billy got fifty-thousand points for swallowing that goldfish, along with the salmonella that nearly took his life. Totally worth it.

2. Also during an internship. It's a wonder I ever got hired anywhere!

The problem wasn't only my cocky attitude about my ability to handle Scripture. The problem in 1 Corinthians was that I was, for the first time in my ministry career, running into biblical enigmas. I just didn't realize it yet.

What Is an Enigma?

An enigma is a saying that defies easy understanding or explanation. An enigmatic verse or passage of Scripture is one that has an abundance of possible *and even probable* interpretations, often without any clear or obvious solution.

I added "probable" interpretations because, as you know, nearly every text has some degree of interpretive issues. Upon entering my second year of Greek, my jaw nearly hit the floor when I learned that there were more than thirty different kinds of genitives.[3] Now, not every possibility works for every genitive, but with most genitives, you have at least a choice or two regarding translation options. Every verse requires numerous small decisions.

But not every verse is an enigma. By "enigmas," I'm talking about the kind of passage where, if you survey ten commentators, you'll get twenty different opinions on the meaning! Enigmas don't just offer several *possible* options but several *probable* interpretations. You know you're looking at an enigma when you see multiple opinions from evangelical commentaries and preachers from the same tradition.

Before we look at a few enigmas and I offer advice on how to navigate them, a reminder is in order: I want to avoid this chapter becoming a "Hard Sayings of the Bible" kind of chapter, where each section reviews a different challenging text. I don't intend to evaluate all the options and then try to sell you my opinion. That's what commentaries are for. This book isn't a commentary.

Instead, the purpose here is to use these examples to show you how to deal with similar examples throughout the New Testament. These aren't the only challenging texts in the Bible. Merely knowing the exegetical and theological options is not enough for preaching and teaching the text well.

---

3. Daniel B. Wallace, *Greek Grammar: Beyond the Basics* (Grand Rapids: Zondervan, 1996), 72, lists thirty-three different kinds of genitives, separated under five broader categories.

A Few Short Examples

Even though this isn't a commentary and my purpose is not to detail every option and convince you of the strongest interpretation, a few quick examples may help clarify the kinds of texts I'm thinking about in this chapter. This will also provide illustrations when I get to the homiletical advice in the second half of this chapter.

Now, two short examples from 1 Corinthians. Though 1 Corinthians has more than its fair share of enigmatic statements, one of the most memorable (and most puzzling) is 11:10: "That is why a wife ought to have a symbol of authority on her head, because of the angels." A quick survey of some opening statements in the best commentaries will reveal why we consider this an enigmatic verse:

> "No interpretation can be held with great confidence."[4]
>
> "By all counts this is one of the truly difficult texts in this letter."[5]
>
> "This verse is fraught with exegetical difficulties."[6]

Do you see what I mean? Statements like these can alert teachers that they are about to encounter an enigma. This verse is really a two-for-one deal. The first half speaks about head coverings, which are a theological challenge of their own. It holds its own problems in translation and interpretation: Does the text mean to have "a symbol of authority *on* her head" or "*over* her head"?[7] Is "authority" understood actively or passively?[8] The issue of interpretation is probably more vexing than the grammatical and

---

4. Garland, *1 Corinthians*, 524.

5. Fee, *1 Corinthians*, 518.

6. Roy E. Ciampa and Brian S. Rosner, *The First Letter to the Corinthians*, PNTC (Grand Rapids: Eerdmans, 2010), 529.

7. The problem relates to both the interpretation of ἐξουσίαν ("authority") and the preposition ἐπί. Also, does "the head" (τῆς κεφαλῆς) mean her own physical head or her husband?

8. Fee, *1 Corinthians*, 519, summarizes the passive sense well: "Some take *exousia* [authority] in a passive sense. To 'have authority *over* her head' means that she 'has' someone else (in this case, her husband) function as authority 'over' her." The active sense, which appears to fit the standard use of ἐξουσία according to Greek grammar, sees the meaning that she has control or the right to do something over her head.

lexical issues: Are the commands about head coverings in 1 Corinthians 11 controlled by cultural norms and thus not directly applicable to modern Christians, or should Christian women wear head coverings to church?

But it's the second part of the verse that holds our attention even more: "because of the angels."

Huh? Thanks for the "explanation," Paul!

Paul's so-called explanation for why women should wear head coverings has stirred up speculation since the days of the early church.[9] Is Paul referring to good or bad angels? If he means bad angels, is this a reference to Genesis 6:1–4, with the (admittedly uncomfortable) meaning that women have a particular vulnerability to fallen angels?[10] Assuming we're talking about good angels, should women veil themselves because angels do so too (Isa 6:2)? Or would unveiling themselves, an expression of immodesty in that culture, distract angels from participating in a worship service (1 Tim 5:21; Heb 1:6; 12:22–23) and thus also distract the men present?[11]

Many other views exist between these positions, and supporters of each would likely make many additional clarifications and specifications. The preceding paragraph should, at best, be taken as a dreadfully brief summary of some of the interpretive options.

Later in 1 Corinthians, Paul drops another enigma during an extended discussion on the future resurrection: "Otherwise, what do people mean by being baptized on behalf of the dead? If the dead are not raised at all, why are people baptized on their behalf?" (15:29).

Allow me to repeat myself . . . *Huh*?

There are, at last count, a minimum of forty different explanations for this verse.[12] The number of focused academic articles and even dissertations on this verse is breathtaking.[13] The problem isn't so much that the

---

9. Thiselton, *1 Corinthians*, 839–40, provides an overview of positions from Ambrosiaster, Tertullian, Augustine, Peter Lombard, Aquinas, and Theodoret, to name a few.

10. This was Tertullian's view. I have not found many modern commentators who hold this view, primarily because, as Garland, *1 Corinthians*, 527, notes, "Paul never uses the word 'angels' with the definite article to refer to bad angels."

11. See Garland, 528–29, for an explanation and defense of this view.

12. Thiselton, *1 Corinthians*, 1240.

13. See especially Michael F. Hull, *Baptism on Account of the Dead (1 Cor 15:29): An Act of Faith in the Resurrection*, AcBib 22 (Atlanta: Society of Biblical Literature,

verse is unclear; the problem is that a straightforward reading of it seems to contradict an understanding of justification by grace through faith and this practice lacks any known historical or biblical precedent.[14]

Gordon D. Fee summarizes it well: "We are left quite in the dark on all the essential questions: (a) *Who* was being baptized? (b) *For whom?* (c) *Why* were they doing it? (d) *What effects* did they think it had for those for whom it was being done? It is impossible to give a definitive answer to any of these."[15]

He goes on to categorize four different approaches to the text: (1) Understand "baptize" metaphorically, such as being "baptized" by martyrdom; (2) understand "for" (ὑπέρ) in a nontraditional meaning, such as "over" (the graves of the dead) or "with a view toward" (their being reunited with dead believers); (3) understand "the dead" to mean something other than the obvious meaning, such as referring to the "(soon to be) dead bodies of the Christians themselves"; and (4) punctuate the text in a creative way, yielding a different meaning.[16] Others, like Thiselton, offer even more explanations and solutions.[17]

In both examples from 1 Corinthians—11:10 and 15:29—expositors can find views that can be easily rejected and views that resist easy dismissal. Clearly, you could spend *years* plumbing the history of research and opinion on just these verses.[18]

2005); and Mathis Rissi, *Die Taufe für die Toten* (Zurich: Zwingli Verlag, 1962), which roughly translated says, "An Entire Book in German Devoted to the Different Interpretations of 1 Corinthians 15:29." One of the most extensive articles on the subject is Bernard Mary Foschini, "'Those Who are Baptized for the Dead,' 1 Cor 15:29," *CBQ* 12 (1950): 260–76, 379–88; and *CBQ* 13 (1951): 46–78, 172–98, 276–83.

14. This summary is adapted from Fee, *1 Corinthians*, 764.

15. Fee, *1 Corinthians*, 764.

16. Fee, 765–66. After this discussion, Fee summarizes the most likely options as either (a) "that it reflects some believers' being baptized for others who either were or were on their way to becoming believers when they died . . . but had never been baptized; or (b) that it reflects the concern of members of households for some of their own numbers who had died before becoming believers" (767). We should note, though, that his final statement on the matter is quite telling: "But finally we must admit that we simply do not know" (767).

17. Thiselton, *1 Corinthians*, 1240–49, summarizes thirteen possible solutions, ten of which he finds are nonstarters. He finally concludes that believers were getting baptized in a desire to be united with their believing relatives who died, thus anticipating the final meeting through the resurrection of the dead at the return of Christ.

18. Of course, other short examples from Scripture can be added to these, such as 1 Timothy 2:15, that a woman "will be saved through childbearing." 1 Peter 3:7,

A Few Lengthier Examples

Sometimes, little verses such as 1 Corinthians 11:10 and 15:29 threaten to stop a sermon dead in its tracks. At other times, we might rightly label entire passages as enigmas.

First Peter 3:18–22 is one example. Bible teachers have used this passage to argue that between Christ's death and resurrection, Jesus went to hell and . . . did *something*. Specifically, he "proclaimed to the spirits in prison." But what did he proclaim? And who are the spirits in prison? And does the passage actually teach that Jesus went to hell? And if so, did it happen between death and resurrection or at some other time?

The interpretation of this passage even impacts a line in the Apostles' Creed:

> I believe in God, the Father almighty,
> creator of heaven and earth,
> I believe in Jesus Christ, his only Son, our Lord,
> who was conceived by the Holy Spirit,
> born of the Virgin Mary,
> suffered under Pontius Pilate,
> was crucified, died, and was buried;
> *he descended into hell . . .*

Some have rightly questioned whether the italicized line is original to the Creed and whether this phrase means "hell" or the grave.[19] Nevertheless, the idea that Jesus may have descended to Sheol or someplace like it after his death continues to linger in theology.[20]

Another example of a large enigma is Hebrews 6:1–8. Hebrews has several "warning" passages (2:1–4; 3:7–4:13; 5:11–6:12; 10:19–39; 12:14–29), with 6:1–8 being the most infamous for its difficulty and elusive interpretation.

---

which calls women "the weaker vessel," may also fall under this category. Or, it may be better dealt with in my chapter on politically incorrect passages.

19. Wayne Grudem, *Systematic Theology: An Introduction to Biblical Doctrine* (Grand Rapids: Zondervan Academic, 2020), 725–36.

20. Other passages that may point to this idea are Acts 2:27; Rom 10:6–7; Eph 4:8–9; and 1 Pet 4:6. See Grudem, 729–34, for a brief counter-explanation of each of these passages.

What does it mean that "it is impossible, in the case of those who have once been enlightened, who have tasted the heavenly gift, and have shared in the Holy Spirit, and have tasted the goodness of the word of God and the powers of the age to come, and then have fallen away, to restore them again to repentance, since they are crucifying once again the Son of God to their own harm and holding him up to contempt" (6:4–6)? Does the author mean that genuinely saved people can lose their salvation? Is he talking about people who only appear saved but aren't, perhaps like Judas? Could he be referring to Jews? Or perhaps this verse has to do with a loss of reward, not a loss of eternal salvation?

This text notoriously presents challenges to anyone's theological system. It's impossible to keep our theological biases from being superimposed on the text. Calvinists will have a hard time accepting any hint of a person's ability to lose their salvation; Armenians cannot fathom the idea that this *doesn't* talk about a loss of eternal life. As one commentator put it, "Since a 'presuppositionless hermeneutic' is impossible, every interpreter comes to the text with preconceived ideas on the theological issues addressed."[21]

I hope by now you catch the gist of the conversation. These are examples—short and lengthy—of enigmas in Scripture: verses or passages that defy easy solutions and quick explanations.[22] They challenge the scholar and layperson alike. How do we handle these kinds of challenges in the pulpit? Here are four steps to take when you encounter an enigma.

Preaching Enigmas

Step 1: Study Hard

I don't mean to patronize, since I'm sure you already do this for every text you teach or preach. But when dealing with an enigma it's even more

---

21. George H. Guthrie, *Hebrews*, NIVAC (Grand Rapids: Zondervan, 1998), 223.

22. One more example of a lengthier enigma: Romans 7. The challenge here is to understand the perspective from which Paul is writing. Does the language of the text represent his current spiritual struggles? Does it reflect on his pre-conversion experience or perhaps get into the mind of the Jews before the Mosaic law? An interpreter must choose between these options (and more!) before ever stepping foot in the pulpit.

critical that you have the right resources and take the time to really understand the debate. This will help you avoid coming to the pulpit unprepared or looking like a fool.

Use good resources. Surround yourself with great resources. The best teachers of God's word regularly study at the feet of great writers—writers of commentaries, articles, books, academic monographs, systematic and biblical theologies, etc.

After working through your normal Bible study steps,[23] it's critical to make sure you work through several *quality* resources.[24] You may want to step up your game and look at a few academic commentaries, not your cheaper, more readable application-oriented books. Those books have a place on the shelf and in the life of a Christian, but they probably won't cut it when you're studying an enigma.

If you don't have a few quality commentaries at hand, ask your pastor. (Or if you are a pastor, ask the more seasoned pastor down the street. Or better yet, buy your own copy and plump up your library so you won't have to ask next time!) Go to your nearest seminary or Bible college library. You're going to want to dig a little bit to make sure you have a good handle on the issue.

Study commentaries that arrive at different opinions. Don't read in an echo chamber. If every resource you read comes to the same final opinion on an issue, then either you aren't actually looking at an enigma or you need to broaden your reading substantially.

I had a professor who said, "Everyone should have their favorite heretic." I'm not sure I would go so far as to encourage that opinion myself, but I do find it helpful to read from different viewpoints, even those outside

---

23. For resources on hermeneutics, the art and science of studying the Bible, a few of my favorites include Howard G. Hendricks and William D. Hendricks, *Living by the Book: The Art and Science of Reading the Bible* (Chicago: Moody, 2007); Fee and Stuart, *How to Read the Bible*; Roy B. Zuck, *Basic Bible Interpretation* (Colorado Springs: Cook Communications Ministries, 1991); and Grant R. Osborne, *The Hermeneutical Spiral: A Comprehensive Introduction to Biblical Interpretation*, rev. ed. (Downers Grove, IL: IVP Academic, 2006).

24. Again, a quality resource is usually one you can't find for free online. That's your baseline starting point. Another indicator of a quality resource is regular footnotes throughout. A book without footnotes (or at least some kind of citation) limits your research to only what the author thinks and hinders further study.

the evangelical faith. We must read these individuals with caution and not allow ourselves too steady a diet of their teachings. But when dealing with enigmas, find a few competing voices. Usually, you gain a better idea of the strengths and weaknesses of each approach than if you just read one or two authors who basically come to the same conclusion.[25]

Step 2: Find Your Opinion

After you've spent enough time studying, it's time to settle on your own tentative conclusion. You're going to have to say *something* from the pulpit. Even if you think you'll get away with sharing only two or three of the strongest viewpoints, undoubtedly someone will ask you after the service, "But what do *you* believe?"

As you think about where you land on the issue, consider the following: *Be humble and charitable.* This advice should sound familiar now. Good. We need it.

Teachers must approach challenging texts—especially enigmas—with a great deal of humility and charity. After hours of careful study and reading, you have settled on the interpretation that you think best reflects the intent of the original author. Good. Now, teach it with humility, recognizing that you may still be wrong.

After two millennia, there are still multiple legitimate ways the passage can be understood. This should develop a healthy humility within you as you explain your preferred interpretation. Others have gone before you—other scholars more intelligent, more studied, and more experienced—and have drawn different conclusions. That alone should humble us as we present our perspective.

Putting forth your interpretation with humility means treating opposing viewpoints with charity. Enigmas rarely center around core gospel doctrines. This means that Christian evangelicals can fall into many different places and still not step outside the realm of orthodoxy.

---

25. This advice, by the way, works across denominational lines as well. It's good for dispensationalists to read covenantal theologies. It's good for Reformed readers to dip into something written by an Armenian from time to time. It's a healthy thing to challenge yourself from different standpoints. You might just like what you're reading.

When discussing such touchy topics, imagine that a friend with a different view is listening. In larger congregations, this very well may be the case. You may have a healthy debate with a friend over a tricky subject, but you'll likely speak with at least a degree of respect and appreciation for their position. Do the same from the pulpit. If your listeners think people on the other side of the table are enemies, then you probably presented your case without humility and charity.[26]

Beware of novel interpretations. If—after having studied your passage, consulting a few commentaries and articles, and maybe even reading a few church fathers on the issue—you find yourself landing on a novel interpretation you have never seen in print, then you may want to reconsider your conclusions!

I'm not suggesting that the Holy Spirit can't give someone fresh insight into a passage of Scripture, even after two thousand years of church history. I *am* suggesting there's not much new under the sun (Eccl 1:9), and most often, a better term for a "novel" interpretation of Scripture is a "wrong" interpretation of Scripture.

It may be quite arrogant to think that you have uncovered the one key to unlocking the meaning of a text that has evaded interpreters for two millennia. Remember, you're not the first one to study your verse. In fact, there's a high likelihood that someone spent *years* studying the history of interpretation of your passage in some dissertation out there. At the very least, someone has devoted several months of research—along with peer review—to write an article or commentary on it. Do you really think that in your several hours of preparation you came up with something brand new?

Novel interpretations are not necessarily wrong. They may even be correct. But their novelty should give us pause. When coming up with a novel interpretation—and realizing its uniqueness after studying secondary resources—our posture should be one of humility and a willingness to admit that maybe we're the one in the wrong, not millions of others throughout the years.

---

26. I recognize that with some enigmas, people can indeed be "enemies" of the cross, depending on where they land. Mormons have a different view than evangelical Christians on what it means to baptize the dead (1 Cor 15:29). We should still speak with charity on these topics, speaking the truth in love, which may keep a door for evangelism open.

Ask yourself: How does this interpretation fit into the larger argument of the passage? Sometimes we can get lost in the forest when we spend too much time staring at one tree. We forget the bigger picture of what's happening.

The point of the passage is *not* your preferred interpretation.

Yes, you may have come across the correct interpretation, one that supports the argument of the biblical author. But always keep in mind the biblical author's larger point. *That* larger argument is the point of your passage. It's easy to get lost in the debate—as fun as it is to talk about it sometimes—and forget to pull things together and show your listeners how the passage fits into the bigger picture.

For example, the point of 1 Peter 3:18–22 is not to determine whether Jesus went to hell between his death and resurrection. The answer to that question certainly has great theological relevance. But Peter's *main* point isn't to settle a debate regarding where Jesus traveled over the weekend. Peter offers his readers hope through the proclamation Jesus gave to the spirits in prison (whoever they are). Peter's readers could likewise trust in a final vindication over their enemies and have greater confidence during their own spiritual exile.[27]

Whatever interpretation you land on must fit the larger argument of the biblical author.

Step 3: Decide on Your Strategy

Now that you've studied your passage and landed on a tentative interpretation that fits the context, you must figure out how you will present your sermon or lesson. You have a few options to do this successfully.

Preach just the enigma or the entire passage. If you study properly, you will likely have more than enough material to fill an entire sermon—and then some. The question is: *should you*? To once again adapt the words of the great philosopher Ian Malcolm, "Just because you can, doesn't mean you should."[28]

---

27. Miller and Murawski, *1 Peter*, 217.

28. The exact quote was "Yeah, yeah, but your scientists were so preoccupied with whether or not they could, they didn't stop to think if they should." *Jurassic Park* (1993).

It takes great restraint, but the best preachers and teachers know how to filter their research and deliver only what their audience needs most. Many times, it's far better to treat the enigma as part of the larger context instead of giving it your full attention for all forty-five minutes. After all, due to the mysterious nature of its meaning, you have to hold all your conclusions with an open hand anyway. And since whatever conclusion you reach should fit within the larger argument of the passage, why not just preach the passage with an extended sidebar treatment of the enigma?

For example, if I were preaching 1 Corinthians 11:10, the "because of the angels" enigma, I could either pause my expository series and preach just that verse, or I could preach all of 1 Corinthians 11:2–16, the main pericope, and give the enigma a little more attention than the other verses.

If I chose to preach just the enigma, I might outline the sermon like this:

1. Introduction
2. Summary of argument in 1 Cor 11:2–16
3. The enigma
    a. Head coverings
    b. The meaning of "authority"
    c. Good or bad angels?
    d. Summarize main theories
    e. Argue for my position
4. Application and conclusion

When we preach only a shorter enigma, we have time to discuss several different views on each phrase or word or grammatical anomaly.[29] Just one caveat: If you spend an entire sermon on a single difficult verse, the application had better be worth it in the end! The payout must be proportional to the effort put into the exegesis. Otherwise, we're just arguing about how many angels can dance on the head of a pin.

If I choose to preach the entirety of 1 Corinthians 11:2–16, here's how I might outline it:

---

29. This entire point assumes we're talking about shorter enigmas—one or two verses at most. If they are longer, it usually makes sense to treat them as their own sermon or lesson.

1. Introduction
2. Summary (1 Cor 1–10)
3. The meaning of "head" (1 Cor 11:2–3)
4. The meaning of "covering" (1 Cor 11:4–6)
5. The meaning of "glory of man" (1 Cor 11:7–9)
6. The meaning of the enigma (1 Cor 11:10)
7. "Judge for yourselves": applicable today or not? (1 Cor 11:11–16)
8. Application and conclusion

When you preach enigmas alongside the broader pericope, you will not be able to say everything you want to or could say about it. That's okay. You may end up simply alerting the masses to the problem, giving your interpretation, and moving on. This has the advantage of keeping the main point the main point. The disadvantage is that it may frustrate your more learned audience members who came wanting to watch a bloody war in the text.

You will have to decide the best approach to the issue for your given context.

Focus on interpretive options that are stronger and more relevant to your audience. When studying an enigma, you may come across twenty different interpretations. This is not an exaggeration! It would do no one any good if you covered all the options. Save that for the academic paper or commentary.

How do we triage which interpretations to mention from the pulpit?

Two factors should rise to the surface: the strength of the interpretation and the relevance of the interpretation.

Interpretations heralded by some obscure scholar in Germany that no one has ever heard of and has no credence among other academics probably won't impress your church audience either. Feel free to leave flawed interpretations on the cutting room floor. Let the strongest interpretations hold your audience's attention.

You should also consider interpretations that are more relevant for your audience. If I were preaching on 1 Corinthians 15:29, the "baptized on behalf of the dead" enigma, I may or may not address the argument that Paul is talking about baptizing in proxy for dead unbelievers. This is a Mormon interpretation of the passage. If my church had a strong Mormon influence, or if I knew of a few believers who actively evangelized Mormons, then it would certainly be worth several minutes of attention, if not only for the apologetic value.

If I were preaching Hebrews 6 to a group of Reformed Presbyterians, I may not need to spend a lot of time disproving the "lose your salvation" view, since I know none of them would hold to it. If I spent ten minutes showing them from Scripture why the Bible doesn't teach a person can lose their salvation, I just wasted ten minutes of my sermon preaching to the choir. Assuming I don't hold that perspective, I may offer a sentence or two of dismissal before moving on to other views that my audience may actually hold.

Simplify your options with a chart. Visuals help, especially when dealing with challenging passages. If you can provide your audience with some kind of graphic—whether a flow chart, a set of images representing different viewpoints, or some other creative option—it could greatly benefit a confused congregant.

Maybe you're not creative. That's okay. Someone in your church is. Find them and ask them for a favor. Chances are that they'll delight in the challenge and the chance to serve the church with their gifts. Sketch out your ideas for them and then allow them to improve them. Give them your outline and ask them to put it into a visual, and then work to incorporate that into your sermon.

When I preached Hebrews 6, I boiled down the interpretive options to five main paths. I charted it like this:

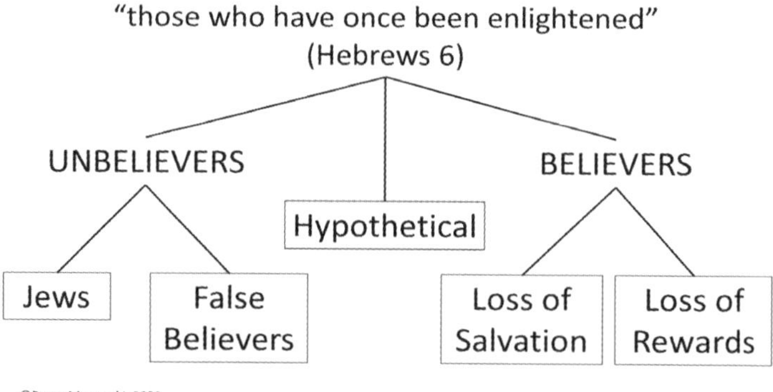

As I explained each "pathway," I bolded that option in a different color so people could more easily follow along. Whenever I eliminated an option (for exegetical or theological reasons), I grayed out the entire pathway and position so that only the more viable options remained. In the end, I was left with my own position, which I then preached.[30]

When preaching 1 Peter 3:18–22, I did not use my own chart, but I modified a chart from Patrick Schreiner.[31] No need to reinvent the wheel. After reading the entire passage and baiting the audience with challenging questions (Who did Jesus preach to? When? Where? What did he say?), I walked through each option. Conveniently, the final option represents my own position, which I then defended. We provided the chart in electronic format so that my listeners didn't feel the need to frantically copy it from a PowerPoint slide.

Using charts like these, or some other creative method, may help simplify a complicated interpretive issue.

Step 4: Preach It!

The final step is to preach or teach your text. You've studied it. You've figured out your approach. Now, take it to the pulpit, or the lectern, or your small group. Here are a few extra points to keep in mind for this final stage.

Don't be afraid to share your opinion. You've done a lot of research leading up to this point. You have an opinion on what your enigma means and how it fits the broader context of your passage. With great fear and trembling, go share it with your listeners.

Don't feel like you need to be a Bible expert to have an opinion on a Bible passage. God doesn't require an advanced degree to understand Scripture or to have a correct opinion about a certain passage. Even if you don't feel like you have it all figured out, it's okay to share where you're at, at least tentatively. I commonly say—mostly tongue in cheek—from both the pulpit and the university classroom, "*Today*, here's where I'm at with this passage . . ."

---

30. Since I know you're dying to know, I believe the passage—like the rest of Hebrews—addresses believers and specifically warns of a loss of future rewards. I found David L. Allen, *Hebrews*, NAC 35 (Nashville: B&H, 2010), closest to my own position.

31. The adapted chart that I further refined for my teaching environment is found in Miller and Murawski, *1 Peter*, 215. Schreiner's chart can be found at https://x.com/pj_schreiner/status/1282667110091587584.

The implication is that my opinion might change tomorrow when I have studied more. And yesterday my opinion may have also been different because I wasn't as studied as I am now. In his excellent book *A Little Book for New Theologians*, Kelly M. Kapic writes, "Anyone who stands at the end of his days and claims never to have changed his mind should not be praised for unwillingness to compromise but rather pitied for naïve pride."[32]

You may feel like there's someone who is smarter than you on this topic. Keep two things in mind: (1) You're correct. There are *plenty* of people who are more knowledgeable about this passage! And there are even people smarter than them. But that shouldn't stop you from saying *something*, even if it's a thought held with confident humility. (2) You may be incorrect, at least in your small context.

You've spent at least a week studying this passage. Maybe you translated it, parsed it (okay, maybe not that one!), read commentaries, and even made a nifty chart. Chances are that you might be the leading expert on that passage in the room on the night you teach. Don't sell yourself short.

But still . . .

Don't forget humility and charity! Teach with humility. Teach with charity.

I know I've said this already, but it bears repeating. We are a prideful people and quite unmerciful at times. We need the reminder to teach and preach with humility, showing grace to the other side. When I preached Hebrews 6, I had an opinion. Secretly, I had been arguing for my opinion for weeks leading up to that sermon. I thought I was building a good case for my thoughts on the passage. I still think that.

But when I preached it, I did my best to preach it with the understanding that there were people within my congregation who disagreed with me. Some very passionately. I wanted to preach it in such a way that I made a good case for my own position, but I didn't make the other positions sound foolish. Good, intelligent scholars and pastors and friends were on the other side of this issue. I had the responsibility to explain their position justly and to treat it with care while arguing why I thought it wasn't the best.

Humility and charity. Enough said on this topic. For now.

---

32. Kelly M. Kapic, *A Little Book for New Theologians: Why and How to Study Theology* (Downers Grove, IL: IVP Academic, 2012), 73.

It's a sermon, not a commentary. One of the most helpful comments I've ever heard in response to a sermon came during my second semester of homiletics. Thankfully, it wasn't directed toward me, though it could have been. After a sermon in 1 Samuel, my professor gave feedback to one student, saying, "That was more of a running commentary than a sermon." Although I'm sure the feedback stung at the time, it was quite helpful for me to evaluate what I was doing in the pulpit.

Sermons are not meant to provide an exhaustive commentary on every option related to every exegetical conundrum in your text. Just because the option is listed in your commentary does not mean you need to speak it into existence in your sermon or Sunday school class. The effectiveness of your Bible study is not directly proportional to the number of interpretive opinions you offer on a text.

Sometimes, teachers or preachers get so caught up in studying a passage that their excitement leads them to share every little detail and discovery from the week. But we must learn to be selective and master the art of preaching and teaching, not just regurgitating facts.

It's much easier to share facts than to preach a sermon. It's much easier to share a PowerPoint full of data than it is to teach an engaging lesson. Strive toward the latter, even if it means not sharing everything you know.

Enigmas are mysteries that can be preached. Your church needs to hear them preached and taught well. Neglecting to treat them properly will lead to confusion at best, division and heresy at worst. But if you handle them well, with proper study and focus, you may just lead your listeners to a place of greater peace and understanding, even in challenging texts.

9

Preaching and Teaching the Politically Incorrect

The year 2020 was tough for ministry. It didn't matter how big or small your church was. It didn't matter where you were in the country, or in the world, for that matter. It was a tough year for ministry.

In March of 2020, the entire world shut down.

COVID-19 rapidly jumped from continent to continent, then from state to state. Everyone's lives changed almost overnight. Governments ordered people to stay at home and work from home. There were toilet paper shortages. Online church services were no longer exclusively for bigger, more technologically advanced churches. They became the norm. The pandemic changed everything.

As a pastor, it seemed that there was no right answer and no winning. Whenever I spoke about any issue, one side loved it, another side hated it. It seemed that any middle ground had vanished, right alongside grace and love for believers with opposing opinions. Choosing to say nothing was not an option either. Everyone wanted the pastor's opinion. Or rather, everyone wanted the pastor to agree with *their* opinion. And there was no shortage of opinions and issues to fight over.

It wasn't just COVID. Along with opinions about the virus came opinions about whether to require masks in church. People had opinions about vaccines, online church services, and any political figure in the spotlight.

As if COVID wasn't enough, on May 25 in Minneapolis, Derek Chauvin, a white police officer, suffocated to death George Floyd, an unarmed Black man. People rioted.

And people had opinions.

COVID. Trump. Black Lives Matter. And let's not forget the Tiger King.[1]

Pastors were accused of saying too much, not saying enough, politicizing the pulpit, not politicizing it enough. Congregations shrunk. Others went online, seemingly never to return. The world was a mess.

That was 2020. Yet as King Solomon once wisely said, there's nothing new under the sun (Eccl 1:9).[2] Controversial issues have plagued churches and pulpits since the time of Peter and Paul. And they will continue to challenge pastors until Christ returns.

"But wait!" you might be thinking at this point. "Isn't this book about preaching and teaching difficult *texts* of the New Testament? Why are we talking about *issues* instead of *texts*?"

People committed to expository preaching and teaching do not have to wait long before Scripture itself presents challenging topics. I don't mean for this chapter to be about "How to address political issues" or "How to preach topical sermons on cultural debates." That may be a good book for another day.

The purpose of this chapter is to help preachers and teachers appropriately handle texts that bring up controversial issues—what I'm calling "politically incorrect" topics. How do we preach a text that potentially threatens to divide the church?

First, let's examine a few examples of these kinds of texts.

Politically Incorrect Texts

You can't spell "politically incorrect texts" without "politics," and that's as good a place as any to begin. Political issues tend to ebb and flow with the decades. Although some issues, like war and foreign policies and the economy, never seem to leave the political fore, many others change as rapidly as the surrounding cultural climate.

Concerns about climate change and the desire for a greener way of life have only grown since the 1970s when Al Gore held the first congressional

---

1. *Tiger King: Murder, Mayhem, and Madness*, a Netflix documentary, dropped on March 20, 2020, and became an international phenomenon, partly because the world was on lockdown and had nothing better to watch.

2. Although Solomon was a connoisseur of exotic animals (1 Kgs 10:22), he could not have foreseen *Tiger King*.

hearings on the issue. Today, if preachers dare say anything for or against such a notion, they will make enemies on one side or the other. When would they encounter such occasions in the text? I remember teaching on eschatology in 2 Peter and reading verses that state the heavens and earth will be burned up and dissolved upon Christ's return (e.g., 2 Pet 3:10). Someone asked, "So what does this mean for all those climate activists? Why do we need to care about the earth if it's all gonna get burned up in the end anyway?"

It was a good question. One that needed a careful, nuanced answer, sensitive to all in the room.

Naturally, I deflected to the senior pastor.

Slavery was a big deal in the late 1800s. Civil rights became the focus a century later. Today, ongoing racial tensions are still plaguing America. The New Testament has much to say in relation to these issues, sometimes in surprising ways. Most obviously, Philemon was written to address Onesimus, a runaway slave who became a Christian through Paul's ministry. Preachers might be surprised to find a lack of overt condemnation against slavery in this letter, though a good case can be made for Christianity's condemnation of such practices.[3] Even a casual read through the book of Acts reveals the Holy Spirit breaking down racial barriers as the church spread from Jerusalem to Judea to Samaria to the end of the world. Philip helps convert an Ethiopian eunuch (Acts 8:26–40). People from multiple nations and languages join the church (2:5–13, 37–41). Multiple statements in the Bible point to the power of the gospel to unite even the most deeply divided racial lines (Gal 3:28; Eph 2:13–14).

If these issues don't press buttons, how about gender roles? This topic impacts several different fronts. Gender roles in the home: In what way is the husband the "head" of the wife/household (Eph 5:23)? What does it mean for a wife to "submit" to him (5:22)? Is she really a "weaker vessel" (1 Pet 3:7)? And is it a sin for a man to stay at home with the kids while the wife is the primary breadwinner (1 Tim 5:8)?

Gender roles in the church: Can a female be a pastor (1 Tim 2:12)? Can a female be a deacon or other kind of church leader (3:11)? Can a woman preach, lead a conference, teach a mixed Sunday school class, or lead a small group?

---

3. See especially the helpful discussion in Kevin W. McFadden, *Hidden with Christ in God: A Theology of Colossians and Philemon* (Wheaton, IL: Crossway, 2023), 83–86, 95–97.

To these we can add a host of other issues: homosexuality, transgender people, abortion, immigration, and so forth. Even issues like what kind of education best suits your family can be ripe for controversy. Do I send them to public school and risk their spiritual lives? Or is public school the best place to train them for evangelism? Do I send them to a Christian school and risk a substandard education while digging into my retirement funds? Or do I homeschool them and risk them turning out socially weird?[4]

But here we go again talking about *issues*. This chapter is about *texts*. Let's bring these things together now. A politically incorrect text is any text that touches on such a controversial issue that you know you're getting an email on Monday morning from someone—either because you said too much, said too little, or said the wrong thing.

We can't avoid the text. We shouldn't avoid the issues the text brings up. So how do we deal with these passages when we come to them?

Preaching and Teaching Politically Incorrect Texts

Three words will be our best friends throughout this chapter that I want you to know well by the time we're done: *sensitive, confident, humility*. That's the secret sauce. That's the recipe for successfully navigating the murky waters of a culturally challenging passage.

The opposite of sensitive, confident humility is callous arrogance. How many people have been won over to the gospel by a street preacher using callous arrogance? How many people have listened to a debate and been swayed because someone uncaringly and insensitively bashed the other position? Let's unpack these three words through a series of homiletical principles.

Sensitive Confident Humility

Consider your text through the eyes of a non-Christian. We tend to think about the text through our own experiences and context. This is natural and healthy. One of the greatest Bible teachers ever did it. Before he ever taught the Bible, Ezra studied it and lived it (Ezra 7:10). Only after the word went through him did it go out to others.

---

4. I am in the position where I can playfully tease about all three of these, having done each with my kids at various times.

But when we *only* consider the Bible through our own situation, it can become unhealthy. Throughout my entire time in vocational ministry, I have been married. More than half of that time, I've had young children. I sometimes forget to give illustrations and applications that speak directly to a divorced person, a lifelong single person, a grandparent, or a couple who can't have children.[5]

We ought to consider how a text impacts people outside of our current station in life, as well as those from different socioeconomic contexts, races, etc.[6] Different levels of belief should also be considered, not just unbelievers versus believers. Even within the category of unbelievers, there are seekers, apostates, the spiritually ignorant, and rebellious teens dragged to church by their parents, to name a few.

It's especially important to consider a few of these unbelievers when preaching a controversial text. Consider 1 Corinthians 6:9, which mentions "passive homosexual partners, practicing homosexuals" (NET) among those who will not inherit the kingdom of God. Again, my purpose here isn't to argue for a position on homosexuality. I have my opinions, and I'm sure you do too.

Let's imagine that you, like the majority of evangelicals, believe that homosexuality is a sin and that 1 Corinthians 6:9 says so. You may have all the biblical proof in the world for your position. Your church probably says something about it in its doctrinal statement. That's all good, but if you preach it like an arrogant jerk, with more yelling than love, you've all but guaranteed that you're shutting out any unbeliever on the other side of the issue.

Think about how an unbeliever would hear you. Empathize. Put yourself in their shoes. Many modern unbelievers have not been raised in church. They've developed most of their opinions through social media and worldly influences. Unbelievers may be enemies of the cross (Phil 3:18),

---

5. See Haddon Robinson, "Preaching to Everyone in Particular," in *The Art and Craft of Biblical Preaching: A Comprehensive Resource for Today's Communicators*, ed. Haddon Robinson and Craig Brian Larson (Grand Rapids: Zondervan, 2005), 117.

6. The trick to doing this effectively is to be a good shepherd—spend time with people from your church in their contexts. You'll quickly get to know their heartbeats.

but we should view them through eyes of compassion and desire for them to know the love of Jesus.

This should not cause you to water down or compromise your message. Sin is still sin and it needs to be preached as such. The starting point of the gospel is a recognition of our sinfulness and need for a Savior.

But we can still preach these controversial issues from a posture of love and compassion instead of arrogance and hate. Pour over your message and consider: How will my unbelieving friend hear this? How will this strike my unbelieving coworker? Again, this doesn't mean you must change the truth if your unbelieving coworker won't like what you have to say. But it *might* mean you should change your approach and demeanor.

I was once asked to visit a public high school, which boasted that their LGBTQ+ club was one of the most popular in the school, to talk about the Bible and homosexuality. The school's Christian club invited me for a voluntary meeting during lunchtime, so students weren't required to be there. But the club did a good job advertising it, so many unbelievers attended.

One of the ways I prepped for this experience was by thinking through the different arguments typically made by the "other side." I even went on a few online forums to read comments from people with opposing viewpoints to get a sense of where they were coming from.

Then, in my opening comments, I tried to anticipate a few of these arguments and explain the biblical perspective. I left plenty of time for Q & A at the end, which led to some great dialogue.

I don't know if anyone converted that day. I don't know if anyone even changed their position on the issue. But we did see a person or two in the youth group later on, and I think they had a different perspective on how Christians talked about such issues. I'd consider that a win.

Consider your text through the eyes of your "opponent." Not only should we think about these texts through the eyes of an unbeliever, but we should also think about them through the eyes of those on the other side of the issue. You have not fully researched a controversial topic until you can articulate the opposing viewpoint in a way that the other side would agree is accurate.

I grew up in a conservative Baptist church. As such, the only thing I ever knew was a complementarian view of gender roles. Only men should be pastors. Husbands should be the leaders of the home. And so on.

It wasn't until I was teaching through 1 Timothy 2 that I was really challenged in my viewpoint on this issue. In our mostly complementarian, mostly Baptist church, there was a female egalitarian who had some seminary training. Boy, did she have questions! Good questions. Challenging questions.

I also had a woman in the congregation who had been severely hurt by an extreme, twisted version of complementarianism. She had grown up under an oppressive machismo that led to abuse and all sorts of dysfunction. She had questions, concerns, and deep pain.

Did those questions and concerns change my position? No. But it did cause me to consider the perspectives of these women every time I preached or taught on the issue. And I wasn't doing this to argue them into oblivion every time the topic arose. I tried to empathize with them. I endeavored to understand not only their position but why they held it. It helped me ensure my own thoughts were clear, loving, and rooted in the truth, not just tradition. By doing that, I gained the respect of those individuals, even though we might disagree about some secondary issues in Scripture.

Be careful of "open sharing" in an interactive teaching context. This is one for the teachers out there. Giving time for feedback, questions, and comments is a regular staple of good teaching ministry. You want to interact with your students, get a sense of how they're processing the material, and give them time to challenge and explore the topic through their own questions and comments. In other words, an open forum can benefit both teachers and students.

Use caution when passing around a microphone during a controversial, politically incorrect text. People's stupidity and terrible opinions tend to come out even in the best of times. The hotter the topic, the faster these offensive traits seem to rise to the surface.

Yes, you want to understand where your students are at. To do this well, you can give time for questions or ask a pointed question and seek their response. But there are other ways to gauge where they are at. Great teachers know how to read body language. (I've become an expert at knowing when people have fallen asleep during my sermon!) You gauge if people are tracking with you and even if they agree with you. Someone standing up and walking out is usually a sign that they disagree. Nods and amens and even excited notetaking probably indicate that you're hitting home.

An insensitive comment on a sensitive issue can lose your audience faster than if you misquote Jesus. Even if the comment is true, it does not mean it is shared in love or with sensitivity for those with opposite viewpoints.

For example, if you're preaching from Matthew 19:1–12, the passage where Jesus challenges the Pharisaical understanding of divorce and marriage, your audience will likely hold a variety of views on these topics. Even Jesus's statement about eunuchs can bring up debates on the issue of gender identity and transgender people.

One old guy with a microphone spouting his opinion on divorce can be just as damaging as a Gen Xer on the same microphone arguing for woke politics. It may be better to control the microphone for the night, letting people know ahead of time that, due to the volatility of the topic, you're changing the format for the evening.

If you choose to allow opinions and questions, be prepared to redirect or even reframe questions to something more palatable or more appropriate. "Why don't the gays understand that God made Adam and Eve, not Adam and Steve?" the angry man barks out, perhaps hoping for a laugh and some support. You might respond, "The question is, why do some people who struggle with homosexual temptations believe their position is biblically admissible?" By rewording the offensive (but relevant) question to something less confrontational, you can diffuse some anger. It lets people know you're willing to have a reasonable conversation and engage with intelligent, helpful questions while also subtly communicating the kind of tone and posture you're expecting. Always respond with patience and truth seasoned in love.

Diffuse the issue whenever possible. One of the problems with talking about politically incorrect topics is that some people tend to elevate their opinions to an unnaturally high level. I've spoken to six-day creationists (of whom I am one) who talk about the topic in such a way that, in their mind, anyone who believes anything other than them is not a Christian. And they speak with such incensed passion that it seems it's the primary issue any Christian will have to face.

Whenever possible, help someone diffuse the issue. First, help them put the issue in the proper category. Can someone believe differently than me and still be saved? Even guiding someone to explore this question may diffuse some of the heat from that conversation.

Speaking about the topic in calm, rational, and controlled tones will also ease the tensions. I'm not saying you can't speak with passion or even with proper force. After all, the prophets sure did! But these issues sometimes call for a more level-headed academic approach than a shouty preacher approach. You may win more people to your side that way.

Sensitive *Confident* Humility

Don't apologize for the text. We don't have to be embarrassed about the truth of Scripture. Sometimes, the truth is painful to hear, or uncomfortable, or difficult. That's perfectly reasonable. When the doctor must break sad news about a terminal disease, it can be painful, uncomfortable, and difficult for all parties involved. But the truth is the truth, and it must be shared with gentleness, candor, and love.

At best, it makes your audience uncomfortable when they hear a stuttering preacher feign an apology for the plain truth of the text. At worst, your apology sounds like you know better than God, who wrote Scripture. "I'm sorry for this next part. . . . This certainly isn't how *I* would've written it."

God is not surprised by our culture's interpretation of biblical truths or morals. Medical advancements do not shock God and reveal something he doesn't already know. Therefore, there's no reason to think that a God outside of time with infinite omniscient knowledge would have written the Bible any differently, if only he had our brains and moral compass!

This holds true for the bigger issues but also for some less obvious texts. When I was preaching Acts 13, I was impressed by the array of individuals mentioned in the church of Antioch. The church had a wealth of talent and people from different socioeconomic classes, races, and backgrounds. I was convinced that's part of the purpose of the text—to let us know about Antioch's abundance of diverse people.

How do I know?

Luke lists them. Barnabas, who we know is a Levite from Cyprus (Acts 4:36). Saul/Paul, an ex-Pharisee and persecutor of Christians (Acts 7:58–8:3). Lucius of Cyrene, who may be the same person Paul mentions in Romans

16:21. Manaen, a lifelong friend of Herod the tetrarch, who probably had considerable political and social standing.[7]

Then we have Simeon, also called Niger. "Niger" is a Latin term meaning "black." What does that mean? It means that Simeon was probably dark skinned. Some scholars think he was of African descent. The fact that his nickname was Latin may indicate he worked with or around the Romans.[8]

When I preached this sermon, I wanted to follow the text's emphasis and highlight the array of individuals ministering in Antioch. Simeon the Black was part of that group. I realized in our congregation of mixed ethnicities that someone could potentially take offense at a dark-skinned person being nicknamed "Black." I also realized the even graver risk of someone associating the word *niger* with another offensive word (which has no etymological connection, as far as I'm aware). But the text stresses that a mix of socioeconomic, political, and ethnic classes ministered together in Antioch. Because of the text's focus, I felt it was necessary to mention this fact.[9]

So, when I preached the text, I addressed these things in a matter-of-fact way. You probably have caught this by now, but I tend to joke around a lot. Since preaching is an expression of God's word through our personality, that tendency comes out quite often in the pulpit (as it should).

As I listed the names of the individuals in Antioch, briefly explaining them, I came to Simeon called Niger. I did not apologize for the text, but instead I said something like this: "I'm going to say something about Simeon's name, and I'm not trying to be funny or offensive. But I think it's relevant. The word *niger* is a Latin term meaning 'black.' Simeon the Black. This probably means he had a darker complexion, possibly that he was African in ethnicity. That it's a Latin nickname may indicate that he worked or had a ministry among the Romans. I point that out because it shows you the diversity of people ministering in Antioch, both in race and

7. The word translated as "lifelong friend" describing Manaen might also mean he was raised with Herod. See Polhill, *Acts*, 289; Bruce, *Acts*, 245.

8. Keener, *Acts*, 2:1984–86.

9. Besides this, most Bibles have a footnote mentioning that "niger" is a Latin word meaning "black" or "dark." I've even found a few translations that translate the word as "black"; e.g., NLT—"Simeon (called 'the black man')."

background." I then reviewed the rest of the individuals, highlighting that diversity. Because I was sincere and forthright instead of apologetic and embarrassed about it, I never received any nasty emails the next day. No one walked out. Everyone seemed to get it.

Don't apologize for the text. Explain it with sincerity and truth, and people will hopefully understand why it's there.

Develop your conviction. Some areas of Scripture are grayer than others. See the chapter on enigmas if you don't believe me.

But many of the texts categorized as "politically incorrect" aren't necessarily gray. They're challenging and convicting. They push against the cultural tide. For most of them, it will help if you develop some convictions.

By "convictions," I mean, wherever possible, grow a spine.

I'm encouraging humility. But I'm also encouraging sensitive, *confident* humility. You will need to study enough to develop a position on the issue in the text. In most cases, this is a real possibility. You probably already have convictions on many of these issues. Few churches hire pastors without convictions on some of the key controversial topics.

The issues mentioned in this chapter have numerous verses and passages—some even have lengthy discourses—devoted to these subjects. Because of this, it won't do to have a position of no position. With most issues, you should be able to study enough to form an opinion one way or the other.

That means you may need to read ahead. It's always a good practice to study ahead of your text. If you're scheduled to preach through Galatians, don't start studying Galatians the week before you're scheduled to preach! Instead, start studying and reading a few months in advance (if possible). This way, you will know what issues are on the horizon.

When you know a more challenging issue is coming, pick out a book or two on that topic to study. This will help you gain expertise in the area and continue to shape your own position. You'll be much more prepared to speak to the text when you get there.

Again, I don't want to discourage humility. And I don't want you to get the impression that you will be an expert in any one area with a few weeks of reading. But for most texts, careful study will yield an informed opinion. Don't be afraid to preach the text in front of you. Stand on the authority of Scripture and deliver the goods. Just don't forget to do so with sensitive humility.

Sensitive Confident *Humility*

Don't make a mountain out of a molehill. You may have heard this saying before. I didn't know people really did this until my mother twisted her ankle on the smallest of molehills while walking to an ice cream store one day. By the end of the week, you would've thought she had fallen into a crater, based on the way she told the story. She literally made a mountain out of a molehill.

Preachers and teachers of Scripture tend to do this, usually with good intentions, and sometimes because the issue is more pertinent to them or a previous context than it is to their current audience. You might carry unreleased steam from your previous church and feel the need to vent some of it to your new parishioners.

For example, I once served at a church that, for a time, had a no-alcohol clause in their membership covenant. To be a church member, you had to promise to be dry. Our leadership spent a lot of time studying Scripture to develop a more biblically centered position on alcohol. One that would've allowed good folks like Jesus (John 2:1–11) and Paul (1 Tim 5:23) to become members.

At the next church where I served, I talked about alcohol as if I were in the past church. I thought that all churches were like my previous one. At some point I realized, *this new church doesn't care*. And at the church after that, the lead pastor served alcohol at his birthday party. Somewhere in between, one of my doctoral professors took us out to dinner one night and had a nice martini with his steak. Shocking!

When preaching and teaching these topics, we need to consider our audience. The no-alcohol crowd might need some extra explanation about John 2, where Jesus turns the water into wine. The crowd that goes out for a drink after church probably doesn't need a whole lecture about why it's not a sin to drink at a wedding (though they may need a different kind of talk!).

Be careful not to blow an issue out of proportion. A good rule of thumb is to give the issue the same weight the text gives it. If Paul goes off on a tangent about it, you should too. If it's mentioned in passing, it's probably best that you handle it in a similar way.

Call people to understanding and charity. You should model both an intelligent grasp of the issue and a gracefulness toward opposing viewpoints, even if you are firm in your opinion. Invite people to do the same.

Understanding an issue involves understanding all sides, at least to some degree. Charity calls us to put that intellectual understanding in a context of grace when we respond.

It's easy to say "Life starts at conception" and start spouting Bible verses to back up your point. It's easy to condemn those who choose abortion. But when I hear the way many preachers talk about the subject, I wonder how many of them clearly understand the decision-making process that a young teenage girl goes through who finds herself in this situation.

Most women who choose abortion do not do so because they relish killing a baby or are callously indifferent toward their decision. Some are victims of rape and some of them are young teenagers whose parents or boyfriends pressure them into choosing something they may not want.[10] Many are scared and unsure of what the future looks like. Many have no way of raising a child and continuing their education at the same time. Some mothers must make painful decisions due to a risky pregnancy. We must also not forget those who have made a sinful decision and then later repented and sought forgiveness, only to now hear their past sins discussed as if they are unforgivable.

Too many who speak against abortion talk as if those who have had one are unfeeling monsters who are hellbent on murdering babies. Charity does not necessarily mean you *agree with* the other position. But it does mean you treat them with love and grace, despite the sin. Jesus didn't affirm the woman at the well's lifestyle, but he treated her as a person made in God's image who needed God's love (John 4).

Stand on the truth. But don't forget to speak that truth in love (Eph 4:15).

Don't forget the gospel. It's easy to get so caught up in an issue that you forget to preach the gospel. Don't forget that God's grace is the bigger picture! It does not excuse sin; rather, it deals with sin. The gospel puts perspective on difficult issues. Every conversation should be filtered through the gospel.

---

10. I heard of one teenager whose mother told her, "If you abort, we'll get you a puppy."

Here is a helpful question to ask yourself: Can a person on the other side of the issue accept the gospel while holding their position? In other words, is this a tier-one, gospel-level issue? Or is it an issue in which we can legitimately disagree and yet both find ourselves in heaven one day? How you answer that question will help you know how to speak on the issue.

For example, some believe that homosexuality is a top-tier issue due to Paul relating it to "sound doctrine" (1 Tim 1:8–11). If that's your position, it will color the way you speak on the subject. It's not a "we can agree to disagree" kind of topic for you. Rather, you will need to speak with open, honest, biblically centered truth and boldness (still seasoned with love!), for where a person falls on that issue will determine their eternal destiny.

Other politically incorrect issues more easily fit into the category of secondary issues. Still important, but not necessarily determinative for salvation.[11] I believe I'll see both Democrats and Republicans in heaven. I believe I'll see flat-earthers in heaven. I believe I'll see complementarians and egalitarians in heaven. The jury is still out on people who like cats, but you get the picture.

This means that when I preach or teach on the gender issue in the church, for example, I'm not bifurcating the audience as those who agree with me and the rest who are going to hell. I might even let the audience know that good people are on both sides. I still share my convictions with proper biblical and theological support, but I don't unduly elevate or denigrate the issue in the process.

The goal of this chapter is not to convince you to remove all passion from the pulpit. It's not to persuade you that all truth is muddy, and it doesn't matter what you believe. That's not the case at all. Rather, study until you have a conviction, then stand firm in it. But speak about it with love and grace befitting a sinner saved by love and grace.

---

11. See Gavin Ortlund, *Finding the Right Hills to Die On: The Case for Theological Triage* (Wheaton, IL: Crossway, 2020). Based on Ortlund's book, I like to categorize doctrine into different tiers for my theology class: absolutes (things you must believe to be saved), secondary doctrines (important but nonessential for salvation; differences may affect fellowship within the same church), and convictions/adiaphora (areas where we can agree to disagree on these and still fellowship together in the same church).

10

Preaching and Teaching the End Times

God's people have always had an interest in eschatology. This is good and natural, as the topic of the "end" begins in the first pages of Scripture (Gen 3:15). "Eschatology" is the theology concerning the end times. From the Old Testament to the New, large portions of the Bible, spanning many different ages and even genres, challenge laypersons and teachers alike to think about the things to come.[1]

In my lifetime, it seems that the interest in eschatology peaked around the time of the *Left Behind* books, a series coauthored by Tim LaHaye and Jerry Jenkins that sold 65 million copies (and counting). This series also spawned a trilogy of direct-to-video movies starring Kirk Cameron, followed by a 2014 reboot with Nicolas Cage that did so well that they recast him almost ten years later with Kevin Sorbo in the sequel.[2] There may even be a few *Left Behind* video games out there.

That was the *height* of eschatological fever in my lifetime!

If Mike Seaver, Nick Cage, and Hercules can't get you excited about the end times, then I don't know who can! Okay, I guess I can think of a few things.

It won't take long for new pastors to get a sense of how hot this fever is in their church. When I took my first senior pastorate, it took about twelve

1. Regarding genres, there are large portions of eschatological-focused Scripture in poetry (Ps 110), Old Testament prophecy (Ezek 38–39), narrative (Matt 24–25), and epistle (2 Pet 3:1–13), to name a few examples.

2. In case you missed my sarcasm, the Nicolas Cage picture has a whopping 0 percent rating on Rotten Tomatoes. Yes, it is that good.

seconds for someone to ask, "When are you going to preach the book of Revelations?" After biting my tongue so I didn't correct them on the book's title (*Revelation*, not *Revelations*!), I carefully explained that I had no intention of avoiding the book, but it wasn't first on my agenda.

It took another twelve seconds for someone else to ask me the same question.

In another church where I served, the pastors had previously preached an extended series on the book, and the sense I got from the congregation was, "We're kind of sick of this!" Eschatology—no thanks!

It's been pointed out that interest in eschatology falls into one of two categories—either an obsessive fascination with it or a terrified avoidance of it.[3] I call these options "prophecy mania" or "prophecy apathy." Prophecy maniacs obsess over the topic to the neglect of all other theological areas, prowling from conference to conference to get their next fix. Prophecy apathetics may not care about it, avoid studying it, feel confused about it, or may even be legitimately scared to delve into it.

We want to avoid both extremes. Preachers and teachers of God's word know that the end times is a challenging topic in the Bible, no matter what our eschatological scheme is.[4] Nearly all end-times passages—especially the extended ones—are difficult texts indeed. Almost every topic within eschatology breeds controversy.

When is the rapture? When and how long is the tribulation? How do we interpret Revelation? Are we living in a "millennium" now or is it still to come? What is 666 and the mark of the beast? Is [fill in the blank] the antichrist? Will there be Oreos in heaven?

You can see why some teachers are afraid to dip their toes into this deep, murky pool. To make matters more challenging, the number of passages that deal with eschatology in the New Testament is quite extensive.

---

3. In their excellent book *Understanding Prophecy: A Biblical-Theological Approach* (Grand Rapids: Kregel Academic, 2015), Alan S. Bandy and Benjamin L. Merkle note, "Prophecy is something with which most people are either obsessed ad nauseam or about which they feel so inadequate they avoid it altogether" (17).

4. By "scheme," I do not intend to be pejorative or demeaning, but I only refer to a system of viewing and dealing with prophetic matters in Scripture.

End-Times Texts

Many New Testament books have significant portions of text focusing on eschatology. Matthew 24–25 has become known as the Olivet Discourse. Most see these chapters as glimpses ahead to events such as the return of Christ (24:27, 29–31, 37) and the final judgment (25:31–46).[5] Both Mark (13:1–37) and Luke (17:20–37; 21:5–36) have parallel texts.[6]

All, or nearly all, of the parables relate to the kingdom of God, many with a specific focus on the end times. Certain speeches and sermons given within Acts have some eschatological seasoning (e.g., 2:16–21; 15:15–18). Pockets of text within the Pauline Epistles directly address issues related to the end times, such as the restoration of Israel (Rom 11), the resurrection(s) (1 Cor 15), the return of Christ (1 Thess 4:13–18), the day of the Lord (5:1–11), the final judgment(s) (2 Thess 1:5–12), and even the antichrist (2:1–12), to name just a few!

The General Epistles also have their fair share of eschatological texts. In Hebrews, the "warning passages" are referred to as such because they warn about coming judgments and rewards.[7] Although James's epistle is not necessarily as explicit as others, it has an eschatological focus throughout (e.g., 1:12; 2:5; 4:13–17; 5:1–3, 7–9). Most of 2 Peter looks forward to the future (esp. 2:1–3:13). John warns of an antichrist and antichrists to come (1 John 2:18–19). Though short, much of Jude speaks of eternal judgment (e.g., 13–15).

And then, there's Revelation.[8]

Besides these larger passages, countless other verses offer glimpses into the future or moral encouragement related to eschatology.

Preachers who take Scripture seriously and teach expositionally through New Testament books cannot and should not avoid these texts. The first step

---

5. Some Bible teachers in the preterist camp believe this text speaks primarily of events that have already taken place, primarily in AD 70 with the destruction of the Jerusalem temple.

6. I use the term "parallel texts" in this context rather loosely, since both Mark and Luke have a different arrangement and, in some cases, unique material.

7. It is debated whether these passages refer to believers or unbelievers.

8. I am not unaware of positions on Revelation that see it as mostly already fulfilled in AD 70 and surrounding events or fulfilled from the author's time until and including our own (and beyond). However, this chapter will treat it as a book that primarily anticipates events still future, as this is my position on Revelation.

to understanding how to teach them, though, is knowing how to understand them and discerning their purpose and function within Scripture.

Characteristics of Eschatological Literature

For some time now, scholars have debated what, exactly, defines apocalyptic literature. Many see a difference between prophetic literature and apocalyptic literature. Are they two separate genres? If so, what characterizes them?

Perhaps the most widely used definition of apocalyptic literature comes from John J. Collins. He writes, "'Apocalypse' is a genre of revelatory literature with a narrative framework, in which a revelation is mediated by an otherworldly being to a human recipient, disclosing a transcendent reality which is both temporal, insofar as it envisages eschatological salvation, and spatial, insofar as it involves another, supernatural world."[9]

Got that?

One of the greatest services you can provide your church as a minister of the gospel is to never repeat that definition from the pulpit!

But a careful read of that definition will reveal several commonly agreed upon elements of apocalyptic literature, such as (1) it's revelatory, meaning the mediator believes it's coming from a divine source; (2) it's usually framed within a narrative; (3) it's mediated to a human being, meaning a prophet or seer receives the revelation from an angel or a deity and passes it along; (4) it relates to future events; and (5) it has a supernatural focus.

Other characteristics have been added to these, including (6) apocalyptic literature tends to be written during periods of persecution or historical crisis; (7) it features extensive symbolism, numerology, and visions; and (8) ethical discourse is often presented in cycles.[10] I'm sure others could be added.

Now, how does that help us understand end-times literature in Scripture? First, many of these texts function as a separate genre. Therefore, they likely have special "rules" that govern how we should read them.

---

9. John J. Collins, "Towards the Morphology of a Genre: Introduction," *Semeia* 14 (1979): 9. This definition has gone through various reworkings, updates, and modifications throughout the years, but this appears to be the one most commonly cited.

10. These additional elements were adapted from Stephen R. Miller, *Daniel*, NAC 18 (Nashville: B&H, 1994), 46; and Osborne, *Hermeneutical Spiral*, 276–80.

To illustrate, you wouldn't pick up a *Goosebumps* book by R. L. Stine and expect a serious, realistic, grounded plot. It's normal to see talking ventriloquist dummies and haunted masks in these stories. Those expectations of otherworldly creatures and events shape how you engage with the literature. I don't expect to see the same kind of thing in a Jack Reacher thriller that I do in a young adult novel set in a dystopian future, even though both fall under the broader category of "fiction."

How does that impact end-times texts? If there's a difference between the genres of prophecy and apocalyptic literature, that will influence the hermeneutical rules that govern your study of that text. When we see a number used in prophecy, our foundational assumption may be that it is literal unless proven otherwise. If we see the same number in apocalyptic literature, our foundational assumption might be that it's symbolic unless proven otherwise.

Clearly, this is not the place to solve such issues. Many other resources offer more detailed summaries of the genre problem.[11] Below, I will humbly offer a few hermeneutical reminders that apply to whatever genre you label your text. I hope this section encourages you to dig a little more into the question of literature and invites further study to develop your presuppositions as you approach the text.

Hermeneutics of Interpretation

Each genre of Scripture presents its own challenges. Narrative cannot be preached like an epistle, nor can a text in Proverbs be preached in the same way as a genealogy.[12] Likewise, eschatological texts have their own unique "rules."[13] Though other texts provide more technical overviews of this literature, allow me to offer a few pointers as you study these difficult texts.

---

11. Such as Paul D. Hanson, "Apocalypses and Apocalypticism," in *The Anchor Bible Dictionary*, vol. 1, *A–C*, ed. David Noel Freedman (New York: Doubleday, 1992), 279–92; and Beale, *Book of Revelation*, 37–43.

12. For more on preaching some of these genres, such as genealogies, see my *Preaching Difficult Texts*. For a helpful overview of these other genres, see Fee and Stuart, *How to Read the Bible*.

13. As noted above, some put Revelation in its own separate category of "apocalyptic literature," with genre conventions different from other prophetic texts in Scripture.

1. Interpret with a Hermeneutic of Humility

This has been one of the drumbeats throughout this book, but once again with these end-times texts, it's important enough to reiterate. Humility must characterize your preaching and teaching.

This may surprise you, but you are human. We have a limited perspective on these issues. Again, that doesn't mean we can't be right in our understanding or that we're necessarily at fault for this darkened understanding, but it should stop us from speaking with supreme arrogance, thinking we've figured it all out.[14]

2. Pay Special Attention to the Use of Other Scripture

If there's any key to interpreting the book of Revelation, it is the use of other Scripture. Though Revelation may not explicitly quote the Old Testament anywhere, there are literally hundreds of allusions and echoes to the Old Testament. The same is true for many other end-times texts in the New Testament, and if modern scholarship has taught us anything, this kind of phenomenon is nothing new.[15]

I've already covered the topic of the Old Testament in the New Testament in chapter 6 of this book, so I won't repeat that information here. But because of the way eschatological texts tend to overlap language and reuse imagery, it's especially important to be aware of this when studying end-times Scripture.

3. Expect Symbolic Language, but Don't Overread It

How much symbolism you interpret from your text will partly depend on the type of literature you believe you're reading. We should expect to see at least some symbolic language. Even in clear "prophetic" genres that predate the "apocalyptic" era (typically understood as roughly 250 BC to AD 250), there are plenty of symbols and signs to be interpreted within the prophecy.

However, a hyper-reading of symbols can lead to a messy interpretation. How do we know where the symbols and signs start or stop? What grounding, if any, do we have in reality?

---

14. We know no more about the second coming than Jesus's Jewish disciples. We must approach this with a "hermeneutics of humility." Grant R. Osborne, *Revelation*, BECNT (Grand Rapids: Baker Academic, 2002), 16.

15. See Schnittjer, *Old Testament Use of Old Testament*.

Conversely, a stubborn insistence that everything is literal unless it has seven heads is also problematic. Symbols and signs are common in this genre (or these genres). Therefore, we should not be surprised when we have a number or an object that might otherwise be literal but here could potentially stand for something else.

Debate will continue about how to read each text. But it's wise to avoid the extremes of hyper-interpretation and under-interpretation.

4. Interpret Against the Historical Background

No New Testament text was written in a vacuum. Eschatological texts are no different. A text had to have *some* meaning to its original audience. Scholars will continue to debate whether a text could have additional meanings for future readers beyond what the original audience would have understood. But no one doubts that each letter or narrative in the New Testament addressed an immediate audience in its historical context. Progressive revelation advances our understanding of older prophecies, but these prophecies still needed to mean *something* to those original readers.

As much as we can discern, knowing the historical background helps. Only once we understand how a prophecy would apply to these original readers can we explore what it means for modern readers.[16]

5. Interpret Through the Lens of Redemptive History

All interpretations should be gospel centered, with Christ clearly in view as the end and goal of all history and prophecy. Bandy and Merkle write, "Christ is the *eschatos* of prophecy who gives meaning to all that has happened or will yet transpire throughout human history."[17] They add, "All prophecy [should be filtered] through the lens of the resurrected Christ."[18]

Keep in mind the overarching narrative of Scripture. The classic formulation of creation, fall, redemption, and restoration helps put any prophecy into perspective. Does your text relate to a restored fallen creation? Does it picture an aspect of redemption? How does it highlight the gospel in terms of its current impact or its future final form?

---

16. Bandy and Merkle, *Understanding Prophecy*, 33.
17. Bandy and Merkle, 27.
18. Bandy and Merkle, 29.

6. Keep in Mind the Prophecy's Application to Both Believers and Unbelievers

We have already discussed the importance of focusing on application in prophecy. But remember, you almost surely won't be speaking only to believers. How should an unbeliever think about your end-times text? What encourages us might terrify them. What we long for might cause them to tremble. At least, it should, if we preach it correctly.

No prophecy is given only to be understood intellectually. Prophecy should challenge, convict, comfort, reorder priorities, inspire worship, and so on.

Why Does God Tell Us About the End Times?

Contrary to the way they are often handled in the pulpit and the classroom, prophetic texts were not written to solve complicated debates over eschatological schemes. Preachers and teachers should consider evaluating any sermon or lesson using the following five reasons for prophecy. If your lesson does not reflect at least one of these, you are likely too focused on the academic aspect of prophetic literature.[19]

1. End-Times Texts Remind Us Who God Is

How do we know that God is God? What proof of divinity separates YHWH from every other so-called deity or idol?[20]

In a nutshell, *prophecy.*

More specifically, it is the aspect of prophecy that accurately proclaims the future before it has happened. Deuteronomy 18:21 asks, "How do we know that a so-called prophetic word is legit?" The answer is that legitimate prophecy from a legitimate God actually comes true, 100 percent of the time (18:22).

---

19. The following list is heavily influenced by and indebted to Paul N. Benware, *Understanding End Times Prophecy: A Comprehensive Approach* (Chicago: Moody, 2006), 13–17. Benware lists five reasons for biblical prophecy: (1) Biblical prophecy reminds us that God is sovereign; (2) biblical prophecy reminds us that God is good; (3) biblical prophecy motivates us to holy living; (4) biblical prophecy helps us establish proper priorities; and (5) biblical prophecy gives us hope.

20. YHWH is God's personal name revealed to his covenant people in the Old Testament.

Isaiah 44:7 puts it like this: "Who is like me? Let him proclaim it. Let him declare and set it before me, since I appointed an ancient people. Let them declare what is to come, and what will happen" (cf. 45:21). The prophet Isaiah presents a challenge to the opponents of God. You think you're like God? Prove it by declaring what is to come, *before it comes.*

In other words, one of the purposes of prophecy is to confirm God exists. He alone is sovereign and true. God's ability to accurately declare the future is a distinguishing feature of him as God.[21] When you teach prophecy, one thrust of your teaching should be apologetic. "See this prophecy? Isn't this cool? Only God can declare something like that before it happens!"

2. End-Times Texts Invite Our Worship

In Revelation, we repeatedly see visions of angelic worship in heaven, often either preceding or following a glimpse into the future. The four living creatures declare the holiness of God and his eternality (4:8). The twenty-four elders cast their crowns before the throne and worship the Lord for his worthiness (4:10–11). In the following chapter, both groups sing again about how worthy God is for dying for us (5:9–10). Their song is followed by the voices of innumerable angels and all creatures (5:12–13).

This isn't the only time worship is the focus in Revelation. Nor is it the only place in Scripture where worship is connected with eschatology (e.g., Dan 7:13–14, 27). When God declares the end from the beginning, it should cause us to recognize our place in relation to his greatness. Truly he is a God worthy of worship!

Preacher, does your sermon reflect this focus? Teacher, does your discussion on eschatology cause others to draw near to the Lord in worship? Or does it leave people confused and frustrated, or worse, angry and contentious?

3. End-Times Texts Motivate Our Sanctification

Many end-times texts directly address issues of the heart and hands, not just the head. First John offers a few helpful examples.

---

21. I prefer the term "declare" to "predict" since "predict" may imply that it's just a guess. I can predict the end of a football game, and I may or may not be wrong. But by no means can I accurately *declare* the end of the game.

In 1 John 2:28, the author writes, "And now, little children, abide in him, so that *when he appears* we may have confidence and not shrink from him in shame at his coming" (emphasis mine). Notice how John ties together the appearance of Jesus with the command to abide in him and live in such a way so as not to be ashamed.

When I was a teenager, my parents would often leave me home alone with my three younger siblings. They would rarely tell me the specific time they planned to return. It was a good strategy (though I hated it as a teen!). They expected me always to be ready for their arrival. Had I known the exact hour of their coming, I would only need to organize the house and keep the kids behaving during that small window. But with only a vague idea of when they would return, I had to always be prepared.

The Lord does the same with his children. Why didn't Jesus say, "I'm coming back in two thousand years?" Because that would have invited 1,999 years of bad behavior! But the vaguer "I'll be back" (in an Aramaic accent, not Schwarzenegger) encourages us to be ready at all times.

A few verses later, John writes, "And everyone who thus hopes in him purifies himself as he is pure" (3:3).[22] The "hoping in him" John speaks of here is the hope in his return and all the benefits believers accrue through it. Hope in Christ's return motivates us to purify our lives so that we are properly prepared for his return.

4. End-Times Texts Help Us Establish Proper Priorities

To quote a rather lengthy passage from 2 Peter 3:10–13:

> But the day of the Lord will come like a thief, and then the heavens will pass away with a roar, and the heavenly bodies will be burned up and dissolved, and the earth and the works that are done on it will be exposed. Since all these things are thus to be dissolved, what sort of people ought you to be in lives of holiness and godliness, waiting for and hastening the coming of the day of God, because of which the heavens will be set on fire and dissolved, and the heavenly bodies will melt as they burn! But according to his promise we are waiting for new heavens and a new earth in which righteousness dwells.

End-times texts should also help us organize our priorities. Notice how Peter relates the "day of the Lord" with how believers ought to live: We

22. Cf. Matthew 24:48–51.

should be waiting for and hastening the coming of that day (v. 12). Again he says it in verse 13: "waiting for new heavens and a new earth."

This waiting is not passive. It's an active waiting, a hastening of the return of the Lord. Everything about our priorities should change, knowing that the Lord can return at any moment. Our urgency to evangelize increases, since we do not know how long others have. We do not store up treasures for ourselves but instead seek heavenly, spiritual treasure (1 Tim 6:18–19; Jas 5:3). Our life is not lived for retirement in this age but for the heavenly rest to come (Heb 4:1–11).

Your congregation should feel the urge to rearrange their priorities after studying an end-times text.

5. End-Times Texts Stir Up Hope and Longing

Some time ago, I read Randy Alcorn's *Heaven.*[23] What a beautiful longing it stirred within me, eagerly awaiting the things to come! Biblical prophecy does that. Paul writes in Romans 8:18, "For I consider that the sufferings of this present time are not worth comparing with the glory that is to be revealed to us." Do we not long for this incomparable glory?

If our congregation leaves without longing for what is to come, then either they're not on the right side of the judgment or you, Teacher, may have taught too much with your head and not enough with your heart. Don't forget to allow the people to *feel* the longing for the end times.

This also gives us great hope. Paul calls the return of Christ "our blessed hope" in Titus 2:13. For believers, knowing that God's return will usher in perfect justice and righteousness is a great hope indeed. We suffer much in this life; we will not suffer at all in the life to come. Every pain, every death, every fractured relationship we endure reminds us of a perfect existence awaiting us for all eternity. Our afflictions are temporary; our hope does not rest in this life alone. As the old adage goes, afflict the comfortable and comfort the afflicted.[24]

---

23. Randy Alcorn, *Heaven: Biblical Answers to Common Questions* (Carol Stream, IL: Tyndale Momentum, 2004).

24. As far as I can tell, this adage originated in Finley Peter Dunne, as noted in Bandy and Merkle, *Understanding Prophecy*, 33.

God has great plans for his people! Make sure you paint people a picture of hope, leaning on the eschatological promises of Scripture.[25]

Preaching and Teaching End-Times Texts

The congregation doesn't need to feel growing pains or put in Herculean effort every time you preach an end-times text. But there are quite a few of those texts, so good preachers and teachers of the Bible will need to increase their comfort level when handling these.

Use Charts or Visuals

For some reason, discussions about end times seem to go hand in hand with endless charts and visuals. Unfortunately, some of these charts are so complicated that I can hardly discern how they are supposed to help.

Some time ago, a friend gave me an old book with the humble title *The Greatest Book on "Dispensational Truth" in the World.*[26] The book has an obvious theological slant. It is renowned for its many elaborate charts. They are too elaborate to reproduce here, but take a minute and do a Google image search of some of the charts.

I'll wait.

Now do you see what I mean? The charts are so enormous and full of activity that you need a chart to understand the chart.

When it comes to visuals, sometimes the simpler the image, the better.

For example, when I teach eschatology in my Introduction to Christian Theology class, I first discuss the end times from the perspective of the New Testament writers. A glimpse at texts like Romans 13:11–12; 1 Corinthians 10:11; Hebrews 1:1–2; 9:26; 1 Peter 1:20; 2 Peter 3:3; and 1 John 2:18 demonstrate that the New Testament writers view the time from Christ's

---

25. Other points can be added to these. Bible prophecy is given to help us understand the future (Rev 1:1). The word "revelation" literally means "unveiling." It indicates revelation is not meant to confuse or confound but to bring to light. End-times texts also bless the believer (1:3). Merely reading the words of Revelation brings blessing to Christians.

26. Clarence Larkin, *The Greatest Book on "Dispensational Truth" in the World* (Glenside, PA: Rev. Clarence Larkin Est., 1920).

incarnation onward as the "last days" or the "end times."[27] So I developed a helpful chart to illustrate this:

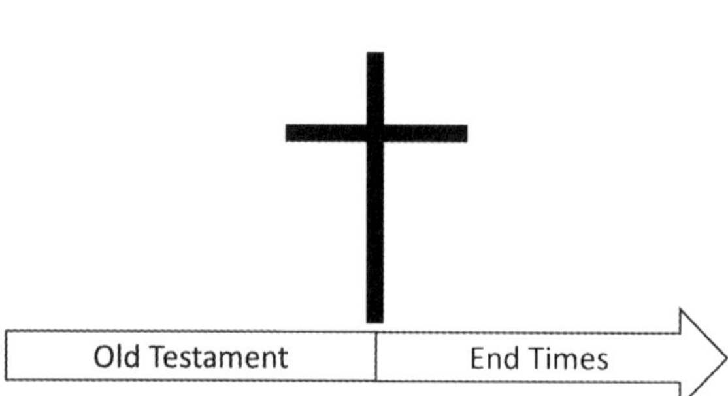

As you can see, charts do not have to be overly complicated to illustrate or illuminate a point. If a chart clarifies, summarizes, or simplifies a viewpoint through a visual means, by all means use it. Put it on a PowerPoint slide, include it as a bulletin handout, or put a QR code on the screen for people to download from a website. Whatever you have to do, do it.[28]

Thankfully, there are a few resources dedicated to this effort, so you don't have to reinvent the wheel.[29]

Speak About Other Views with Proper Respect

The "other side" in most eschatological issues is not the enemy. Most end-times discussions are in-house, family discussions. Those who disagree with you are likely also evangelical Christians who see the text from a different point of view. People who think that we're living in a spiritual millennium and people who think a literal millennium is still to come will both share eternity one day. Someone will be right, and someone will be wrong, or both will be wrong. But either way, we're not talking about issues that

---

27. I see the "end times" specifically beginning with the incarnation, mainly due to Hebrews 9:26 and 1 Peter 1:20, which associate that time with the manifestation/appearance of Christ.

28. This discussion assumes, by the way, that you are using legal methods to distribute or reproduce a chart. At the very least, give attribution to whatever source you display.

29. One of the most helpful is H. Wayne House and Randall Price, *Charts of Bible Prophecy* (Grand Rapids: Zondervan, 2003).

determine salvation. Those who disagree with you on most eschatological issues are also not heretics.[30]

Along with this, those on the "other side" are not idiots. In fact, even if you don't want to admit it, many of them are far smarter than you. This doesn't make them right, but they didn't come to their position through ignorance or purposeful biblical malpractice. They too have studied for years, have advanced theological degrees on their walls, and have written commentaries and theologies. They see their position just as consistently as you see yours.

They are not enemies, not idiots, and not heretics. So speak of them and their stance with proper respect. If you believe 1 Thessalonians 4 speaks of a pretribulation rapture, don't villainize those who hold a mid- or post-tribulation position. When you speak of the other side like they're all a bunch of fools, the only one who sounds like a fool is you.

Benjamin L. Merkle is helpful here: "When we don't understand others' theological systems, it is easy to dismiss their views or, worse, demonize them. It is far too easy to attach some impure motives to those who disagree with us and question their spirituality."[31] He goes on to say, "By learning the systems of others, we are able to understand and even value that which we don't necessarily affirm."[32]

Remember Your Audience

Preachers, you're preaching a sermon, not teaching a seminary class.

Teachers, you're teaching a Sunday school lesson, or a Bible study, or a small group, not giving a lecture at an academic conference.

---

30. I say "most" because there are issues that we cannot deny, such as the return of Christ. To deny the return of Christ is to deny clear, consistent, voluminous Christian doctrine and therefore would be considered heretical.

As a side point, consider how this idea applies to church membership covenants. I believe far too many people are kept from church membership due to issues that will not keep someone from heaven. If we're going to spend eternity together, why can't we spend the next few decades in local church ministry together?

31. Benjamin L. Merkle, *Discontinuity to Continuity: A Survey of Dispensational and Covenantal Theologies* (Bellingham, WA: Lexham, 2020), 2.

32. Merkle, 2. Helpfully, Merkle also notes a fourfold result of studying other theologies and their hermeneutics: It helps you solidify what you believe, appreciate the viewpoint of others, recognize your own theological system is not perfect, and strive to become a person of the book (1–4).

Don't get me wrong—I'm all for meaty theology and good biblical teaching in a local church setting. But we must remember that our goal is not simply to add knowledge or help people understand eschatological schemes. Our goal is edification (1 Cor 14:26); our goal is to bring glory to God (1 Cor 10:31); our goal is discipleship and sanctification (Matt 28:18–20; 1 Pet 1:14–16); our goal is evangelism (2 Tim 4:5).

These things are not mutually exclusive to a good intellectual sermon or lesson. But knowledge tends to puff up (1 Cor 8:1). Remember that Johnny Teenager in the pew didn't show up today to figure out the mysteries of Daniel's seventieth week. Johnny Teenager is there because Joe Daddy dragged him to church. He needs to hear why this is important. He needs the gospel.

Grandma Ethel didn't get up early because she wanted to fill in her chart with how many judgments there will be. Grandma Ethel is there because she's been there every Sunday for the last eighty years. She still needs edifying. She needs hope at the end of a long and fruitful life.

Auntie Ann just went through an ugly divorce after two decades of an abusive marriage. She cares little about eschatology. She needs a broken heart mended.

Never forget who you're preaching to.

Preach the Text, Not a Systematic Theology

Before you brand me a heretic, allow me to clarify. Again, teaching systematic theology in church is important. It's not done often enough, in my opinion. I regularly teach 100-level systematic theology to college students who grew up in church and often exclaim with annoyance, "Why wasn't I ever taught this before?"

However, many preachers who tackle end-times texts seem to think they need to fit every event into every passage. As if you might miss the rapture if you don't mention the rapture, even in passages that don't talk about the rapture!

To use an Old Testament illustration (forgive me!), I was preaching through the book of Isaiah. We eventually got to what is sometimes called Isaiah's "Little Apocalypse" in chapters 24–27. Over the course of five weeks, as we followed Isaiah's text, we uncovered topics like the eternal state, the final restoration, the tribulation, the millennium, and even the marriage supper of the Lamb. As we went, I showed the congregation a few charts.

Eventually, toward the end of that five-week miniseries, I had a few end-times nerds ask me after church, "What about the rapture? Don't you believe in the rapture? Where does that fit into all of this? Why haven't we heard anything about the rapture?"

I heard the question so often that I eventually decided to address it from the pulpit. One of the last weeks in the series, I said, "Many of you have wondered where the rapture fits into all of this. I haven't addressed the rapture simply because *Isaiah doesn't address the rapture*. When Isaiah speaks about the Lord's return, it seems to me that he's clearly referring to the second coming of Christ. I've tried to speak only about the events that we see in this part of Isaiah.

"And guess what? If you're wondering where the rapture fits in, I'm happy to once again disappoint you this morning! Isaiah 27 doesn't speak about the rapture either.

"But here's the good news: If you want to know what my position is on that subject, and if you want to know about other views on that subject, we have a class starting up in a few Wednesdays from now . . ."

You may not be as snarky as I am in the pulpit (that's probably a good thing!), but I hope you see my point. Preacher, you are under no obligation to preach about every possible end-times event in every eschatological text.[33] Sometimes you have the time and a good reason to throw in an extra event or two that the text does not directly address. Sometimes you don't, and you shouldn't.

Feel free to stick with the text.

Define Your Terms

I recall the first time I heard the word *eschatology*. I mistakenly thought it had something to do with bathroom humor. It didn't. But for a time, it was a *very* confusing sermon.

As preachers, pastors, and Bible teachers, many of us have had the privilege of attending Bible college and seminary, giving us time to study and teach these concepts, many of us for decades. Words like eschatology and dispensationalism and preterism might roll off our tongues, but for many in our congregation, that's not the case.

33. It would be a perversion of Acts 20:27 to say that every aspect of theology must be discussed in every text in order to preach the whole counsel of God.

I remember one time as a teenager when I was teaching a Bible study in my home. Our topic was the end times.[34] About halfway through the lesson, one of my classmates interrupted and exclaimed, "Wait? What is the 'rapid' again?" She was talking about the rapture. The entire time I spoke about it, she was thinking a different word.

Define your terms. Maybe even put the term itself on the screen behind you so that people can see how it's spelled. Don't assume everyone knows what you're talking about, even with seemingly "simple" things like our future resurrection or the final judgment. Explain the terms, then explain them again the next week, and then again the week after that. It's no trouble to those who are familiar with this terminology to hear it repeated; it's a great help to those who don't remember the terms to hear them again.

Simplicity Is Your Friend

Become a friend of the simple. There's no need to overcomplicate an already complicated system of theology. If possible, unite your church or study group with a basic overview of eschatology. Then fill in the details as needed.

I was recently reading a book on different views of heaven.[35] In the introduction, the editor writes, "When it comes to eschatology, the Christian Scriptures teach the three Rs: the Return of Christ, the Resurrection of the body, and the Restoration of all things."[36] I can't imagine someone could disagree with that big-picture overview!

It's surely not *all* we need when it comes to eschatology. But presenting your text with that reminder may help people categorize your discussion appropriately. If you're preaching on 2 Peter 3—that wonderfully encouraging passage about the Lord returning and burning up all the heavenly bodies—it could benefit your audience to review the three Rs and then let them know that the final chapter of 2 Peter touches on the first and third of those Rs.

Again, it's not all you'll say about this subject. But one mark of a great Bible teacher is the ability to simplify the complex so that those who are less familiar with it can understand it. This does not mean watering anything

---

34. Foolish me. I think I broke about every principle in this chapter over the course of several months!

35. It is creatively titled *Four Views on Heaven*, ed. Michael E. Wittmer (Grand Rapids: Zondervan Academic, 2022).

36. Wittmer, 9.

down or patronizing your audience. It's just another method of communicating challenging texts with the goal of clarity.

Don't Be Afraid to Preach the Text

If you come from a background that values dogmatic preaching and teaching, even on secondary and tertiary issues, you might come to the end of this chapter with a degree of frustration. You may think of me as a sniveling wimp who would rather keep things so general that I avoid saying anything of substance or anything that might offend.

This is not the case. My wife tells me I can be quite offensive on a regular basis.

Your responsibility is to preach and teach the text. If the text leads you to preach a view mostly in line with a pretribulation rapture, then preach it. Show your class where you got there from the text and then teach it with conviction. If the text leads you to a preterist view of Matthew 24, then take courage, be honest, and again, make sure you show your church how you got there.

We ought not be afraid of preaching and teaching the text. As ministers of God's word, we stand behind the authority of the text. The text guides us and informs us. We don't impose our will on the text. We certainly shouldn't shoehorn the text into our own systems of theology. Rather, the text tells us what to say and even how to say it.

You'll want to include a dash of practical wisdom in your teaching, especially if it rubs against your church's official position on that topic. If your church holds an amillennial position in its doctrinal statement and after your studies you believe Revelation 20 teaches a literal future millennium, you need to be honest with your leaders. Bringing that kind of surprise from the pulpit will likely lead only to division, mistrust, and possibly an abuse of your position. Your leaders may choose to have someone else preach it. Or they might suggest another route. Either way, be humble enough to accept their counsel without a battle.

Be Strategic About Teaching These Texts

As I mentioned earlier in the chapter, one of the first questions I received when taking a lead pastor position was, "When are you preaching the book of Revelations?"

Again, Revelation, not Revelations.

I'm sure my answer frustrated many die-hard eschatology fanatics. "I'm not sure I'd want to teach Revelation until I teach Exodus, Daniel, Ezekiel, and Zechariah, at least."

That was usually met with a look of exasperation. But if much of the imagery from Revelation rests on events and theology in these Old Testament books, I thought it would be most edifying for the congregation if they had a greater foundation in those other books before attempting to figure out the end.

Reading Revelation without the Old Testament would be like watching the third Marvel Spider-Man movie (*Spider-Man: No Way Home*) without watching the Sam Raimi trilogy or the two *Amazing Spider-Man* movies. You might get the bigger picture, but you'll be lost in all the details. For you older, more mature readers, it would be like watching the last episode of *Seinfeld* without ever having watched the rest of the series. You won't get the joke.

Now, some preachers might balk. Add up all the chapters in Exodus, Daniel, Ezekiel, and Zechariah and you have 114 chapters of Scripture to preach. That's probably more than two years of preaching, assuming you don't have a few New Testament book series sprinkled in between. Two years of preaching before Revelation?

Yes. That's *exactly* what I mean.

And also, so what? Even if you have only a ten-year tenure in your church, that's easily doable, twice over! Why rush what might be the capstone of your preaching career? If other preachers can spend half a decade just preaching Romans, why can't you spend half a decade leading up to Revelation? Think about how enriched your faithful members will be once they get there with you.[37]

---

37. You may also object, "But what about those people who show up a few years in?" This is why it's necessary to regularly review the broader context. You may want to point them to your sermon archive or give people your previous notes. People binge television shows all the time to catch up with season five of the latest cultural craze. Why not encourage people along the way to do the same with your sermon series?

Conclusion

As I sit at my desk and write these closing thoughts, a collection of fossils and gems I have amassed over the years stares back at me behind the glare of my laptop.

There is a fossilized clamshell, dug out of the clay in the shores of the Calvert Cliffs in Maryland. Next to it sits a tiny claw of an extinct sloth, no longer than an inch, found by sifting through hundreds of pounds of stone and sand in a brook in Colts Neck, New Jersey.

A large Herkimer diamond, still embedded in the matrix, catches the light and glistens. It was freed from a slab of rock bigger than my car in upstate New York.

A shadowbox full of shark teeth and dolphin bone rests above a large concave fragment of a whale's skull, all unearthed from the ground in South Carolina.

Belemnites, trilobites, horse teeth, and all kinds of other ancient remnants decorate my bookshelves, attesting to the strange and wonderful treasures God has seen fit to bury under our feet . . . but only for those who do the hard work of digging.

Preaching and teaching the Bible is difficult work. When we take it seriously and study as we ought, it brings great reward. We find treasures on every page—some of the surface-hunt variety, scattered in plain sight among the pages of Matthew and Romans and James. Other biblical treasures take significantly more effort to uncover. Both varieties may end up on display in the sermon.

I have had the privilege of preaching through all of John, Galatians, Hebrews, 1 Peter, and much of Acts. In various ministry contexts, I have also taught through nearly every book of the New Testament cover to cover. In my experience, some books can be preached and taught more easily than others. Some passages require extra digging to yield their meaning and application.

It's all worth the effort. Every word of Scripture is inspired and useful for teaching, reproof, correction, and training in righteousness to equip believers for every good work (2 Tim 3:16–17). Every passage of Scripture—even the difficult ones—can and should be preached (4:1–2). If we know where to look and how to dig, significant treasure awaits the adventurous preacher and teacher.

The only thing left now is for you to put in the effort.

Appendix

Lists of Difficult Texts

Note: In many cases, it is impossible to exhaustively list all passages in certain categories. Such categories therefore ought to be considered starting points rather than comprehensive lists.

1. People Lists

Rom 16:1–16, 21–23; 1 Cor 16:10–18; Col 4:7–17; 2 Tim 4:9–21; Titus 3:12–14; Phlm 23–24; 1 Pet 5:12–13

2a. Entrances

Rom 1:1–7; 1 Cor 1:1–3; 2 Cor 1:1–2; Gal 1:1–5; Eph 1:1–2; Phil 1:1–2; Col 1:1–2; 1 Thess 1:1; 2 Thess 1:1–2; 1 Tim 1:1–2; 2 Tim 1:1–2; Titus 1:1–4; Phlm 1–3; Jas 1:1; 1 Pet 1:1–2; 2 Pet 1:1–2; 2 John 1–3; 3 John 1; Jude 1–2

2b. Exits

Rom 16:25–27; 1 Cor 16:19–24; 2 Cor 13:11–14; Gal 6:18; Eph 6:21–24; Phil 4:21–23; Col 4:18; 1 Thess 5:23–28; 2 Thess 3:16–18; 1 Tim 5:20–21; 2 Tim 4:22; Titus 3:15; Phlm 23–25; Heb 13:22–25; 1 Pet 5:12–14; 2 Pet 3:14–18; 1 John 5:20–21; 2 John 12–13; 3 John 13–15; Jude 24–25; Rev 22:21

3a. Well-Worn Stories: General

Feeding of the Five Thousand (Matt 14:13–21; Mark 6:30–44; Luke 9:10–17; John 6:1–15)

The Good Samaritan (Luke 10:25–37)
Jesus Walking on Water (Matt 14:22–33; Mark 6:45–52; John 6:16–21)
Jesus Turning Water into Wine (John 2:1–12)
Jesus Raising Lazarus from the Dead (John 11:1–57)
The Ethiopian Eunuch (Acts 8:26–40)
Conversion of Saul/Paul (Acts 9:1–19; 22:1–21; 26:12–23)

3b. Well-Worn Stories: Communion/Lord's Supper

Matt 26:26–28; Mark 14:22–24; Luke 22:14–23; 1 Cor 11:17–34

3c. Well-Worn Stories: Holidays

Christmas: Matt 1:18–25; 2:1–12; Luke 1:26–38; 2:1–7, 8–21
Good Friday/Easter: Matt 27:32–66; 28:1–10; Mark 15:21–47; 16:1–8; Luke 23:26–56; 24:1–53; John 19:1–42; 20:1–10

4. Nuggets

Rom 1:16–17; 12:1–2; Gal 2:20; Eph 5:1–2; Phil 4:8; Heb 13:2; 1 Pet 3:15

5. Textual Nightmares

Long Examples: Mark 16:9–20; John 7:53–8:11
Short Examples: John 5:4; 20:30; Acts 8:37; 9:5–6; Eph 1:1

6. New Testament Use of the Old Testament

Acts 2:17; 7:7 (7:2–53); Heb 1:5 (1:5–14)

7. Apocryphal Texts

Matt 19:1–12 // m. Gittin 9:10
John 5:8–10 // m. Shabbat 7:2
John 7–8 // m. Sukkah
John 12:3 // m. Ketubbot 7:6
Acts 4:19–20 (cf. 5:29) // Socrates (in Plato, *Apol.* 29D)
Acts 17:24 // Seneca

Acts 17:28 // Epimenides of Crete and Aratus of Cilicia

Acts 26:14 // various ancient sources

1 Cor 15:33 // Menander's *Thais*

2 Cor 11:24 // m. Makkot 3:10–14

Titus 1:12–13a // Epimenides of Crete

Heb 11:35 // 2 Macc 7

Jude 9 // Assumption of Moses (Testament of Moses?)

Jude 14–15 // 1 Enoch 1:9

8. Enigmas

1 Cor 11:10; 15:29; Heb 6:1–8; 1 Pet 3:18–22

9. Politically Incorrect Texts

1 Cor 6:9; Eph 5:22–33; 1 Tim 1:8–11; 2:12; 5:8; 1 Pet 3:7

10. End-Times Texts

Matt 24–25 (Mark 13:1–37; Luke 17:20–37; 21:5–36); Rom 11; 1 Cor 15; 1 Thess 4:13–18; 5:1–11; 2 Thess 1:5–12; 2:1–12; 2 Pet 2–3; Rev 1–22

Bibliography

Alcorn, Randy. *Heaven: Biblical Answers to Common Questions*. Carol Stream, IL: Tyndale Momentum, 2004.

Allen, David L. *Hebrews*. NAC 35. Nashville: B&H, 2010.

Aune, David E. *Revelation 1–5*. WBC 52A. Grand Rapids: Zondervan, 1997.

———. *Revelation 6–16*. WBC 52B. Grand Rapids: Zondervan, 1998.

———. *Revelation 17–22*. WBC 52C. Grand Rapids: Zondervan, 1998.

Bandy, Alan S., and Benjamin L. Merkle. *Understanding Prophecy: A Biblical-Theological Approach*. Grand Rapids: Kregel Academic, 2015.

Bauckham, Richard J. *2 Peter and Jude*. WBC 50. Waco, TX: Word, 1983.

Bauckham, Richard, James R. Davila, and Alexander Panayotov, eds. *Old Testament Pseudepigrapha: More Noncanonical Scriptures*. Grand Rapids: Eerdmans, 2013.

Beale, G. K. *The Book of Revelation: A Commentary on the Greek Text*. NIGTC. Grand Rapids: Eerdmans, 1999.

———. "The Cognitive Peripheral Vision of Biblical Authors." *WTJ* 76 (2014): 263–93.

———. *Handbook on the New Testament Use of the Old Testament: Exegesis and Interpretation*. Grand Rapids: Baker Academic, 2012.

Beale, G. K., and D. A. Carson, eds. *Commentary on the New Testament Use of the Old Testament*. Grand Rapids: Baker Academic, 2007.

Benware, Paul N. *Understanding End Times Prophecy: A Comprehensive Approach*. Chicago: Moody, 2006.

Blomberg, Craig L. *Matthew*. NAC 22. Nashville: B&H, 1992.

Bock, Darrell L. *Acts*. BECNT. Grand Rapids: Baker Academic, 2007.

Bock, Darrell L., and Mikel Del Rosario. "The Table Briefing: Engaging Challenges to the Reliability of the New Testament Text." *BSac* 175 (2018): 96–105.

Bruce, F. F. *The Book of the Acts*. Rev. ed. NICNT. Grand Rapids: Eerdmans, 1988.

Carson, D. A. *The Gospel According to John*. Grand Rapids: Eerdmans, 1991.

———. *The King James Version Debate: A Plea for Realism*. Grand Rapids: Baker, 1979.

———. "Jude." Pages 1069–1079 in *Commentary on the New Testament Use of the Old Testament*. Edited by G. K. Beale and D. A. Carson. Grand Rapids: Baker Academic, 2007.

———. *New Testament Commentary Survey*. 7th ed. Grand Rapids: Baker Academic, 2013.

Carson, D. A., and Douglas J. Moo. *An Introduction to the New Testament*. Grand Rapids: Zondervan, 2005.

Chapell, Bryan. *Christ-Centered Preaching: Redeeming the Expository Sermon*. Grand Rapids: Baker Academic, 2005.

———, ed. *The Hardest Sermons You'll Ever Have to Preach: Help from Trusted Preachers for Tragic Times*. Grand Rapids: Zondervan, 2011.

Charles, J. Daryl. "Jude's Use of Pseudepigraphical Source-Material as Part of a Literary Strategy." *NTS* 37 (1991): 130–45.

Charlesworth, James H., ed. *The Old Testament Pseudepigrapha*. 2 vols. Peabody, MA: Hendrickson, 1983.

Ciampa, Roy E., and Brian S. Rosner. *The First Letter to the Corinthians*. PNTC. Grand Rapids: Eerdmans, 2010.

Collins, John J. "Towards the Morphology of a Genre: Introduction." *Semeia* 14 (1979): 1–20.

Cranfield, C. E. B. *A Critical and Exegetical Commentary on the Epistle to the Romans*. 2 vols. ICC. New York: T&T Clark, 1975, 1979.

Danby, Herbert. *The Mishnah*. Peabody, MA: Hendrickson, 2011.

Davids, Peter H. *The Epistle of James: A Commentary on the Greek Text*. NIGTC. Grand Rapids: Eerdmans, 1982.

Dawson, Nancy S. *All the Genealogies of the Bible: Visual Charts and Exegetical Commentary*. Grand Rapids: Zondervan Academic, 2023.

Dodd, C. H. *According to the Scriptures: The Substructure of New Testament Theology*. New York: Fontana Books, 1953.

Edwards, James R. *The Gospel According to Mark*. Grand Rapids: Eerdmans, 2002.

Eriksson, Anders. *Traditions as Rhetorical Proof: Pauline Argumentation in 1 Corinthians*. Stockholm: Almqvist & Wiksell International, 1998.

Evans, Craig A. *Ancient Texts for New Testament Studies: A Guide to the Background Literature*. Peabody, MA: Hendrickson, 2005.

Fee, Gordon D. *The First Epistle to the Corinthians*. NICNT. Grand Rapids: Eerdmans, 1987.

———. *Paul's Letter to the Philippians*. NICNT. Grand Rapids: Eerdmans, 1995.

Fee, Gordon D., and Douglas Stuart. *How to Read the Bible for All Its Worth*. Grand Rapids: Zondervan, 2003.

Fee, Gordon D., and Mark L. Strauss. *How to Choose a Translation for All Its Worth*. Grand Rapids: Zondervan, 2007.

Foschini, Bernard Mary. "'Those Who are Baptized for the Dead,' 1 Cor 15:29." *CBQ* 12 (1950): 260–76, 379–88.

———. "'Those Who are Baptized for the Dead,' 1 Cor 15:29." *CBQ* 13 (1951): 46–78, 172–98, 276–83.

France, R. T. *The Gospel of Matthew*. NICNT. Grand Rapids: Eerdmans, 2007.

———. *Jesus and the Old Testament: His Application of Old Testament Passages to Himself and His Mission*. Vancouver: Regent College Publishing, 1998.

Garland, David E. *1 Corinthians*. BECNT. Grand Rapids: Baker Academic, 2003.

Geisler, Norman L., and Thomas Howe. *The Big Book of Bible Difficulties*. Grand Rapids: Baker, 1992.

Geisler, Norman L., and William E. Nix. *From God to Us: How We Got Our Bible*. Chicago: Moody, 2012.

Gibson, Jonathan. *Covenant Continuity and Fidelity: A Study of Inner-Biblical Allusion and Exegesis in Malachi*. LHBOTS. New York: Bloomsbury T&T Clark, 2016.

Grassmick, John D. "Mark." Pages 95–197 in *The Bible Knowledge Commentary: New Testament*. Edited by John F. Walvoord and Roy B. Zuck. Colorado Springs: Cook Communications Ministries, 2000.

Green, Gene L. *Jude and 2 Peter*. BECNT. Grand Rapids: Baker Academic, 2008.

Grudem, Wayne. *Systematic Theology: An Introduction to Biblical Doctrine.* 2nd ed. Grand Rapids: Zondervan Academic, 2020.

Guthrie, George H. *Hebrews.* NIVAC. Grand Rapids: Zondervan, 1998.

Hanson, Paul D. "Apocalypses and Apocalypticism." Pages 279–92 in *The Anchor Bible Dictionary*, vol. 1, *A–C*. Edited by David Noel Freedman. New York: Doubleday, 1992.

Hays, Richard B. *Echoes of Scripture in the Letters of Paul.* New Haven: Yale University Press, 1989.

Hendricks, Howard G., and William D. Hendricks. *Living by the Book: The Art and Science of Reading the Bible*. Chicago: Moody, 2007.

Hixson, Elijah, and Peter J. Gurry, eds. *Myths and Mistakes in New Testament Textual Criticism*. Downers Grove, IL: IVP Academic, 2019.

Hoehner, Harold W. *Ephesians: An Exegetical Commentary.* Grand Rapids: Baker Academic, 2002.

House, H. Wayne, and Randall Price. *Charts of Bible Prophecy*. Grand Rapids: Zondervan, 2003.

Hull, Michael F. *Baptism on Account of the Dead (1 Cor 15:29): An Act of Faith in the Resurrection.* AcBib 22. Atlanta: Society of Biblical Literature, 2005.

Instone-Brewer, David. *Divorce and Remarriage in the Church: Biblical Solutions for Pastoral Realities.* Downers Grove, IL: InterVarsity Press, 2003.

Kapic, Kelly M. *A Little Book for New Theologians: Why and How to Study Theology*. Downers Grove, IL: IVP Academic, 2012.

Keener, Craig S. *Acts: An Exegetical Commentary*. 4 vols. Grand Rapids: Baker Academic, 2012–2015.

Kristeva, Julia. *Desire in Language: A Semiotic Approach to Literature and Art.* New York: Columbia University Press, 1980.

Kuruvilla, Abraham. "Time to Kill the Big Idea? A Fresh Look at Preaching." *JETS* 61 (2018): 825–46.

Larkin, Clarence. *The Greatest Book on "Dispensational Truth" in the World.* Glenside, PA: Rev. Clarence Larkin Est., 1920.

Longenecker, Richard N. *The Epistle to the Romans: A Commentary on the Greek Text*. NIGTC. Grand Rapids: Eerdmans, 2016.

Longman III, Tremper. *Old Testament Commentary Survey.* 5th ed. Grand Rapids: Baker Academic, 2013.

Mathewson, Steven D. *The Art of Preaching Old Testament Narrative.* Grand Rapids: Baker Academic, 2002.

———. *The Art of Preaching Old Testament Poetry*. Grand Rapids: Baker Academic, 2024.

McDowell, Josh, and Sean McDowell. *Evidence That Demands a Verdict*. Nashville: Thomas Nelson, 2017.

McFadden, Kevin W. *Hidden with Christ in God: A Theology of Colossians and Philemon*. Wheaton, IL: Crossway, 2023.

Merkle, Benjamin L. *Discontinuity to Continuity: A Survey of Dispensational and Covenantal Theologies*. Bellingham, WA: Lexham, 2020.

Metzger, Bruce M. *A Textual Commentary on the Greek New Testament*. New York: United Bible Societies, 1971.

Miller, Stephen R. *Daniel*. NAC 18. Nashville: B&H, 1994.

Miller, Timothy E., and Bryan Murawski. *1 Peter: A Commentary for Biblical Preaching and Teaching*. Grand Rapids: Kregel, 2022.

Millman, Dan. "On Courage." Pages 27–28 in *Chicken Soup for the Soul: 101 Stories to Open the Heart and Rekindle the Spirit*. Edited by Jack Canfield and Mark Victor Hansen. New York: Guideposts, 1993.

Moo, Douglas J. *The Epistle to the Romans*. NICNT. Grand Rapids: Eerdmans, 1996.

———. *The Letters to the Colossians and to Philemon*. PNTC. Grand Rapids: Eerdmans, 2008.

Morris, Leon. *The Gospel According to John*. Rev. ed. NICNT. Grand Rapids: Eerdmans, 1995.

Mounce, William D. *Pastoral Epistles*. WBC 46. Grand Rapids: Zondervan, 2016.

Murawski, Bryan. *The Preacher's Hebrew Companion to Isaiah 1–39: A Selective Commentary for Meditation and Sermon Preparation*. Peabody, MA: Hendrickson, 2024.

———. *The Preacher's Hebrew Companion to Isaiah 40–66: A Selective Commentary for Meditation and Sermon Preparation*. Peabody, MA: Hendrickson, 2025.

———. *Preaching Difficult Texts of the Old Testament*. Peabody, MA: Hendrickson, 2021.

———. "'To Study the Law of the Lord': The Use of Deuteronomy in Ezra–Nehemiah." PhD diss., Westminster Theological Seminary, 2020.

Ortlund, Gavin. *Finding the Right Hills to Die On: The Case for Theological Triage*. Wheaton, IL: Crossway, 2020.

Osborne, Grant R. *The Hermeneutical Spiral: A Comprehensive Introduction to Biblical Interpretation*. Rev. ed. Downers Grove, IL: IVP Academic, 2006.

———. *Revelation*. BECNT. Grand Rapids: Baker Academic, 2002.

Peterson, David G. *The Acts of the Apostles*. PNTC. Grand Rapids: Eerdmans, 2009.

Piper, John, and Wayne Grudem. "An Overview of Central Concerns: Questions and Answers." Pages 60–92 in *Recovering Biblical Manhood & Womanhood: A Response to Evangelical Feminism*. Edited by John Piper and Wayne Grudem. Wheaton, IL: Crossway, 2006.

Polhill, John B. *Acts*. NAC 26. Nashville: B&H, 1992.

Quinn, Jerome D. *The Letter to Titus*. AB 35. New York: Doubleday, 1990.

Rissi, Mathis. *Die Taufe für die Toten*. Zurich: Zwingli Verlag, 1962.

Robinson, Haddon W. *Biblical Preaching: The Development and Delivery of Expository Messages*. 3rd ed. Grand Rapids: Baker Academic, 2014.

———. "Preaching to Everyone in Particular." Pages 115–20 in *The Art and Craft of Biblical Preaching: A Comprehensive Resource for Today's Communicators*. Edited by Haddon Robinson and Craig Brian Larson. Grand Rapids: Zondervan, 2005.

Schnittjer, Gary Edward. *Old Testament Use of Old Testament: A Book-by-Book Guide*. Grand Rapids: Zondervan, 2021.

Schnittjer, Gary Edward, and Matthew S. Harmon. *How to Study the Bible's Use of the Bible: Seven Hermeneutical Choices for the Old and New Testaments*. Grand Rapids: Zondervan, 2024.

Schreiner, Thomas R. *1, 2 Peter, Jude*. NAC 37. Nashville: B&H, 2003.

———. *Romans*. 2nd ed. BECNT. Grand Rapids: Baker Academic, 2018.

Schultz, Richard L. *The Search for Quotation: Verbal Parallels in the Prophets*. JSOTSup 180. Sheffield: Sheffield Academic Press, 1999.

Scott, J. Julius, Jr. *Jewish Backgrounds of the New Testament*. Grand Rapids: Baker Academic, 1995.

Strauss, Mark L. *Four Portraits, One Jesus: A Survey of Jesus and the Gospels*. 2nd ed. Grand Rapids: Zondervan, 2020.

Taylor, Mark. *1 Corinthians*. NAC 28. Nashville: B&H, 2014.

Thiselton, Anthony C. *The First Epistle to the Corinthians: A Commentary on the Greek Text*. NIGTC. Grand Rapids: Eerdmans, 2000.

Thomas, Robert L. *Revelation 1–7: An Exegetical Commentary.* Chicago: Moody, 1992.

———. *Revelation 8–22: An Exegetical Commentary.* Chicago: Moody, 1995.

Tov, Emanuel. *Textual Criticism of the Hebrew Bible.* 3rd ed. Minneapolis: Fortress, 2012.

Turner, Ian. "Going Beyond What Is Written or Learning to Read? Discovering OT/NT Broad Reference." *JETS* 61 (2018): 577–94.

Wallace, Daniel B. *Greek Grammar: Beyond the Basics.* Grand Rapids: Zondervan, 1996.

Wegner, Paul D. *The Journey from Texts to Translations: The Origin and Development of the Bible.* Grand Rapids: Baker Academic, 1999.

Weima, Jeffrey A. D. *Neglected Endings: The Significance of the Pauline Letter Closings.* JSNTSup 101. Sheffield: Sheffield Academic, 1994.

Wilhoit, James C., and Leland Ryken. *Effective Bible Teaching.* Grand Rapids: Baker Academic, 2012.

Wittmer, Michael E., ed. *Four Views on Heaven.* Grand Rapids: Zondervan Academic, 2022.

Yarbrough, Robert W. *The Letters to Timothy and Titus.* PNTC. Grand Rapids: Eerdmans, 2018.

Zuck, Roy B. *Basic Bible Interpretation.* Colorado Springs: Cook Communications Ministries, 1991.